GOD'S STORY

The Bible Epic from Abraham to Exile

MARK RONCACE

ISBN-13: 9781517723354

TABLE OF CONTENTS

INTRODUCTION

This book is intended to help you understand the Bible; it is not meant to replace the Bible or improve upon it. *God's Story* is designed to facilitate and enhance your enjoyment and knowledge of Scripture. And let me tell you, there is a lot to enjoy and learn. The Bible is much more than you ever thought! You have no idea what you are missing. Yes, you probably know the Bible contains many stories, but were you aware that the first part of the Bible—the books of Genesis through 2 Kings—features one continuous and amazing epic narrative? Hardly anyone knows the story is there, much less how remarkable it is. The purpose of this book, then, is to tell the greatest story never told in a clear, straightforward, and engaging style.

This project emerges from years of experience watching my students struggle through these Old Testament narratives. As a university professor, I believe that struggle yields much fruit. But I have also come to realize that readers must first understand the story in order to embrace its enduring beauty and power. My students and people everywhere, I thought, should have the opportunity to sit down and read this astonishing divine saga without all the elements that make the Bible so intimidating.

To that end, I present the narrative from Genesis 12 to 2 Kings 25 in an appealing and highly accessible format by removing chapter and verse numbers, laborious genealogies, long lists of laws, poetry, confusing names, frustrating repetition of information, and other extraneous parts that make the central storyline difficult to follow. I have also gently and lightly elaborated in order to knit together a coherent story, animate the characters, and clarify and enliven the plot. The result is something a bit unique in that this book is neither a translation of the Bible nor a fictionalized account "based on the Bible." It is something in between. You might call it an "abridged and expanded paraphrase." Perhaps think of it as *The Message Bible* squared, or a children's Bible for grown-ups.

The book, however, is very different from a children's Bible in two important ways, which correspond to two main objectives. First, the book is one continuous story, not a series of isolated vignettes. Hopefully it reads like a novel of sorts. It has been my experience that most people, even if they are quite familiar with Scripture, do not have a good grasp and appreciation of this epic narrative in its totality. They may know many of the individual tales—Joseph sold into slavery, Moses and the ten plagues, Joshua and the battle of Jericho, Samson and Delilah, David and Goliath, and so on. But all of these are part of one grand story of God and His people. A main goal of this book is to help you see how it all fits together.

The second way in which this book differs from a children's Bible is that there are many riveting scenes we never find in children's Bibles because, well, they are not fit for children. Here is just a sample of what you are about to read, stories straight from the Bible:

- A woman disguises herself as a prostitute in order to seduce her father-in-law.
- A man burns his daughter to death as a sacrifice to God.
- A woman is gang raped and then her body sliced up and sent throughout the land.
- A king takes ten women and has sex with each of them in public.
- A woman decapitates a rebel and throws his head over the city wall.
- A king dances wildly and exposes himself.
- Bears maul to death forty-two children for making fun of a bald prophet.
- Women kill and eat their children to survive a famine.
- A queen is pushed from a second story window and then stomped to death by a horse.
- A king displays two piles of seventy bloody heads.

The Bible indeed can be complicated and unsettling. So while this book makes the Bible easier to comprehend, it does not mean it will be an easy read. On the contrary, you may find the uncensored biblical story challenging and difficult. But that is a good thing, because life itself is challenging and difficult. We do not want to censor God's word, thereby robbing it of its richness and complexity, for that robs it of its authenticity, its ability to speak to us. The Bible is eminently relevant. It is real. It is true to life, which means it is sometimes messy and ugly. God's Word comes to us in the form of a sophisticated story, not a neat little lesson book.

Accordingly, a second objective is to facilitate a genuine encounter with *all* elements of the Bible story. This will invite us to wrestle with Scripture's complexity, which in turn will help us to imaginatively attend to the stories of our own intricate lives alongside the biblical one. It is precisely this juxtaposition of biblical story with personal story that creates new possibilities for exploring our faith and for living transformed lives in light of that faith. The exploration of one's faith is the purpose of the five discussion questions for each chapter, found at the back of the book. These prompts are constructed to stimulate a fresh and meaningful study of Scripture as you negotiate questions and tough issues in your own life.

In a sense, this book is nothing new. Christians and Jews have been retelling Bible stories for centuries in a variety of forms: artwork, songs, poems, movies, novels, commentaries, children's Bibles, sermons, and so on. Contemporary pastors and priests, Bible study leaders and Sunday school teachers seek to apply the Word in such a way that it speaks anew in our time and place. They adapt the ancient text so that it ministers to and inspires us in our particular context today. They keep Scripture alive by making it relevant, practical, and applicable.

When they do so, they are adhering to the model set forth in the Bible, for reshaping the Bible takes place *within* the Bible itself. Scripture is already in the process of reinterpretation. Believe it or not, the story in Genesis through 2 Kings was first retold by the writer of 1-2 Chronicles. It is rather easy to see how the Chronicler took the material in 1-2 Samuel, such as the stories about King David, and revised them for his own audience. In the New Testament, it is widely believed that Matthew and Luke used the Gospel of Mark as a source for their own Gospels. There are numerous places where we can observe Matthew and Luke edit the text they find in Mark. Google "synoptic gospels" or "gospel parallels" and you will see what I mean. We could discuss many more examples of inner biblical interpretation. But suffice it to say, it is quite common for later biblical writers to creatively rework earlier biblical texts. Thus, you might say that all attempts to faithfully retell Scriptural stories—like this book—are following the biblical tradition itself by reframing God's Word for a new generation.

Finally, a thought or two about the geography of the story you are about to read and how the story fits into the Bible as a whole. One map is provided for your general reference; many biblical places are difficult to identify with certainty. Do your best to follow the movement of the story and consult other resources, many good ones online, as needed. We begin with Abraham (Abram) in Genesis 12. Abraham is the father of God's people Israel. The story starts with him, so that is where we start, skipping over Genesis 1-11, which is sometimes called the "prehistory." The epic runs to the end of 2 Kings; thus we too conclude there. If you want to know what happens subsequently, you can piece things together by consulting the books of Ezra and Nehemiah, as well as portions of Ezekiel, Isaiah, and a few other prophets. I encourage you to do that. I also encourage you to check the Scripture and to critique and challenge the way I render it. If you do, then you are engaging God's Word for yourself, which relates directly to the aims of this book.

Or you can simply sit back, relax, and enjoy reading a new and invigorating version of the Bible's opening books. Whichever approach you take, may this presentation be a blessing to you on your journey through His story.

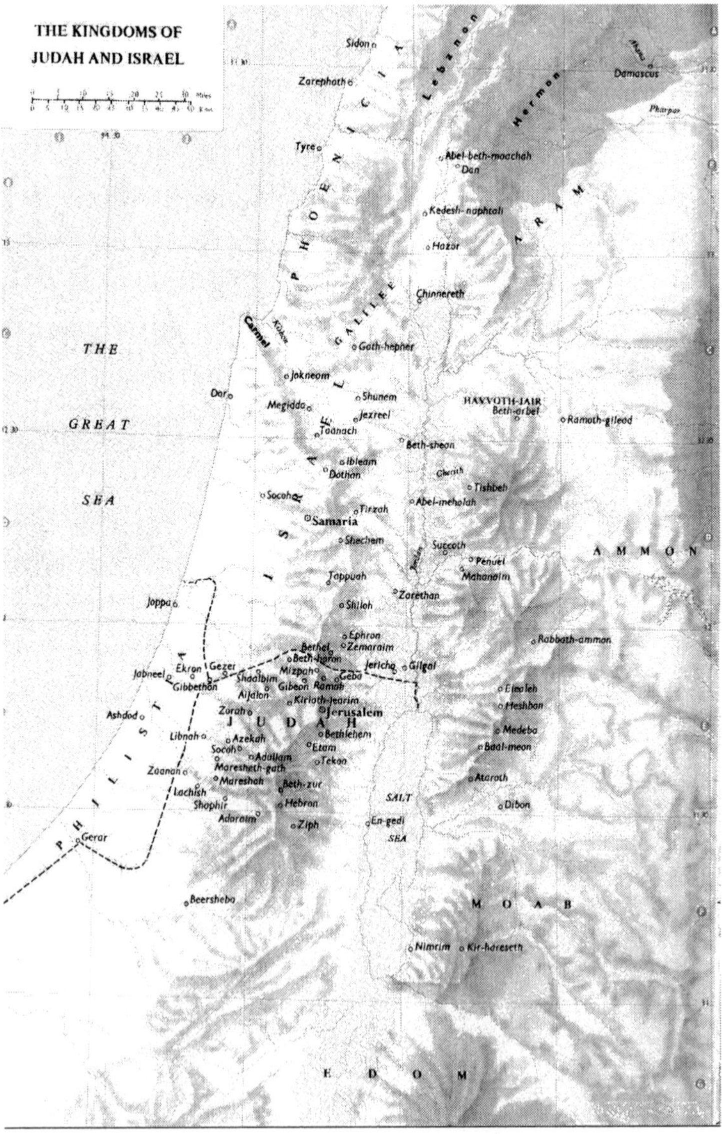
THE KINGDOMS OF
JUDAH AND ISRAEL
Miles
Kms
THE
GREAT
SEA
PHOENICIA
Lebanon
Hermon
ARAM
GALILEE
ISRAEL
JUDAH
PHILISTIA
AMMON
MOAB
EDOM
HAVVOTH-JAIR
SALT
SEA
Carmel
Kishon
Jordan
Cherith
Pharpar
Sidon
Zarephath
Damascus
Tyre
Abel-beth-maachah
Dan
Kedesh-naphtali
Hazor
Chinnereth
Gath-hepher
Jokneam
Dor
Megiddo
Shunem
Jezreel
Taanach
Beth-arbel
Ramoth-gilead
Beth-shean
Ibleam
Dothan
Tishbeh
Socoh
Tirzah
Abel-meholah
Samaria
Shechem
Succoth
Penuel
Mahanaim
Tappuah
Zarethan
Joppa
Shiloh
Ephron
Bethel
Zemaraim
Rabbath-ammon
Beth-horon
Jabneel
Ekron
Gezer
Mizpah
Geba
Jericho
Gilgal
Gibbethon
Shaalbim
Gibeon
Ramah
Aijalon
Elealeh
Kiriath-jearim
Heshbon
Ashdod
Zorah
Jerusalem
Libnah
Azekah
Bethlehem
Medeba
Socoh
Adullam
Etam
Baal-meon
Zaanan
Moresheth-gath
Tekoa
Mareshah
Ataroth
Lachish
Beth-zur
Shaphir
Hebron
Dibon
Adoraim
Ziph
En-gedi
Gerar
Beersheba
Nimrim
Kir-hareseth

1. THE COVENANT OF GOD

Abram relaxed under a sprawling oak tree near his home in Haran. He crunched on a midday snack of nuts and raisins. At seventy-five, he was old and gray; but he was not tired. His hands were strong, his body lean, his eyes sharp. "Well, I'm going on my walk," Abram said, slipping on his sandals.

Sarai nodded and smiled, working a thread expertly through a rent seam. She was about ten years younger than her husband. And still beautiful. Her straight black hair fell about her olive complexion. She was at once soft and sturdy.

A fresh afternoon breeze greeted Abram as he set out on his usual route. It was not his habit to walk briskly. Walks were a time for quiet meditation, reflection, and rejuvenation. He often sensed a divine presence.

"Leave your home in Haran," God said to Abram as he strolled along. Abram knew the voice. He came to an abrupt stop, listening. "Pack up and depart from your native land, and I will lead you to another land, a new place to call home."

Abram's brow wrinkled, his jaw tightened. "Me? Go? Why?" he asked.

"Go," God commanded. "I promise I will take care of you. I will multiply your descendants into a great nation and I will give them the land to which I am leading you. I will bless those who bless you and curse those who curse you. But you must go."

Abram eased himself onto a nearby rock. His head swirled: Where on earth is God sending me? And what's this about many descendants and a great nation? I don't have any children—not one. How can I just pick up and go? What will Sarai say?

Abram was on that rock for a while, the questions rushing through his mind. There were not many answers.

But he had to do it.

• • •

That evening over a bowl of steaming goat stew, Abram told Sarai what God said. She listened, her eyes wandering, her pulse quickening.

"So what do you think?" Abram asked with raised eyebrows.

"You know I've never been able to conceive," she reminded him. But it was clear his mind was made up, so she added, "Where are we going?"

"Canaan," Abram said without hesitation. "That's the land where my father once planned on moving when I was young. But we never made it; we ended up here in Haran instead. Maybe Canaan is the land God has in mind for us."

She took his hand, and the two sat together in silence.

The next morning they gathered up their possessions—servants, animals, food, clothes. Everything. They also asked Lot, Abram's nephew, and Lot's wife to accompany them. After several days of packing and goodbyes, they left Haran in the chilly dawn air, walking south.

The journey had begun.

• • •

Three months later, they arrived in Canaan, their faces streaked with the dust of travel. They pitched their leather tents near a large oak tree—just like the one back home. The village of Bethel lay to the west and Ai to the east.

"This indeed is the land I have chosen for you and your family," God announced as Abram rested in the oak's shade. "It is the land I will give to your descendants who will come after you. Yes, now the Canaanites live here, but in time this is the place where I will make you a great nation."

Abram arose. He stood gazing up at the sky and out across the vast land. To mark the spot and the occasion, Abram began to build a small earthen altar. As he scraped together the mud and dirt, bricks and stone, he could not help but notice the dry ground. It was very different from the fertile black soil in Haran. Soon the humble monument was erected and Abram worshipped God. Then he hurried home to share the news with his wife: This was the Promised Land.

"Promised, but also famished," Sarai said. "There's no food here. I've looked everywhere and talked to the people around. There's nothing. They say it's the worst drought in years. We will run out of grain in the next few weeks."

"This is the right place—God said so—but perhaps it's not the right time," Abram granted.

Sarai's face twisted with frustration.

"This is our home, our new and final home," Abram reassured her. "But for now, we must move again. Egypt. There we will find food."

● ● ●

So Abram and Sarai and Lot and his wife and their whole company loaded their animals and headed south once more. In Egypt they found an abundance of food. And an altogether different kind of crisis. Abram soon learned that the king of Egypt, Pharaoh, took beautiful women to be his wives, and their husbands—if they had one—mysteriously vanished. Word of Sarai was bound to make its way to the throne, and Abram's life would be in jeopardy.

Abram took Sarai in his arms. "You are a very pretty woman. I'm incredibly lucky to have you. But now I fear your beauty is threatening our safety. Sooner or later someone will come to take you to Pharaoh. And I . . . well, they will kill me. I think the best thing we can do is pretend you are my sister. That way my life will be spared. And who knows, they might even treat me with special favor because of you—as long as they think I'm your brother. If nothing else, they won't murder me in order to take you."

"But what about me?" Sarai said, pulling away sharply. "I don't want to be taken into Pharaoh's harem. Think of what will happen there. How can you just give me to another man?"

"It's not just another man. It's Pharaoh, the king of Egypt. Do I—we—really have a choice?" Abram insisted. "Maybe news of your arrival won't make it to Pharaoh. Maybe we won't have to deal with any of this. But if we do . . ." He shook his head and kicked at the dirt.

Pharaoh's men arrived a few days later. Sarai was grinding wheat.

"We are here to take you to Pharaoh. Tomorrow you will be royalty," the captain of the guard said to her. "Where is your husband?"

"I am not married. He is my brother," Sarai replied, pointing to Abram who stood in the shadows.

"Very well, then. Collect your things and prepare to leave," the man commanded. Then turning to Abram, he added, "The king will send his regards very soon. It will be a handsome sum, I'm sure. She is a lovely woman." Abram said nothing.

So Sarai went to live in the house of Pharaoh. Shortly thereafter, Abram received a large herd of cattle, sheep, donkeys, and all kinds of servants, as well as silver and gold. He was now a wealthy man, and Sarai was a queen.

"But what about the land of Canaan, the promise of protection, and the vow of a great nation?" Abram cried out to God. "Now I don't even have a wife. Is this all part of the plan?"

God did not answer. He did, however, inflict Pharaoh and everyone in Pharaoh's house with a terrible disease. Everyone but Sarai.

"What's going on here?" Pharaoh demanded of Sarai. "We're all sick and dying. Except you! You must have something to do with this!"

"I don't know," she answered. "But I can tell you Abram is my husband, not my brother."

Pharaoh spun around and threw his hands in the air. "Send for Abram!" he shouted.

"Why did you do this to me?" the king roared when Abram entered. "Why did you let me think she was your sister? You could've told the truth. I thought you were her brother, so I took her. Now we're all about to die. Take your wife and go before we perish. And take the gifts with you. Just leave. Now!"

Abram opened his mouth to speak, but Pharaoh motioned him away. Sarai hurried to his side. He took her by the hand, and the two quickly departed from the palace.

The next day Abram and Sarai, along with Lot and his wife, left Egypt—much richer than when they arrived—and began the journey home to Canaan, though they had barely been there long enough to call it home. The rains also returned to Canaan and food was again plentiful. The two families settled in the same place between the towns of Bethel and Ai. The oak tree and the altar welcomed them back.

● ● ●

It soon became evident that Abram and Lot each had accumulated too many animals in Egypt and there was not sufficient pasture to support all the livestock. Their shepherds were beginning to quarrel.

"Look, I don't want any tension between you and me, or between your herders and mine," Abram said to his nephew. "We are family, after all. The best thing to do is spread out, move away from one another. There's plenty of land, even with the Canaanites here. Why don't you choose where you want to go, and I will move in the opposite direction."

Lot agreed. He surveyed the land in the region and decided to move east, toward the well-watered plains of the Jordan River. There his flocks had plush grasses, and he and his wife made a home for themselves near the city of Sodom. The plains of the east were indeed rich and fertile. But the people in Sodom were wicked—horribly wicked.

● ● ●

Several years passed. Lot flourished in the east and Abram in the west. But then war broke out.

"Sodom has fallen," a messenger reported to Abram. "Lot and his family have been captured."

Abram frowned knowingly. Without delay, he summoned his men to arms—now a formidable brigade of over three hundred well-trained warriors. He led them with a secret speed in pursuit of Lot's captors. In the night, he divided his forces and surprised the enemy from two sides at once. He routed them and rescued Lot and his family and all their possessions from the armies who had plundered Sodom.

That evening Abram spoke quietly to Lot by firelight. "You must leave Sodom. You and your family are not safe there. Pick another place to live. There are plenty of options. If you stay, you're bound to get into more trouble."

"We've moved enough already," Lot disapproved. "Plus, we've got two little girls now. We're a growing family and need to put down some roots."

Abram was too exhausted to argue. Besides, Lot's words drained the life from him. For he knew he and Sarai were not a growing family. The promise remained unfulfilled.

When he returned home, Abram fell on his knees and entreated God. "I have no children. My servant Eliezer will inherit everything I own. Yes, I've acquired much, thanks to your hand of blessing. But you've given me no offspring, so a mere house servant is going to get it all."

"Don't worry," God replied. "He won't be your heir. A son of your own flesh and blood will be your heir. Look up at the sky. Count the stars. Number them one by one. You can't do it, can you? I promise your descendants will be as numerous as the stars of heaven. And remember, I'm the God who led you from your home in Haran and gave you this land."

"Yes," Abram acknowledged. "I am living in the land now. But what will happen when I die? How do I know that my children—which I still don't have, mind you—will possess this land and own it forever?"

"Bring me a heifer, a goat, and a ram, each three years old," God answered.

Abram fetched the animals.

"Now kill each one and cut their carcasses in half and lay each half opposite the other, with a narrow path down the middle."

So Abram slaughtered each of the beasts with a quick slash to their necks. Then he took the knife and ripped the blade down the breastbone of each carcass, slicing the animal in two. Blood drenched the earth. Soon, birds of prey circled overhead and descended on the freshly butchered meat. But Abram drove them away.

As night fell, a deep, thick sleep overcame Abram and terror filled his soul. Then God spoke to Abram:

"I hereby establish a covenant between you and me. I promise to make you the father of many nations. To mark this covenant, I am changing your name from Abram to Abraham. I will make you very fruitful. Nations and kings will come from you. Thus, this covenant is also with your descendants, a covenant that will last forever and ever. I vow to be your God and the God of all your offspring who will come after you. I will give to you and your descendants this land where you are now living, this whole country of Canaan, to own forever.

"You and your descendants who will come after you have one requirement in order to demonstrate your loyalty to the covenant: Each male among you must be circumcised. You must cut off the flesh of your foreskin as a sign of the covenant between me and you. From generation to generation, every male child must be circumcised. Therefore, your bodies will bear the mark of my everlasting covenant. Any male who fails to be circumcised will be cut off from the covenant family. Thus I have spoken."

When it was pitch black, God sent a flaming torch that passed between the severed animal corpses. By this sacred sign God sealed his covenant with Abraham.

2. A SON, A PROMISE, A FIRESTORM

When Abraham awoke from his sleep, he felt a strange sense of tranquility and a quiet confidence in God's promise. But the next morning when he explained to Sarai the reason for the dried blood on his clothes and told her all that occurred and everything God revealed to him, she was not so quiet or so confident.

"Do we have children? Have I ever even been pregnant? . . . No and no!" Sarai said, her voice rising. "God made this covenant with you back in Haran. But that was ten years ago. Nothing has happened so far. Doesn't God understand that in order to have a nation of descendants, you must first have *one* descendent?" Sarai sighed, closing her eyes. "Look, I know God said he would make your children into a great nation, but God has prevented me from having children. So I don't understand how he plans to keep his covenant." There was silence as they both gazed at the dew on the green pasture.

"Abram—I mean Abraham—I think maybe," Sarai continued cautiously, "I think maybe your new name means we should find a new way to have children."

Abraham tilted his head to one side, his brow furrowed. He only knew of one way.

"My servant Hagar, the one we acquired in Egypt, is a young, strong woman. I'm sure she could conceive. Why don't you sleep with her and perhaps we can have a child through her."

Abraham looked at his wife incredulously.

"I had to, you know, do things in Egypt with Pharaoh to keep you alive. Now it's your turn to do things with Hagar to keep my hopes alive," she said. "It's for the sake of the covenant."

So that afternoon they told Hagar of the plan. A week later, when the time was right, Abraham and Hagar slept together, and she conceived.

As soon as she announced her pregnancy, Hagar's attitude and demeanor changed, for she knew her status had changed. She was no longer a servant girl; she was the bearer of the divine promise. And she would be treated as such. She ignored Sarai's requests, talked constantly about the joys and trials of pregnancy, and took every opportunity to show off her new condition.

Sarai was furious. "This is your fault!" she screamed at Abraham when he returned home one afternoon. "I'm suffering this abuse because of you. I put my servant in bed with you, and the minute she knows she's pregnant, she treats me like I'm nobody. I'm not going to stand for this! We'll let God decide who's right here—me or you."

"She's your servant," Abraham said calmly. "Do whatever you want with her. It was your idea in the first place."

So Sarai resolved to make Hagar's life miserable. And she did. Every day. She made Hagar carry twice as much water from the well, replaced her afternoon nap with extra chores, and limited her meals, taken alone, to bread and a few vegetables.

It was not long before Hagar ran away. "This physical and emotional stress," she muttered, "is going to kill the child in my belly."

Hagar had not gotten far when the angel of God met her. "Where are you going? What are you doing?" he asked the disheveled and distraught woman as she sat near a spring of water.

"I am escaping from Sarai—she's bent on destroying me and my baby. I was only doing what she asked me to do."

"Go back to Sarai and submit to her," the angel instructed.

Hagar's head sunk.

"I will give you more descendants than you can count," the angel continued. "You are carrying a little boy. When he is born, name him Ishmael, for God has heard your cries of distress. This Ishmael will be something of a wild man—a real fighter—always stirring up trouble and always at odds with all his relatives."

Hagar raised her eyes. Her countenance brightened. "God really does see me. And I see him!"

So Hagar did as the angel commanded. A few months later, Hagar bore a son for Abraham, and he named him Ishmael. Abraham was eighty-six years old.

● ● ●

Over the next thirteen years, Ishmael grew into a strong, fierce, and independent young man. Hagar was a proud, happy, and good mother.

Sarai remained childless.

Abraham prospered and was pleased to have a son through whom God could build his family.

One day as Abraham tended his crops, God spoke to him. "Your wife Sarai is also part of my covenant with you. She will no longer be named Sarai. But Sarah. I will bless her and give you a son by her. Yes, I will bless her abundantly. She will become the mother of many nations. Kings of nations will be numbered among her progeny."

Abraham bowed to the ground. But inwardly he laughed, How can I father a son at one hundred years of age? And how will Sarah conceive at ninety? Then he said to God, "Please continue to bless Ishmael. Keep him alive and well."

"Are you hearing me?" God asked. "Do you understand what I'm telling you? Your wife Sarah will bear you a son. You will name him Isaac. I will establish my covenant with him and all his descendants—a covenant that lasts forever. And as for Ishmael, yes, I will bless him too, as you've requested. I will multiply his offspring and he will become a great nation. But Isaac, not Ishmael, is the son through whom I will fulfill my covenant with you. Isaac will be born to you and Sarah in a year's time."

Abraham stood there alone among the stalks of grain. "What am I to do now?" he wondered aloud. "Should I tell Sarah? Should I let it be a surprise? What if it never happens?"

A few days later, God appeared again. The sun was high and hot in the clear blue sky as Abraham reclined at the entrance to his tent. He looked up and saw three men approaching. He recognized one as God himself. The other two, he thought, were angels. Abraham got up and ran to meet them. He bowed and said, "Please stay here with us. Rest under this tree while I get water for you to clean up and food to refresh you."

"Yes, please do," the three men said.

Abraham rushed back into the tent. "Hurry," he said to Sarah. "Get some of our best flour and make bread." Then he hastened to the cattle pen and picked out his best calf and gave it to his servant who quickly prepared it. As soon as the meal was ready, Abraham served the freshly baked bread and roasted meat, along with some yogurt and milk. As they ate, the visitors asked, "Where is your wife?"

"She's inside the tent," Abraham answered.

Then God said to Abraham, "I am coming back about this time next year. When I do, Sarah will have a son."

"Yes, I believe your word, God. But are you going to tell Sarah?"

God gestured toward the tent. Abraham turned to see his wife standing in the doorway, her fingers covering her parted lips. She said nothing, but laughed to herself, How can an old, dried out woman like me have a baby, especially when my husband is even older?

Abraham looked back toward God, who asked him, "Why did Sarah laugh? Why does she think she's too old to become pregnant? Is there anything too difficult for me? Mark my words, I will return this time next year, and Sarah will be carrying a little boy in her arms."

"I didn't laugh," Sarah spoke up, her hands trembling.

"Yes, you did laugh," God replied.

Sarah turned and disappeared into the tent. Abraham remained with the three guests until they finished eating. Then they got up to leave.

"We are going to Sodom," God told Abraham.

"I will see you off," Abraham said.

So the four of them left Abraham's house, walking toward the cities of the plain. God was considering how much he should tell Abraham about why they were going to Sodom. I will make Abraham a strong and mighty nation, and all the nations of the world will be blessed through him, God said to himself. He will be the one to teach his family to observe my way of life by living rightly and justly. He is the one with whom I have made my covenant. Yes, I must reveal to him my intentions.

God sent the two angels on ahead while he and Abraham turned off the road. "The sins of Sodom and the neighboring Gomorrah have come to my attention," God explained. "The wickedness in those cities is immense, so I'm going there to see for myself. Then I will decide what to do."

"What if it's as bad as you fear?" the old man asked.

God looked Abraham squarely in the eye.

Abraham knew the answer. He closed his eyes and set his jaw. "Will you destroy the righteous along with the wicked? What if you were to find fifty righteous people living there—would you still sweep away the whole city and not spare it for the sake of the fifty? Far be it from you to destroy the good and bad alike as if there were no difference between them. Don't you—the judge of all the Earth—judge with justice?"

"If I find fifty worthy people in Sodom, I will spare the whole city for their sake," God answered.

Abraham took a deep breath and spoke again. "I know I'm a mere human, made only of dust and ashes. But, please, let me continue speaking. What if there are only forty-five good people? Would you destroy the entire city then?"

"No, I won't destroy it if there are forty-five."

"What if there are forty?"

"No."

Abraham pressed further. "Alright then, what if there are thirty decent people?"

"Then I would save the whole city for the sake of the thirty."

"Please don't get upset with me, God. But I must ask, what about for twenty?"

"Same thing. No destruction."

Abraham's heart pounded. "If there are only ten virtuous people in the whole city of Sodom, what then?"

"Again, for the sake of those ten, I will not destroy it," God replied.

Abraham wiped sweat from his brow. God looked at him intently for a moment and then turned and went on his way. Abraham stood there watching. He was worn out, for it had been an exhausting day. A visit from

God. The promise of a miraculous new life in Sarah's womb. The pending destruction of Lot and everyone in Sodom. Abraham wasn't sure how to feel. And he wondered what God was thinking on his way toward Sodom.

• • •

About the time Abraham arrived back home that evening, the two angels reached Sodom. Lot happened to be sitting by the gate of the city. When he saw the angels, he arose to welcome them. Doing obeisance, he said, "Please come to my house and stay the night."

"No," the angels said. "We will spend the night in the city square." But Lot insisted they come home with him—the city streets were no place for strangers in Sodom—and so the angels agreed. Lot and his wife and their two daughters prepared a meal for their guests, and they all ate together.

As they were about to retire for the evening, there was a loud bang on the door. Men from Sodom, both young and old, surrounded the house. "Where are the men who are staying with you tonight?" they shouted. "Bring them out here so we can have our way with them—in every imaginable way." The crowd was rowdy and ravenous.

Lot stepped outside and shut the door behind him. "Please, my friends, don't do this wicked thing! Look, I have two virgin daughters. Let me bring them out to you, and you can do whatever you want to them. But these men are my guests, and I am responsible for protecting them."

"Get out of the way! You're a foreigner and now you're going to tell *us* what to do? We'll treat you far worse than those visitors of yours!" Several men attacked Lot and tried to break into the house. Suddenly the two angels reached out, pulled Lot back inside, and bolted the door shut. Then the angels struck the mob of men with blindness. They were instantly disoriented and confused, and groped their way back to their dark abodes.

Lot lay on the floor, his chest heaving; a trickle of blood dripped from his nose. His wife and daughters huddled in the corner.

"God knows about the wickedness of this place and he's sent us here to destroy the entire city," the angels said to Lot. "Do you have any other relatives in town? If so, you need to get them out of here now."

"There are only two others—the young men pledged to marry my daughters."

"You must find them tonight," the angels urged.

So a few hours before sunrise, Lot slipped out of his house and awoke the two men. "We've got to get out of Sodom immediately. Hurry up and come with me. God is about to break forth!"

But they thought he was only joking and went back to sleep.

At dawn, the two angels commanded Lot, "Quick! Take your wife and children and flee before it's too late and you get swept away in the annihilation."

Lot hesitated.

So the angels grabbed Lot, his wife, and his daughters and rushed them to safety outside the city. "Run for your life! Don't look back! Don't stop anywhere on the plain. Run for the hills or you'll be swept away in the destruction."

The four of them obeyed and fled in the early morning light. But as they went, Lot's wife looked back. There was her home. In that instant, she turned into a pillar of salt.

Her husband and daughters never stopped. It was midafternoon when Lot and the two girls reached the foothills. When they did, God rained down burning sulfur and fire on Sodom and Gomorrah. The sky filled with every shade of red and orange. Smoke and ashes billowed from the earth; glowing rock spewed from the burnt towns. So God utterly destroyed Sodom and Gomorrah, incinerating all the people and every plant of the ground.

3. PARENTS AND CHILDREN IN CRISIS

Early the next day Abraham went to the place where he had talked with God just two days before. He looked down on the plain towards Sodom and Gomorrah and saw clouds of smoke and cinders rising into the air. It was all gone. The once bustling and verdant plain was black with death. Abraham slumped to the ground. Sorrow and questions filled his heart. What had happened to his nephew Lot and his family? Dead, he presumed. And what about everyone else—could there not have been ten righteous people in Sodom? Impossible, he reasoned.

Abraham never learned the fate of his relatives in Sodom. He never knew God spared them on his account. Lot and his daughters were alive, but barely; for their life soon became a miserable one. They made their home in the lonely and desolate caves among the hills. With his wife dead, Lot fell into despair, as did his daughters who had lost the men they were to marry. The depression numbed them. They wasted away.

After a few months, the older daughter said to her sister, "There isn't one man anywhere in this entire area we can marry. The only chance of keeping our family name alive is to have children with our father, and soon he will be too old to procreate. Let's get him drunk and sleep with him so we can get pregnant. That's the only way to preserve our lineage."

That night, as the candles flickered and the darkness grew, the two young women poured glass after glass of wine for their father. When it was time for bed, the older daughter undressed and slept with him. Lot was oblivious to all that took place.

"We had sex," the older sister said to the younger the next morning. "Tonight is your turn. We can do the same thing this evening." And so they did.

Nine months later, almost a year to the day after the destruction of Sodom, the older daughter gave birth to a son and named him Moab. The younger also had a son and named him Ammi. The boys would later become the fathers of the nations of Moab and Ammon.

● ● ●

About the same time Lot's daughters conceived nations in their womb, Sarah conceived one in hers. For God kept his word and did for Sarah exactly what he promised. Sarah became pregnant and, in the early hours of a cool spring morning, gave birth to a son for Abraham. The midwife brought the infant to Abraham, who was now a century old. He held the tiny baby in his arms, nuzzling his soft, pink cheek.

"Your name will be Isaac, a reminder that God has not held our laughter against us," Abraham whispered. "And may he fill your life with love and laughter." He then fell asleep with his son on his wrinkled chest.

When he awoke, Sarah was swaddling the boy, overcome with joy. "God has blessed me with laughter, and all who hear about Isaac's birth will laugh with me. Who would've thought that I would one day nurse a baby? Yet here I am—I've given a son to the old man!"

Isaac was a healthy and happy baby. When he was several years old and about to be weaned, Abraham planned a grand feast to mark the occasion. But on the morning of the celebration, Sarah saw Ishmael poking fun at Isaac.

Now Sarah had come to terms with Hagar and her son, who had grown into a rugged boy of fourteen. But seeds of resentment and discontent had begun to flourish in Sarah's heart. She and Hagar both knew Ishmael would forever be Abraham's firstborn son, with all the special rights and blessings that went with such a position. So when Sarah saw Ishmael making sport of her son, it sparked a venomous rage.

"Get rid of that slave woman and her son!" she screamed at Abraham as he waited for the guests to arrive. "No child of a lowly servant will share the inheritance with my son!" She stood glaring at her husband. "Banish them! Kick them out of this household now!"

Abraham remained motionless, his face deadpan. Inside he recoiled in pain—Ishmael was his son. All along he had been afraid this moment might come, but the timing could not have been worse.

That evening after the feast, God spoke to Abraham. "Don't be upset about Ishmael and his mother. Do whatever Sarah tells you. Your descendants will come through Isaac. But rest assured I will also make a nation from the descendants of Hagar's son, for I know you love him too. But you must do as Sarah said."

Twice Abraham opened his mouth to protest, but no words came out.

The next morning Abraham prepared food and a jug of water and strapped them on Hagar's back. Hagar knew what was happening, for she had heard Sarah's outburst. With a lump in his throat, Abraham embraced his son goodbye. Then he sent away the boy and his mother, just as Sarah ordered.

Hagar and Ishmael went south into the desert toward Egypt. Soon the little bit of bread and water were gone. They were tired and listless; death was imminent. Hagar left her son sitting under a shrub, shaded from the noonday blaze, while she trudged a short distance away. She slumped to the ground and burst into tears. "I can't watch my boy die. I can't. How could it come to this? I gave Abraham a son and raised him well. Now here I am sent off to die for no reason."

Then the angel of God called out from the skies, "Hagar, Hagar, what's wrong? Do not be afraid. God has seen you and your son. Now get up. Go get Ishmael and take care of him. Remember, I will make him into a great nation."

Hagar looked up and in the distance saw a spring. She hurried to it and eagerly gulped the cool water; she then filled her jar and ran back to Ishmael. "God is with us; God is with us," she murmured, cradling his sweaty head against her chest.

And so God was with Ishmael as he grew up in the wilderness. Ishmael became an expert hunter with the bow. When the time came, Hagar arranged for him to marry an Egyptian girl.

Abraham never learned any of this. He had forever lost his firstborn son. He mourned for Ishmael for a long time. But he took solace in God's promise to bless the boy. Plus, he still had Isaac who was becoming a delightful child. Just the same, Ishmael was his son. It had been a trial for Abraham.

● ● ●

As Abraham slowly adjusted to life without Ishmael—the hands of time doing their work—God laid on him another trial.

"Abraham!" God called.

"Yes, here I am," he replied looking up from the fence he was mending.

"Take your son, your only son, Isaac whom you love so dearly, and go to the region of Moriah. Sacrifice your son to me as a burnt offering on one of the mountains which I will point out to you."

Abraham bent over, hands on his knees. After a few moments he slowly straightened up. "God," he sighed, "I've done everything you've asked of me. I've left my homeland, put faith in your covenant, waited years for a child, banished one son from my household. And now . . ." his voice trailed off. He waited for God to say something. But God did not.

The next morning, Abraham arose very early and saddled his donkey. He summoned two servants and his son Isaac; then he gathered wood for the burnt offering, and they set out for the region of Moriah, several days off.

When they arrived, God showed him the mountain on which to make the sacrifice. "Stay here with the donkey," Abraham instructed his servants. "The boy and I are headed up to worship. Afterwards we will come back." Abraham took the logs for the burnt offering and gave them to Isaac, while he himself carried the knife.

As the two of them walked on together, side-by-side, Isaac said, "Father?"

"Yes, my son."

"We have the kindling to make a fire, but where is the sheep for the burnt offering?"

"God will provide the lamb," Abraham answered. And they continued walking together.

Finally they came to the designated place. Abraham built a small earthen altar while Isaac ate a snack in the shade of a nearby tree. Abraham laid the wood on the altar. Then he sat down next to his son to rest. And to wait. The breeze blew; the late afternoon clouds thickened; the birds soared overhead. And he waited.

Then Abraham turned abruptly, and, taking some cord, bound Isaac's hands and feet and laid him on top of the wood on the altar. He clutched the knife. Then he raised his hand to slaughter his son.

At that instant, the angel of God called from the skies, "Abraham, Abraham! Stop! Don't lay a hand on the boy!"

Abraham, shaking, dropped the knife and crumpled to the ground.

"Now I know you are truly obedient and faithful," the angel said, "for you have been willing to sacrifice your son, your only son, as an offering to God."

Abraham looked up and there, directly in front of him, was a ram caught by its horns in a thicket. He got up quickly and untied Isaac. Then he took the ram and sacrificed it as a burnt offering instead of his son. As the flesh roasted on the altar, the angel again called from the sky, "This is what God himself says: Because you have obeyed and not withheld your son from me, I solemnly swear I will bless you and make your descendants as numerous as the stars in the sky and as countless as the grains of sand on the seashore. Your children's children will take possession of this land, and through your offspring, all nations of the earth will be blessed, because you've heeded my word."

Abraham held Isaac tightly. "See, God has provided," he whispered hoarsely. "God has provided."

Then the two of them descended the mountain together.

4. ISAAC AND REBEKAH

Some time later, Sarah died. Abraham purchased a large plot of land from the Canaanites near the city of Hebron to the south so he could give her an honorable burial. "You will be the mother of many nations. Our descendants will be as numerous as the stars of the sky and the sands of the sea," Abraham said as he laid Sarah to rest. "Your name and heritage will live on forever, your legacy to eternity." He wiped a tear from his eye, lingering at her grave.

He and Isaac mourned for weeks.

"Isaac, my son," Abraham said one day as the two prepared dinner together, "my days are numbered. Soon you will bury me alongside your mother. God has blessed me in countless ways. Now it's time to find for you a good wife so that through you God can fulfill his covenant."

The next day Abraham summoned his servant Eliezer and said to him, "I have put you in charge of all that I own. You've earned my respect and confidence, and so now I'm entrusting you with the most important matter of all. Swear to me in God's name that you will go back to my homeland, to Haran, and find a wife for Isaac. I do not want him to marry a girl from here in the land of Canaan."

"I swear I will do as you say," Eliezer said solemnly. "But what if the woman is unwilling to leave her home and family and return with me? Should I then take Isaac back to your native land?"

"No. Never. Under no circumstance are you to take Isaac back there. Look, God took me from my native country years ago and he promised to give this land, the land of Canaan, to my children. God will be with you in your search for a wife for Isaac. If the woman is unwilling to come back, then you're free from your oath. But, I repeat, do not ever take Isaac to Haran."Then with arm outstretched and finger pointed firmly downward, he added, "This here is the land where God will build his nation through Isaac."

Immediately Eliezer began preparations. He loaded ten camels with lavish gifts for the family of the future and unknown bride and then headed off.

He arrived on the outskirts of Haran about dusk. He and his animals were parched, for the trip had been a long one. The women of the town, as they did every evening, came to the main well to draw water. Eliezer whispered a prayer, "O God, God of my master Abraham, please make my mission a success. Show me which girl is to be Isaac's wife. Let this be the sign. When I ask a young woman, 'May I please have a drink,' have her say, 'Drink, and I'll water your camels as well.' Then I will know she is the wife you have chosen for Isaac."

As he looked up from his prayer, a beautiful girl—elegant and dignified—arrived at the well with a jug on her shoulder. She drew water and was about to leave. Eliezer hurried over. "May I please have a drink of water?"

"Yes, drink," she said with a pleasant smile. When Eliezer had taken all he wanted, the girl said, "Let me fetch some water for your camels too, until they've had all they need." She poured the remaining water into the large stone trough for the animals and scurried back to the well. To and fro she went, filling her jug and emptying it into the trough, her long brown hair blowing in the wind. Eliezer watched, marveling at her grace and strength. Surely this is the woman, he thought. But will she be willing to return with me to be Isaac's wife?

As the last camel finished, Eliezer approached her. She was breathing deeply, perspiration glistening on her forehead. "I present to you this gold nose ring and these two gold bracelets," he said extending his hand toward her. "What is your name? And whose daughter are you? And is there room in your father's house for us to stay the night?"

"I am Rebekah, the daughter of Bethuel," she said cupping the jewelry in her hands. "And, yes, there's plenty of space in our house, and lots of straw and feed for the animals too."

She stared at him for a moment and then, leaving her pitcher at Eliezer's feet, turned and sprinted home. Eliezer knelt to the ground and breathed a prayer, "Thank you, God, for your faithfulness to my master Abraham, for you've led me straight to the woman who is to be Isaac's wife."

● ● ●

Now Rebekah's father, Bethuel, was old, so her brother Laban was in charge of the household affairs. When Laban, a tall man with a narrow face, heard Rebekah's report of the evening's events and saw the beautiful ring and bracelets, he hurried out to meet Eliezer who remained at the well. "Please do come stay with us. There is more than enough room for you and your camels."

"I'm glad to see you. I did not know where to go," Eliezer grinned.

When they arrived at the house, servants unloaded the camels, fed them, and brought water for Eliezer to wash. Afterwards they all sat down for a meal.

"Wait," Eliezer said. "Before we eat, I must tell you why I am here."

"Please do," Laban said. Rebekah leaned in.

"I am the servant of Abraham who lives in the land of Canaan," he began. "God has blessed my master abundantly, and he has become very wealthy. He has countless sheep and cattle, camels and donkeys, silver and gold, and many servants. Sarah, his wife, gave birth to a son Isaac, their first and only child, when she and Abraham were quite old. Sarah has since died. Abraham too is nearing death, so he's sent me back here to Haran to find a wife for Isaac. He insisted his son not marry a woman from Canaan. As I approached your city this afternoon, I asked God to give me a sign showing me the right girl. The one who offered not only to give me a drink, but also to water my camels was to be God's chosen one."

Eliezer paused and looked at Rebekah. Then turning back to Laban, he said, "I believe you know the rest of the story." They all gazed in silence at one another—the old father was as alert as he had been in days. "Now, my master has also insisted that the bride-to-be return with me to Canaan. Abraham will not allow his son to come and live here." He stopped again, sat back, and folded his hands in his lap. "That is my story. What do you think? Will you allow Rebekah to come with me? I realize it's a big decision, but I ask that you please make it quickly so I can determine what to do next."

"This is all clearly from God," Bethuel said slowly. "You have said more than you know. For my father, Nahor, is Abraham's brother—though we knew him as Abram. He left here many years ago. And now, after all this time, our families will be reunited in marriage. God has led you not only to Abraham's homeland, but even to his extended family. God is indeed behind all this."

Rebekah sat transfixed.

"My father is right," Laban said. "You may take Rebekah to be Isaac's wife. How could we possibly say no, for this is God's doing."

At this, Eliezer bowed to Laban and Bethuel, and in thankfulness to God. He hurried out to the camels and soon returned with a beautiful boxful of expensive silver and gold and a stack of fine garments which he presented to Rebekah. He also gave costly gifts to Laban, Bethuel, and Rebekah's mother. Then they ate and drank and celebrated into the night.

Eliezer arose before dawn the next morning to prepare for the long journey home. Rebekah's mother tiptoed to him. "Please let Rebekah stay a while, say another ten days or so. Could you do that?" she demurred. "This has been so sudden and we may never see her again."

"I understand," Eliezer replied. "But I am eager to return home. Please do not delay us. God has worked out everything perfectly so far."

The frail woman grimaced. "Can we at least ask Rebekah what she wants?"

Eliezer nodded reluctantly.

So they called Rebekah. She looked tenderly at her mother. "I am ready to go now."

Later that morning, Laban, Bethuel, and his wife said their last good-byes. "May you be safe and prosperous," Laban said, putting his hands on Rebekah's shoulders. "May your descendants be numerous and triumphant, countless and mighty." Rebekah smiled, her eyes moist.

Then she mounted her camel and headed south under the giant sky, following Eliezer on the same road Abraham had taken out of Haran more than sixty years before. And so Rebekah went to Canaan and became Isaac's wife. And Isaac loved her.

Abraham was overjoyed. And it was not long before the ancient patriarch, happy and content, expired peacefully in his sleep. Isaac sent word to Ishmael who came to pay his last respects to the father he had not seen in years. Together Abraham's two sons buried him next to his wife Sarah.

● ● ●

"We are nearly out of food," Rebekah said to Isaac one morning soon after Abraham's funeral. "I'm not sure I'll have enough flour after this week. A wife has to have flour to bake," she said wryly, not grasping the gravity of the circumstances. She always had all she needed in Haran.

Isaac filled his cheeks with the parched air and slowly exhaled. "When my father and mother arrived here years ago—long before I was born—they had to leave almost immediately because of a famine. It looks like we might be forced to do the same thing. There is one difference, though. God told me we are not to go to Egypt, as my parents did. No, we are to stay here in Canaan; there is no famine in the region of Gerar, not too far south of here. We will go there, and soon."

About a week later, Isaac and Rebekah arrived in Gerar. Isaac, like his father years before him, fretted that his beautiful wife would be stolen by the local men. He knew what his father had done, and he planned to employ the same risky ruse if need be. After all, he was reminded many times how well it turned out for his father. "See that herd over there?" Abraham would say. "It all came from one bull I got from Pharaoh." Then he would laugh.

Isaac and Rebekah settled in Gerar. Time passed, and Isaac nearly forgot about the initial fear for his life on account of Rebekah's splendor. But one day when several men from the area inquired about her, the words rolled off his tongue with ease and confidence. "She is my sister."

"I see," one of the men said. "Perhaps we should give first dibs to our king, Abimelech. I'm sure he will want to have a look."

"I might like to take a look myself," another man said salaciously. "If she's your sister, presumably you'd be happy to have her married off."

Isaac gave a quick nod before turning to escape the encounter. He did not tell his wife what happened.

The next afternoon, Isaac and Rebekah lay together in the shade, playfully touching and fondling one another. The vagrant wind and soft caresses distracted them from the sound of Abimelech and his men drawing near.

"So she's really your wife!" the king called out when he saw them.

Isaac jumped up, pulling his clothes around him.

"Why did you let on that she was your sister?" Abimelech demanded.

"I thought someone might murder me," Isaac answered. "You kill a husband to have his wife, but you don't kill a brother to have his sister."

"Yes, but what about us?" Abimelech exclaimed. "I or any one of these men here could've have taken her and slept with her. In that case, it would've been your fault for whatever bad things might've befallen us."

Isaac said nothing. Rebekah sat still in the wavy grass.

Abimelech turned around and faced his company of men. Then he said loudly, "I hereby decree that anyone who bothers this man or his wife in any way will surely be put to death." With that, he glanced over his shoulder at the couple and rode off.

Isaac felt Rebekah tugging at his coat from the ground behind him. He turned and fell into her arms. Laughing.

So Isaac and Rebekah remained in Gerar, and God blessed them there. They planted crops that yielded a huge harvest. They accumulated flocks and herds and many servants, so much so that the people began to envy their vast wealth. Thus, like his father Abraham, Isaac became rich in a foreign land. And like his father, he had a barren wife whose infertility threatened the fulfillment of God's covenant. For Rebekah was unable to conceive.

5. TWIN BOYS

Early one morning after they moved back to their home territory in Canaan, Isaac rose and walked along a winding path that ended atop a rocky hill. The mound was his special place of respite and meditation. On this day, his heart was burdened for his wife who longed for children. Isaac pleaded with God on Rebekah's behalf. Several hours passed before he made his way back home.

God heard Isaac's prayer, and Rebekah soon conceived.

Her initial joy, however, was replaced by crushing pains of pregnancy. She was either about to miscarry or die from the agony in her womb. In desperation, she went to Isaac's holy hill, dropped to the ground, and cried out to God, "If this is the way it's going to be, I cannot go on living! Please, God, tell me what's happening. The pain is too much."

"Two nations are wrestling within you, two peoples are struggling in your womb, and they will forever be divided," God answered. "One will overcome the other, and the older will serve the younger."

Rebekah breathed slowly. God had spoken directly to her. Though the sickness and discomfort would persist, so would her resolve.

When the time came for Rebekah to deliver, she gave birth to twin boys, just as she anticipated. The first one came out with a reddish hue and covered in thick hair as if wearing a furry coat. The other baby came right behind, clutching his brother's heel. The older boy they named Esau on account of his color; the younger they named Jacob because he grasped his brother's foot.

As the boys grew, Esau became a skilled hunter, a true outdoorsman. He would go away on his own for weeks at a time, living off the land. Esau was barrel-chested, ruddy, strong, and given to few words. Jacob, on the other hand, preferred to stay near the house. He enjoyed cooking and lively conversation. His face was soft and smooth, his mind witty and sharp.

Their father Isaac loved Esau. Their mother Rebekah loved Jacob.

One cold, blustery evening Esau returned from a long and unsuccessful hunt. He had barely eaten in days; he was weary and ravenously hungry. The smells of stew—Jacob's stew—wafted in the air.

"Please give me some of that red stuff," Esau said, barging into Jacob's quarters and pointing to the boiling pot. Jacob sized him up as he continued stirring the meat. "I'm starving. Please, something to eat now," Esau groaned, hardly able to form the words.

Jacob worked the broth a bit longer. Then he looked up and said, "Let's make a deal." A smile widened across his face.

Esau stared at the steaming stew.

"I will give you all the food you want," Jacob said, "if you sell me your birthright—the double portion of the inheritance you are to receive as the firstborn."

"I'm about to starve to death," Esau grunted. "What good is a birthright to a dead man?"

"Good point. So it's a deal then." Jacob scooped a heap of stew into a bowl. "I save your life now. You give me your birthright. And we are even."

"Yes, yes," Esau replied, reaching frantically for the bowl.

Jacob pulled it back, his face suddenly dead serious. "Swear it to me, Esau."

"I swear it! I swear it!" the older brother yelled in one gasping fit of energy.

"Good," Jacob said, extending the bubbling stew and warm bread to his brother.

Esau ate and drank greedily. Then he arose and left.

And so it was that Esau sold his birthright. But he remained in line to receive the special paternal blessing bestowed on the firstborn. And Esau knew his father's blessing would indeed be special, for it was based on a sacred covenant with God—a covenant that began with his grandfather Abraham. Esau had lost the birthright, but the blessing of countless descendants who would one day possess the land of Canaan was still his. He thought of it often on his solitary hunts.

One autumn day Isaac summoned Esau and said, "I am an old man. My eyes have failed me and death is near. Now, my son, go into the field and hunt me some game. Then prepare the animal—seasoned to taste just as I like—and bring it to me to eat. Then I will bless you before I die."

Now Rebekah was never far from her husband, since his blindness left him in need of assistance with the basic tasks of life. As a result, she overheard Isaac's directions to Esau. As soon as her older boy had gone off in search of the desired meat, Rebekah hurried to Jacob who was sewing a garment. "Listen to me carefully, son," she began. "Your father has instructed your brother to hunt some game and prepare a meal so he can bestow upon him the special blessing." She pulled Jacob up by the elbow. "Listen to me, Jacob. And do exactly as I tell you. Go to the flock and slaughter two young goats. Pick out the best ones. I'll prepare a savory meal with them, the kind your father loves. Then you can take it and serve it to your father, so that he blesses you first."

"But Mother," Jacob dissented, "Esau is a rough, hairy man, and I have smooth skin. When my father touches me, he will think I'm tricking him, and I will bring down a curse on myself instead of a blessing."

"If it comes to that," Rebekah replied coldly, "then I will take the curse on myself. Now, just do what I say. Go get the two goats." She took Jacob's face in her hands and kissed his brow.

Obediently, Jacob ran out, killed the two small animals, and brought them to his mother. "While I cook the meal," Rebekah ordered, "you take the goat skins and clean them up; we can put them on you when you serve your father."

As soon as the food was ready, Rebekah fastened the skins to Jacob's hands and neck. Then she draped one of Esau's hunting coats around him. She placed the hearty meal with fresh bread into Jacob's hands and whispered, "Hurry. Go."

"My father," Jacob said as he entered Isaac's room.

"Here I am," he replied. "Which son are you?"

"I am Esau, your firstborn. I did what you asked of me. Sit up and eat of my game so that you may give me your blessing."

"How have you returned so quickly, my boy?"

"God was with me."

"Come here, son," Isaac said. "Let me touch you—are you really Esau?" Jacob held his breath as his father stroked the goat fur and tugged at the coat. "The voice is the voice of Jacob but the hands are those of Esau," Isaac deliberated. "Are you truly Esau?"

"Yes. I am," Jacob said.

"Well, then, bring the food so I can eat of the game and bestow upon you the special blessing."

Jacob fidgeted as his father slowly slurped the juicy meat.

After he had eaten the meal and drunk the wine, Isaac said, "Come close, son, so I can kiss you." Jacob bent down stiffly as his father kissed his hands and head.

"Ah, yes, it is the smell of Esau," Isaac affirmed, holding the coat to his cheek. The scent evoked the words of the blessing. He extended his hands over the head of Jacob who knelt to the ground. "The smell of my son is like the smell of the field, the land that God has blessed and will give to your descendants. May God be with you and make you fruitful and increase your offspring until you become a great nation. May he give you and your descendants the blessing given to Abraham, so that you may take possession of the land, of this soil that is engrained in your garment.

"May God grant you the dew of heaven and fruits of the earth. May peoples serve you and nations honor you. Your mother's sons will bow down before you, your brothers will be ruled by you. Those who curse you will be cursed, and those who bless you will be blessed. Forever and ever. Amen."

And so the blessing was bestowed.

Jacob had scarcely left the room when Esau came in from his hunt. He prepared a meal and brought it to Isaac. "Father, arise and eat of the game I have cooked for you; then you may bless me as you promised."

"Who are you?" Isaac grimaced.

"What do you mean? I am your son Esau, your firstborn."

"Esau?" Isaac choked, starting to tremble.

"Yes, I am Esau. I've done just as you said."

"Then who was it who just left?" Isaac stammered. "I blessed him—he's blessed forever! The words cannot be revoked."

Esau broke into a wild, uncontrollable weeping. "Oh, my father! Bless me! Bless me too, please! How can this be?"

"Your brother," Isaac said bitterly, "has deceitfully stolen your blessing."

"He wears his name well," Esau cried, "for twice he has grasped at everything that was rightfully mine. First he took my birthright and now he's taken my blessing."

"And I've made him your master," Isaac said shaking his head. "I've given it all away."

Esau crumpled to the ground and sobbed inconsolably, "Don't you have any blessing left for me, Father? Please bless me, my father! Give me something!"

The old man sat quietly. Then he stretched his hands over his older son and spoke gently, "You will live far from earth's bounty, remote from the dew of heaven. You will live by your sword, and you will serve your brother. But in time, you will break the yoke of your brother, and it will indeed be broken."

Esau arose and stormed from the room, seething with anger. "I will wait until our father dies, and then I will kill Jacob. Then we'll see who gets the birthright and the blessing. It will indeed be as I said: Dead men get nothing."

Rebekah, again, overheard the conversation between her husband and older son. Later that night, she slinked into Jacob's quarters. "Jacob, Jacob," she said stirring him awake. "You must listen to me once more. Esau is plotting revenge. He's going to kill you. You must get out of here now. Go back to Haran, to my brother Laban. Stay with him awhile until your brother cools down and his wrath subsides. In time he will forget what you did to him. Then I will send a message for you to come back. . . . Why, oh why, should I lose both of my sons in one day?"

Jacob obeyed. He gathered a few provisions, kissed his mother, and disappeared into the darkness. Tears filled Rebekah's eyes. She would never again see her younger son.

6. JACOB IN THE HOUSE OF LABAN

Jacob ran the rest of that night and most of the next day—the sound of his pounding feet massaging his sadness, loneliness, shame, and, yet, cautious optimism. It was an odd combination of emotion, punctuated with questions. Had he seen his father for the last time? What good was the birthright now? And where was Esau?

When nightfall came, his legs were wobbly and his mouth raw. He lay down on the ground, resting his head on a smooth, flat rock. Sleep overtook him instantly. And while he slept, he dreamed. In his dream he saw a staircase set on the ground, with its top reaching to the sky. Angels were going up and down the staircase. At its very top sat God himself.

And God spoke to Jacob, "I am the God of your grandfather Abraham and your father Isaac. I will give you and your descendants the land on which you are resting. Your descendants will be like the dust of the earth—stretching from west to east, and from north to south. All peoples on earth will be blessed through you and your offspring. I am with you and will watch over you wherever you go and I will bring you back to this land. I will never leave you until I have done all I have promised."

Suddenly Jacob awoke from his sleep, quivering with fear. "God is surely in this place. And I did not know it!" He rose to his knees. "How sacred is this place. This is none other than the house of God. And that," he said, lifting his eyes to the sky, "must be the gate of God."

When morning came, Jacob took the rock on which he had slept and turned it upright, so that it stood as a pillar. He poured oil over it to mark it as a holy memorial. Then he said, "God, if you will be with me and protect me and take care of all my needs; and if you bring me back safely to my father's house, then you will be my God. And this pillar will be a sign of the place where you spoke to me."

After a light breakfast, Jacob continued his flight to Haran—thinking of Esau, on the one hand, and God's promise on the other. About two weeks later, he arrived in the vicinity of his mother's hometown.

He could see a well in the distance. Three flocks of sheep and goats lay in an open field beside it, waiting to be watered. The shepherds sat nearby in a circle, talking idly. Jacob walked straight toward them, imagining their conversation was now about the approaching stranger. "Where are you from, my friends?" he asked heartily.

"Haran," one of them answered without getting up.

"Yes, I figured as much," Jacob said. "The city itself is just a bit north of here, right?"

"Yes. What brings you to these parts?" the same slim shepherd asked.

"Do any of you happen to know a man in Haran named Laban, the grandson of Nahor?"

The shepherds looked at one another. "Yes, we do."

"Really?" Jacob asked, hardly able to fathom his luck. "Is he doing well?"

"Yes, he's doing quite fine," the thin one answered. "And, as a matter of fact, here comes his daughter Rachel with her flock now." The man pointed into the distance.

Jacob peered into the glaring sun. He saw the girl. His blood rose. Then he turned back to the circle of men. "Why are you all just sitting here?" he asked with a smile. "It's still broad daylight—too early to round up the animals. Why don't you water the sheep and goats so they can return to pasture this afternoon?"

"We wait until all the flocks have arrived and then we water them at one time," a round-faced man explained. "That's just the way we do it here. Plus, it takes several of us to move the stone." He gestured at the boulder over the mouth of the well.

As Rachel and her flock came closer, Jacob turned and stared. Her brown hair curled around dimpled cheeks. Her gait was steady and graceful, her eyes gentle and kind. Filled with a sudden rush of energy, Jacob ran to the well, leveraged both hands under the huge stone, and heaved it from the opening. He then grabbed an empty jar nearby, filled it with water, and poured it into one of the troughs. He beckoned Rachel, and she led her flock to the watering bins, which Jacob continued to fill with frantic speed. Rachel stood by watching quietly. The other shepherds stared curiously.

"Thank you," Rachel said, walking toward Jacob as the last of the sheep took their water.

Her voice sent a surge of emotion through Jacob. He tried to steady himself. "Rachel, I am Jacob, the son of Rebekah, your father's sister." He embraced her, weeping aloud.

"Jacob?" she said, returning his embrace guardedly. "My cousin Jacob?"

"Yes, yes," he whispered, squeezing her tightly. Then he kissed her.

Rachel brushed her hand lightly against his cheek. Then she hastened to Haran to tell her father Laban. When she was gone, the shepherds turned and led their flocks to the troughs.

Later that afternoon, Jacob, alone by the well, looked up and saw Rachel and Laban running together. He bolted to meet them.

"Jacob, my boy," Laban said breathlessly as he threw his arms around his nephew, "I'm so glad to see you!"

Jacob beamed—it was a rare moment of speechlessness.

"You are my own flesh and blood," Laban said. "You must stay with us, for at least a month."

"Yes, at least," Jacob said, thinking of Esau's ire. Then the three of them walked back to Haran, talking happily the whole way.

● ● ●

And so Jacob lived and worked in the house of his uncle Laban, just as his mother had enjoined. At the end of that month, Laban said to him, "This arrangement is splendid. Why don't you stay awhile longer? But, listen, just because you're family, you shouldn't work for me for nothing. Tell me what you want to be paid and it's yours."

Jacob swallowed. He hesitated. He knew what he wanted. But it would require a lengthy commitment.

"Rachel," Jacob said.

"You what? Who?" Laban replied.

"I'd like the hand of Rachel in marriage. I will work seven years for you in order to have her as my wife."

Laban bit his lower lip. Jacob couldn't tell if he was suppressing a grimace or a grin. "What about Leah, my older daughter?" Laban asked.

Jacob shook his head. "I'm in love with Rachel. I have been ever since I first saw her at the well. I will do anything to have her."

"It's a deal," Laban said, slapping Jacob on the back. "I would rather give her to you than to any other." Then he turned the young man's shoulders toward him and looked him level in the eye. "But seven years is quite some time, especially for a man who was intending to go back home." His tone made Jacob uneasy.

"I know," he answered confidently. "I know."

So Jacob settled in as one of Laban's employees and family members. He was given charge of many household tasks, which he handled with skill and aplomb. Laban and his family thrived. And to Jacob, the seven years seemed but a few days because of the love he had for Rachel.

When the time came, Jacob met with Laban. "I've upheld my end of the deal. My years of service are complete. Now I get Rachel as my wife. I'm ready to consummate the marriage." He meant to be more eloquent, but his fervor stunted his speech.

"Yes, it is time for a marriage ceremony," Laban announced. So a date was set, invitations were sent, and preparations made.

It was a grand celebration, with much eating and drinking, singing and dancing. Jacob was honored and congratulated by the guests, whose hugs and kisses soon grew tiresome to the groom who found it surprisingly difficult to wait through the final hours. Wine helped. In the evening, Laban escorted his daughter Leah, fully veiled in the fanciest raiment, to Jacob. He then led the couple through the reception line and to the door of the honeymoon quarters. There he hugged the bride and bowed to the groom. The couple went inside the purposely darkened lodging.

"Rachel, Rachel," Jacob breathed as they tumbled to the bed.

The bride eagerly proceeded with the expected activity, but said nothing. Soon, they were both fast asleep.

Jacob awoke groggily the next morning. He rolled over and looked at his wife.

It was Leah!

His heart thumped with confusion and rage. What had happened? Where was Rachel? He dressed and dashed madly to Laban's house. "What have you done to me? I worked for Rachel! Beautiful Rachel. Not cross-eyed Leah. Where's my rightful bride? You've deceived me, you fraud!"

Laban's brow wrinkled. "Look, we have a custom in our land," he said matter-of-factly. "I assumed you knew. We always marry off the firstborn daughter first. Leah is the firstborn. So you married her."

"But that was not the deal!"

"You can have Rachel too. Just finish the honeymoon week with Leah. Then you can marry Rachel." He paused, a cunning gleam in his eye. "Of course you'll have to work another seven years for Rachel."

Jacob's face reddened. "Seven years for the ugly older sister," he fumed. "And now seven more. I will do it, old man. But you'd better give me Rachel in one week."

"It's just the tradition in our country. We honor the firstborn," Laban said as Jacob thundered out.

One week later, Jacob and Rachel were married. Jacob loved her deeply. He tolerated Leah.

● ● ●

When God saw Leah was unloved, he opened her womb and she bore a son, Reuben. "God has seen my suffering and blessed me," Leah said to her servant, Zilpah, a robust woman. "Surely now my husband will love me. For I have given him a son—a son to carry out the covenant." Jacob loved Reuben, but he did not love the boy's mother. He only did what was required of him as a husband. He spent most of his time with Rachel, who rarely saw her older sister.

Several months later—by dint of those marital duties—Leah was again pregnant and soon gave birth to another boy, Simeon. "God has once again seen that I am hated and blessed me with a second son," she exclaimed. Zilpah nodded.

Yet a third time Leah conceived and gave birth to a son, Levi. "Three sons," she announced. "How can Jacob not love me now? Sarah had one. Rebekah two. But I have borne three male offspring for my husband and the covenant."

Still Jacob did not love her. Even the fourth son, Judah, did not change that.

Rachel was cherished. But also devastated, for she had been unable to conceive. Her infertility and growing jealousy of her sister were slowly killing her. The morning after she got word of Judah's healthy and happy birth, she cried inconsolably. "Please give me children like Leah," she said clinging to Jacob. "If I don't become a mother, I will die."

Jacob's heart hurt for her. But his words did not portray his pain. "Die?" he asked. "You have everything you could possibly want—a comfortable, easy life, a husband who adores you. Just because you've not . . ." Rachel pushed away from him, a venomous fury flashing across her tear-stained face. "Look, don't get mad at me," Jacob said nonchalantly. Then suddenly his demeanor changed to match hers. "Am I God?" he blurted. "Am I the one who's prevented you from conceiving? Take it up with him!"

Rachel buckled to the floor in sorrow. After a few moments, she managed to speak. "Take my maid Bilhah and sleep with her. Maybe she can conceive and I can have children through her. That's what your grandmother did with her servant girl." Jacob did not answer—he was thinking of the stories of his grandmother Sarah.

So Jacob slept with Bilhah, and she gave birth to a son. Rachel named him Dan. "God has vindicated me. He's heard my prayer and given me a son through my maid," she sang joyously.

One day soon after, with Dan gurgling contentedly in her arms, Rachel said to her husband, "Sleep with Bilhah again. I would like another child." Jacob did. And once more Bilhah produced a son. Rachel named him Naphtali, saying, "I have struggled hard with my sister, and now I'm winning."

Jacob was happy because Rachel was happy. And because, with six sons, the promise of descendants as numerous as the sands of the sea did not seem as absurd as it once had.

"Rachel thinks she's winning?" Leah laughed when she was told of Rachel's declaration. She looked at her four boys heartily devouring their evening meal. "It is true I've not been pregnant in several years now," she said to Zilpah, her mood a bit more serious. So the next time it was her turn to sleep with Jacob, she told him to spend the night with Zilpah instead. The fruit of that union was another boy, Gad.

Leah gave Zilpah to Jacob a second time, and she gave birth to another son for Jacob, Asher. "How fortunate I am. My happiness has been multiplied yet again," Leah told all the women who came to see her.

● ● ●

Rachel was not happy for long, for she wanted a child of her own. One day during the wheat harvest, Leah's oldest son Rueben found some mandrakes, a magical plant which bestowed fertility. "Look what I came across, Mother," Reuben called as he ran toward her. "I pulled up the whole plant—roots and all. Take it. Perhaps it will help you have another baby."

"Thank you, my boy," Leah said, tousling his hair. "But not so loud."

It was too late. Word was out. Leah had the love plant.

"Please let me have your mandrakes," Rachel begged Leah later that afternoon. It was the first time in months the sisters had spoken.

"You already stole my husband," Leah retorted. "And now you want my mandrakes too?"

"I will let Jacob sleep with you tonight if you give me the mandrakes," Rachel offered. Leah hesitated. Then she set the mandrakes on the ground and hurried off.

That evening, as Jacob was coming in from the fields, Leah ran out to meet him. "You are sleeping with me tonight. I have traded some mandrakes for you." Jacob looked at her curiously and then followed her home.

Once again, God answered Leah's prayers. She became pregnant and gave birth to a fifth son, whom she named Issachar. Soon a sixth boy, Zebulun, followed. Leah was overjoyed. "God has given me a great gift. Surely now my husband will honor me, for I have given him six sons. Eight, really, including Zilpah's boys."

Then Leah gave birth to a girl, Dinah. She was Jacob's only daughter, and he loved her. Leah had no more children after that.

The mandrakes, as it turned out, did not help Rachel conceive, but God did. For just prior to Dinah's birth, God looked on Rachel and saw her plight. He opened her womb, and she conceived and gave birth to a son, Joseph.

"I have borne a child of my very own. I am a mother. God has taken away my humiliation and misery," she said to Jacob as he swaddled the infant. "I am now part of the covenant too. And who knows, maybe God will give me another son someday."

Jacob wiped his eyes. "Joseph, Joseph," he crooned, "son of my forever and treasured bride."

7. HOMEWARD BOUND

Jacob was fulfilled, but he was also growing restless. Thoughts of home—his mother and father, and Esau—regularly occupied his mind. One evening, he cradled Joseph in his arms and went to his father-in-law's house.

"Laban, I have something I'd like to discuss," he said. Laban cooed with delight at the sight of his eleventh grandson. "I have worked very hard for you for a long time. It's been almost twenty years. Hard to believe. It was supposed to be a month. Remember? And then seven years; then fourteen; and now it's been two decades. It is time for me to take my wives and children and return to my home country. I ask you to bless my going."

"Leave? Now?" Laban said. "But I . . ." He paused and looked once more at the sleeping baby. "God has blessed me richly since you've been here, Jacob. God has blessed us both. I want you to stay. We have a very good arrangement."

Jacob took a deep breath. "Yes, it is an especially good arrangement for you. What little you had before I came has increased greatly. I've made you wealthy—and a grandfather many times over. God has indeed blessed you with everything I've done. But what about me and my family? When do we get something for ourselves? All the flock and livestock and silver and gold are yours. We are just living here."

"What do you want?" Laban asked. "Tell me, and it's yours."

Jacob thought for a moment. "How about this: Let me have all the speckled and spotted sheep and goats for myself and my family. You can keep the rest. That way it will be easy to know what's mine and what's yours. The solid-colored animals are yours; and the multicolored cattle are mine. I will stay here and continue, as usual, to manage all the flocks and other affairs as they arise. The only difference is that now some of the animals belong to me." He stopped to let his proposal sink in. "I don't desire anything else."

"Are you sure that's all you want? We divide things up like that, and you'll stay and work, and little Joseph and the others will remain here?"

"Yes, I am sure."

"It's a deal, then," Laban replied, pulling Jacob toward him in a warm embrace.

But as soon as Jacob left, Laban summoned his sons and instructed them to separate all the animals with any hint of color and to herd them that night at least a three-day journey away. The next morning when Jacob went to gather the speckled and spotted animals for himself, he found none. "It's not the first time he's tricked me," Jacob mused. "What else should I have expected from him?"

"Those mandrakes might not have helped Rachel and me when we mated," Jacob said crudely to a servant as they walked toward the pasture where Laban's solid white, black, and brown animals grazed. "But I know some mating magic that will in fact work with these livestock. I'm going to need some branches from poplar and almond trees."

The servant fetched them, and Jacob made white stripes on them by peeling off strips of bark exposing the inner wood. Whenever strong females from Laban's solid-colored flocks were ready to breed, Jacob placed these partially peeled branches in their watering troughs. When the time came for them to give birth, they dropped speckled, spotted, or striped young. When the weak animals mated, Jacob did not put the rods in the water. Within a few years all the multicolored animals were vigorous; and the solid-colored ones feeble. In this manner Jacob grew exceedingly prosperous and came to own large flocks of sturdy, healthy animals, while Laban's flocks dwindled.

It was not long before Laban's sons began grumbling amongst themselves and casting aspersions at Jacob. "That traitor has robbed our father of everything! He's gained his wealth at our father's expense. What's going to be left for us to inherit?"

Jacob, for his part, perceived that Laban's disposition toward him had changed markedly for the worse. So one morning, Jacob sent word for

Leah and Rachel to join him in the fields. The sisters hurried out together, stressed by the urgent and unusual summons. Jacob greeted each with a kiss and instructed them to sit on two nearby rocks. "I've noticed your father's attitude toward me has deteriorated," he began. "You know how hard I've worked for him over the years; but he has cheated me. Or at least he's tried to cheat me. But God has been with me. Indeed, God has not allowed him to do me any harm." The two wives looked at each other.

"God appeared to me in a dream," Jacob continued, "and showed me how to breed the flocks so that my share increased and your father's decreased. And that's exactly what has happened." Jacob knelt on one knee before them. "And God told me something else in the dream. He said, 'Return home to the land of your father and grandfather, and I will be with you.'"

Leah burst forth. "Neither we nor our children will inherit our father's wealth anyway! He's reduced our status and rights to those of foreign women. Surely everything God has taken away from our father and given to you belongs to us and our children. So I say do whatever God has told you."

"That is true," Rachel concurred bitterly. "Our father has little regard for us. He sold us for fourteen years of labor, and now he has nothing to show for it. Yes, you should follow God's word."

Jacob reached for his wives. "Prepare the children to leave," he said, their heads pressed against his chest. "Pack up everything that is ours; take nothing that belongs to your father. The day after tomorrow, your father and brothers will be away shearing their sheep. This is when we will depart, secretly."

Two days later, Jacob and his family—Leah, Rachel, Zilpah, Bilhah, and all the children—climbed onto camels and, along with their cattle and possessions, began the journey to Canaan. They took everything that belonged to them, and nothing more. Except for Rachel who slipped into her father's house and stole his sacred talismans.

Laban and his sons returned to Haran three days later. Silence and stillness replaced the usual hullabaloo and bustle.

"They've stolen away!" Laban cried, falling to the ground. "They're gone! They're gone! He's taken everything and left!"

Laban's initial shock and sorrow soon turned to anger. He gathered a few of his servants and set out in pursuit of Jacob's entourage.

When he caught them, he snapped. "Why have you deceived me like this? How could you drag away my daughters like prisoners of war? Why did you run away like a coward? Why did you trick me?"

Jacob remained stone-faced.

"Why didn't you just say you were leaving?" Laban continued. "I would've given you a grand farewell feast with singing and dancing. You didn't even let me kiss my daughters and grandchildren goodbye. You've been a fool. I could destroy you right now, little man. But God appeared to me last night and warned me not to hurt you. So I won't."

The two men glared at one another. "And one other thing," Laban said. "Why did you steal my talismans? You know how important those are to me."

"I left secretly because I was afraid," Jacob answered. "I did not think you would let me go. And I knew you wouldn't allow your daughters to leave. So we had no choice but to escape when you were gone. But, listen, as for your talismans, we do not have them." He turned his palms up and shrugged. "You can look everywhere. If you find them with us, the person who took them will die. And if you find anything else that belongs to you, show me, and I will give it back."

Laban wavered, not sure what to say. Then he turned and began searching for the sacred objects. He went through Jacob's belongings, then Leah's, Zilpah's, and Bilhah's. He found nothing. Finally, he approached Rachel who had hidden the talismans in her camel saddle on which she was now sitting. "Please forgive me, father, for not getting up for you," she said. "I'm having my monthly period." So Laban continued his search, but he could not find the talismans.

Jacob grew agitated. "What's my crime? What wrong have I done to you that you chase after me as though I were a criminal? You've rummaged through everything I own. Now show me what you found that belongs to you. Set it out here in front of us so we all can see."

Laban cast his eyes downward and shifted from one side to the other.

"For twenty years I slaved in your house and cared for your flocks," Jacob said. "I worked for you through the scorching heat of the day and through cold and sleepless nights. In all that time, I never stole anything. Not one thing. And you prospered mightily. If it were not for God's intervention you would've sent me back home with nothing. But God has seen my hardships. That's why he appeared to you last night and told you not to touch me."

Laban stretched his arms wide. "These are my daughters, and these children are my grandchildren, and these flocks are my flocks. Everything here is mine. But what can I do. It's all yours now." He dropped his hands and exhaled. "So let's make a covenant, you and I."

Jacob looked carefully into Laban's face.

Then together the two men took a stone and set it up as a monument to their treaty. "If I harm you or if you harm me or my daughters in any way, let the judgment of God fall on that man," Laban said.

"Indeed, God will be watching over us," Jacob replied.

To seal their pact they shared a meal by the stone. In the morning, Laban returned to Haran, and Jacob continued his journey home to Canaan.

8. BROTHERS REUNITED, A DAUGHTER DEFILED

As Jacob neared the land of his birth, he sent two messengers to Edom southeast of Canaan where his brother Esau lived. Jacob told the messengers, "Find Esau and tell him this: 'Greetings from your servant Jacob. I've been living with our uncle Laban all these years. I own cattle, donkeys, flocks of sheep and goats, and many servants. I am sending this message to inform you, my lord, of my arrival, hoping you will receive me peaceably.'"

The next day, the messengers came racing back to Jacob. "We found your brother Esau and delivered the message," they said frantically. "And he's already on his way to meet you. With an army of four hundred men!"

Jacob dropped to the ground and cried out, "O God of my grandfather Abraham and my father Isaac, you were the one who told me to return to my homeland and family. You promised to take care of me. I'm not worthy of all the love and kindness you've shown to me. When I left home years ago, I owned nothing except a walking stick. Now you've made me a wealthy man. So please save me, O God, from the hand of my brother Esau, for I fear he's coming to attack me and my wives and children. He's bent on violent revenge. Remember, God, you have sworn to protect me and to multiply my descendants until they become as numerous as the sands of the sea."

Jacob arose, dusted himself off, and summoned twelve servants. "I'm going to divide my livestock into four groups and send them in successive waves to Esau," he told them. "Three of you will lead each group of animals. When you meet Esau, here's the message you are to give him: 'This drove of animals belongs to your brother Jacob, and he is sending them to you, his master, as a gift. Jacob himself is following right behind.'"

Early the next morning Jacob split up his animals. Each group had numerous goats, lambs, rams, cows, donkeys, and camels. "Be sure to keep some distance between you and the herd in front of you," he instructed as the first envoys left camp. The last party departed late in the afternoon.

"I'm trying to appease him by sending these gifts on ahead," he told Rachel. "Then when I see him myself, face-to-face, perhaps he will welcome me home warmly."

"Or perhaps such an impressive display of wealth will intimidate him," she remarked. Jacob smiled.

That evening Jacob sent his two wives and his eleven sons and Dinah, along with the rest of their possessions, south across the Jabbok River toward Edom. Jacob remained behind, standing alone on the northern bank of the Jabbok.

Darkness soon swallowed him. A steady breeze blew across the waters. Suddenly Jacob felt a man attack him and shove him to the ground, pressing his face into the stony mud. He fought back with all his strength, bucking off the assailant. The struggle waged into the night, both men writhing and twisting furiously, neither able to gain the upper hand. When the man knew he could not overpower him, he touched Jacob's hip and wrenched it out of its socket. But Jacob continued to grip the attacker's arm.

Then the man said, "Let me go, for it is daybreak."

"I will not release you unless you bless me," Jacob replied with jaws clenched.

"What is your name?" the man asked.

"Jacob."

"Your name will no longer be Jacob," his foe told him. "From now on you will be called Israel, because you have wrestled with God and with people and have prevailed."

"Who are you?" Jacob questioned.

"Why do you ask?" the man replied. Without waiting for an answer, he blessed him, before vanishing into the morning mist.

Jacob collapsed, his hip throbbing, his heart pounding. Beads of sweat rolled down his face. He began to tremble, for he now knew who the man was. "I have seen God face to face—and I have survived."

Jacob got to his feet and limped off toward the Jabbok as the sun began its slow ascent.

● ● ●

That same afternoon, Jacob looked up and saw Esau and his four hundred men approaching. He quickly divided up his family, each mother with her children. He placed Zilpah up front, followed by Bilhah, and then Leah. Rachel and Joseph were at the back. He himself hobbled out in front leading them all.

As he neared his brother, Jacob stopped and bowed to the ground six times. Esau kept coming. When he was within ear shot, Jacob bowed slowly one more time. Esau jumped off his donkey and sprinted to meet him, arms waving and face glowing; he threw himself around Jacob and kissed him. They laughed. They cried. Esau could hardly speak.

"Seeing your face is like seeing the face of God," Jacob said. "Thank you for receiving me so kindly."

"Who are all these people with you?" Esau asked, wiping his cheeks.

"This is the family God has blessed me with," Jacob answered humbly. "Come meet my brother," Jacob shouted to those behind him. They all came and bowed before Esau who greeted each one.

"And what were all the herds and flocks I kept meeting yesterday?" Esau queried.

"They are gifts, my lord, in hopes of securing your friendship."

"Jacob, my brother, I have plenty. You can keep them for yourself."

"No, please take them," Jacob insisted. "If you want to truly welcome me home, please accept them as a gift. For God has been very gracious to me."

Esau shook his head, a grin of wonder spread across his face. "I cannot."

"Yes, you can," Jacob persisted, embracing his brother again. "It is truly incredible to see you after these many years."

"Alright," Esau relented. "But first thing tomorrow we all head back to Edom where my family and I live."

Jacob nodded. "That is fine. But as you can see, my lord, some of the children are small, and the flocks and herds also have their young. If they are driven too hard, even for one day, all the animals could die. So, please, you go ahead and return home. We will follow slowly and meet you in Edom."

Esau reluctantly agreed. "Let me at least leave some of my men to guide and protect you."

"There's no need for that," Jacob said, a touch of impatience in his voice. "You've already done more than enough by receiving me with open arms."

The next morning, Esau and his men began the return trip south to Edom. The following day Jacob and his family turned west, crossed the Jordan River, and headed toward the village of Shechem in the heart of Canaan. They made their home there, not far from the place where his grandfather Abraham had died and where his father Isaac now lived.

Jacob had finally returned to the land of his birth. But he would never again dwell with his twin brother. Nor would he see his beloved mother Rebekah who had passed away in his absence.

● ● ●

Jacob and his household built a prosperous life in Canaan. The oldest boys, Rueben and Simeon, grew into strong, intelligent young men who were soon able to handle the herds and flocks on their own. The eleven sons, as different as their personalities were, blended their talents in masterful harmony to form one successful, thriving family under Jacob's headship. The boys loved their only sister, Dinah, who matured into a beautiful and precocious young woman. While the men were at work in the fields, Dinah adroitly managed many of the domestic affairs. She developed a special connection with her grandfather Isaac, who now lived with them. She tended dutifully to the blind and feeble old man.

Dinah would sometimes leave the homestead to carry on business with the locals. When she did, Isaac was visibly weaker and depressed. And Jacob worried. On one such occasion Dinah went out to visit some of the young women in the area. As she walked through the village of Shechem with her friends, the prince of the city, who was named after the city itself, saw her. He was instantly obsessed. He followed the girls at a distance throughout the morning, watching Dinah's every move, and then, as the sun reached its peak, he drew closer.

"Please stay here in the city tonight," Shechem said, taking her by the arm.

Dinah shook her head and tried to pull away.

"Yes, you will," he said, tightening his grip. The other girls quickly disappeared, for they knew he was the prince.

Shechem led her to a quiet part of the city, and there, when she refused his advances, he violated her. Then he took her home and tried to win her affection with gentle words. The normally gregarious Dinah remained mute. But Shechem was not deterred. He said to his father, King Hamor, "Get me this girl as my wife. I must have her."

About the same time Shechem was speaking with his father, Jacob received word from Dinah's girlfriends.

"Where is she now? Do you know where he took her? What happened?" Jacob panicked. The maidens did not answer, but their faces confirmed his worst suspicions. Jacob sat down, his forehead resting on his hands. "My daughter has been defiled!" he cried.

Jacob was paralyzed. Even if he had wanted to do something, he could not; for he was alone. His sons were herding the flocks a few miles away and were not scheduled to be back for three days. Jacob sent word for them to return immediately. When they arrived the next afternoon, they found King Hamor conversing with Jacob.

"My son Shechem is truly in love with your daughter," Hamor explained. "Please let him marry her. Their marriage can mark a treaty between your family and our people. You have lived here for a while now, but we've never really been allies. This is the perfect opportunity to establish a mutually beneficial relationship in business, trade, and good will."

Dinah's brothers listened with shock and outrage. Their sister had been violated, their family name dishonored.

Then Shechem himself spoke to Jacob and his sons. "Please be kind to me, and let me marry her," he begged. "I will give you whatever you ask. No matter how large a dowry you demand, I will gladly pay it. Only give me the girl as my wife."

Reuben stepped forward. "We couldn't possibly allow you to have her." He paused, a crafty glimmer in his eye. "For we cannot give our sister to a man who is not circumcised as we are. It is the sign of the covenant with our God. Any man who marries our sister must thus be cut. Otherwise, it would be a disgrace to us and a breach of our sacred oath. Furthermore, the same is true for all men who enter a formal treaty with our family: They must be circumcised. So there is an easy solution for you, Shechem. If every man in your village will be circumcised like we are, then you can have Dinah, and we will enter a pact with your people."

"Yes, yes, we will do that," Shechem answered with alacrity. Hamor nodded his affirmation. Then the king and prince departed and returned home to present the proposal to their city.

"These men are our friends," Shechem said to the village council. "Let's encourage them to carry on business with us, trading freely. You know how wealthy they are—countless flocks and many possessions. Eventually it will all be ours, if we establish good relations with them now. But they will consider entering such an arrangement with us only if our men are circumcised, just as they are. This will be a very good deal for us. We would be wise to consent to their terms."

The men of the council assented. So the next day, every male in the town underwent the bloody and painful procedure. Two days later when they were still recovering from their wounds, Simeon and Levi—Dinah's full brothers—took their swords, entered the unsuspecting village, and slaughtered every man there. The carnage was massive, for the place was defenseless. They also rescued Dinah from Shechem's house.

When the rest of Jacob's sons heard what Simeon and Levi had done, they rushed to Shechem and plundered it, seizing the livestock in the town and surrounding fields. They ransacked every home and took captive all the women and children. No one escaped.

When Jacob learned of it, he confronted Simeon and Levi who were watching their brothers greedily divide the loot. "You have ruined me!" he screeched. "This will make us utterly hated by all the Canaanites. There are so few of us and so many of them. They will simply crush us. I am ruined! We will be wiped out!"

"Nobody is going to treat our sister like a whore and get away with it," Simeon rasped with squinted eyes. "Nobody." Then he turned to count the captured women.

As for Dinah, she was never the same. She slowly withdrew. Depression overtook her.

Her decline, however, dramatically halted about a year later when Rachel became pregnant for a second time. There had not been a newborn baby in the family for years, and Dinah's spirits brightened at the thought of having a helpless infant to care for. She tended diligently to her aunt Rachel who struggled through a difficult pregnancy. Joseph, too, often stayed home from his work to care for his mother. Jacob watched in anguish as his darling wife moaned from the pains in her womb.

Rachel spent the final three months of her pregnancy in bed. When it came time for her to deliver, it seemed unlikely that both she and the baby would live. Dinah held Rachel's hand through the harrowing screams of labor that pierced the night.

"You have another son—it's a boy," Dinah whispered into Rachel's ear as the midwife washed the newborn. Rachel opened her eyes and gasped, "Name him Benoni, for he is the son of my sorrow." Then she breathed no more.

Dinah took the baby boy to his father.

Jacob held his son and kissed him delicately. "He will be called Benjamin."

"But his mother named him—"

"And how is his mother?" Jacob interrupted worriedly.

Dinah's eyes lowered, and Jacob knew.

He wept for many days.

Soon thereafter, Isaac passed away. When Esau received word, he journeyed from Edom, and together Jacob and Esau buried their father.

9. JOSEPH

Jacob loved all his children, but he had a special affection for Joseph because he was the firstborn son of his dear Rachel. The bond between the two of them had been strengthened as they cared for Rachel in the final days of her tumultuous pregnancy. When she passed, they helped each other cope. Baby Benjamin's presence also helped.

Joseph, now a sturdy boy of seventeen, worked in the fields alongside his ten older half-brothers. He was the only one not to have at least one full sibling. While no one ever talked about it, this was an unavoidable fact which made Joseph different. And different in a way his brothers did not like. Joseph also had the annoying habit of reporting to his father every little thing that reflected poorly on his brothers. He was a tattletale. Whatever was done or said in the fields—business or personal—Joseph was sure to tell Jacob.

"Things have never been the same since Simeon and Levi ransacked Shechem," Joseph liked to remind his father. "I fear those Canaanites will seek revenge." And when Jacob found out that Reuben had had sex with Bilhah, well, everyone knew who told him.

So when Jacob presented a special, beautiful robe to Joseph for his eighteenth birthday, it fanned the flames of hatred and jealousy smoldering among the brothers. "He is father's favorite alright," Levi muttered bitterly, as Joseph showed off his new garment. "None of us have ever received anything like that."

"Listen to this," Joseph said to his siblings at breakfast a few days later. "Last night I had a dream. We were all out in the field tying up bundles of grain. Suddenly my bundle stood up, and your bundles circled around and bowed down to mine."

"What is that supposed to mean?" Judah asked with a scowl. "So you think you will be our king? And you will reign over us?"

Joseph just smiled. His brothers scoffed.

The next morning Joseph donned his robe for breakfast. "I've had another dream," he announced. "The sun, moon, and eleven stars bowed down before me." His brothers ignored him this time.

"What kind of dream is that?" Jacob scolded. "Will your mother and I and your eleven brothers come and bow down before you?" Joseph shrugged. His brothers stewed. Dinah lamented that she was not in the dream, even if it meant bowing down to her younger brother. Jacob wondered what the dreams meant.

Soon Joseph received the privilege of remaining at home while his brothers toiled in the fields. He rarely went with them on trips in search of pasture. On one such occasion, Jacob called Joseph and said, "Go see how your brothers and the flocks are doing. Then come back and give me a report."

The following day Joseph gathered a few provisions, kissed his little brother Benjamin goodbye, and set out north toward Dothan. Late in the afternoon, Joseph's brothers saw him coming in the distance, for they recognized his robe.

"Here comes the dreamer," Judah said. "This is our chance. Come on, let's kill him and throw him into a cistern. We can tell our father a wild animal devoured him. Then we'll see what becomes of his dreams."

"No, let's not kill him," Reuben spoke up. "Then his blood will be on our hands. Let's just throw him into a cistern—he'll die there sooner or later." He said this hoping he could convince his brothers to save the boy.

Joseph came closer, waving and shouting warm greetings. "How is everybody?" he said slapping some of them on the back and hugging others. "Our father wants to know if everything is alright."

"I bet he does," Judah sneered.

"Let me take a look at that robe," Levi said, grabbing a sleeve.

"No, not right now," Joseph replied, jerking back.

"Yeah, I think we should," Simeon grunted, seizing the collar.

"What are you doing?" Jacob yelled as they ripped off the cloak and shoved him to the ground.

Judah laughed menacingly. "We just wanted to see the pretty coat of Daddy's favorite."

They pushed and dragged and kicked Joseph to an empty well nearby. They thrust him over the edge, and he tumbled to the mucky bottom. Joseph cried for help, but the brothers only walked silently back to their campsite.

A band of traders inched toward them in the fading sun.

As they sat down to the evening meal, Judah said, "What will we gain by killing Joseph? We'd have to cover up the crime, and besides, he's our brother—our own flesh and blood. Let's sell him instead to these spice traders headed to Egypt." They all agreed, except Reuben.

So several of them ran to stop the caravan, while others went back to the cistern and, tossing down a rope, pulled Joseph out. Reuben buried his face in his hands and did not move.

Joseph's brother's sold him to the traders for twenty pieces of silver.

The next morning they ripped up Joseph's robe, slaughtered a goat, and smeared its blood on the robe.

"Take this back to our father," Judah instructed a servant, handing him the stained and tattered garment. "Tell him we found it, and ask him if it's the one that belongs to Joseph."

When the courier arrived with the message, Jacob broke into tears. "It is Joseph's!" he wailed clutching the robe against his chest. "My son! My son! He's been killed by wild beasts. Torn to pieces. Oh, Joseph!" He pressed his face into the cloth and howled.

Leah and Dinah and the others heard the commotion and came running. They tried desperately to comfort him. But he was inconsolable. When his sons returned home a few days later, Jacob was pale and dehydrated. "We've nearly killed our father too," Reuben said sadly to his brothers. They too tried to soothe Jacob, but could not.

"I will go to my grave mourning for my son," Jacob would say, and then he would weep some more. He cried bitterly for days on end.

As his father lamented and his brothers carried on with life in Canaan, Joseph arrived in Egypt, lonely and frightened. He was placed on the auction block and sold to Potiphar, a high ranking official of Pharaoh, the king of Egypt. I've been sold twice in two weeks, Joseph thought to himself as he was led to his new home.

Everything was different in Egypt—the color of people's skin, their dress, their food, their language. But, like his father, Joseph was a determined, sagacious, and protean man. And God was with him. So it was not long before Joseph was transferred from the slave quarters to Potiphar's private residence.

"Have you noticed Joseph's competence and intelligence?" Potiphar asked his wife one day. "He is successful at everything he does. I mean everything."

"Yes, I have," she answered, not looking at her husband.

"I'm going to promote him to my personal assistant. He will be in charge of the household affairs and will oversee everything we own," he stated.

From that day on, God blessed Potiphar's home. All domestic dealings ran smoothly, and his crops and livestock flourished. With Joseph in complete administrative control, Potiphar did not worry about a thing—except what to have for dinner.

Now Joseph was a well-built, handsome young man, with striking eyes and wavy brown hair. Potiphar's wife noticed. She was a slender, genteel woman, not too much older than he. She never missed an opportunity to speak with Joseph, holding her gaze at him as they bantered, and when she would take his hand to dismount from her horse, she squeezed it firmly, her thumb rubbing the back of his fingers. With time, her flirting became bolder. Joseph tried to ignore it.

One afternoon, she came into the room where he was working alone. She cupped his face in her hands. "Have sex with me," she whispered longingly.

Joseph stepped back. "My master trusts me with his entire household—he's put me in charge of all he owns. The only thing he hasn't turned over to me is you, his wife. How could I violate his trust and sin against God?"

She stared into his eyes lustfully, her hands sliding down his chest.

Joseph took a stride backwards. "I can't. I won't."

"Why not?" she breathed. "No one will know."

"Please, no," he said, glancing towards the door.

She slowly withdrew and left.

Joseph took a deep breath. That will put an end to her teasing, he thought.

But it did not. The next day she again found him at the same time and place and expressed her carnal desires. The following afternoon Joseph varied his schedule to avoid her. But she found him nonetheless. And she did so nearly every afternoon for several weeks, her advances and touches becoming more direct. Joseph refused them as politely and firmly as he knew how.

Finally, one day when the house was especially quiet, she slipped into his quarters, grabbed his collar, and began kissing him. "Come to bed with me now. All the servants are gone. Make love to me, just this once." Joseph tried to push her away, but she held him fast. He turned violently to one side, trying to shake her off, but still she clung to him. He jerked in the other direction. This time his shirt ripped off and Joseph darted out of the house bare-chested.

She stood there for a moment, her bosom heaving. Then she shrieked, "Get out! Get out, you filthy Israelite!" She staggered from the room, calling for the servants. "Look!" she screamed as several of them hurried towards her. "He tried to rape me! He came at me and forced himself on me. I fought him off. His shirt ripped in my hands before he ran away."

Then the woman composed herself and summoned Potiphar to come home immediately. "Joseph tried to rape me!" she burst out crying when her husband arrived. "You know you shouldn't buy foreign slaves and bring them into our house! I kicked and screamed, but he wouldn't stop. His shirt tore off in the struggle. See, here it is." She shoved the garment into Potiphar's chest and fell into his arms.

"That scoundrel! I had faith in him. He betrayed me," Potiphar seethed.

He called the palace police. They came at once and arrested Joseph and led him to prison. Joseph did not resist.

That night Joseph lay on the cold, hard floor, shackled, despondent, and lifeless. He drifted off to sleep with thoughts of home, his father, and happier days.

• • •

Life was again difficult for Joseph. But God was with him. The captain of the guard soon took a liking to Joseph and put him in charge of all the inmates. About a year later, Pharaoh's chief butler and chief baker offended their royal master. Pharaoh imprisoned them, and the ward assigned their care to Joseph. After the two men had been there awhile, much longer than they anticipated, they each had strange dreams on the same night.

"Why do you look so haggard today?" Joseph asked when he saw their frightened faces the next morning.

"We have dreamed dreams, and we don't know what they mean," the butler answered.

"Don't interpretations come from God? Tell me the dreams," Joseph said without missing a beat.

The chief butler looked askance at Joseph. But, with nothing to lose, he began. "In my dream, I saw a grapevine dangling in front of me. The vine had three branches, each of which budded, blossomed, and produced clusters of ripe grapes. I took a cluster and squeezed the juice into the royal cup. Then I placed the cup in Pharaoh's hand."

"This is what your dream means," Joseph said. "The three branches represent three days. Within three days Pharaoh will pardon you and restore you to your position as his chief butler."

"Are you sure?" the man asked, a grin tugging at the corners of his mouth.

"Yes, I am," Joseph replied. "Please remember me when you return to your position. Mention me to Pharaoh; perhaps he will get me out of this place. For I was kidnapped from my homeland, Canaan, and now I've been wrongfully accused and put in prison unfairly." The butler bowed to Joseph and promised to tell Pharaoh.

When the chief baker heard the interpretation, he spoke right up. "In my dream three wicker baskets were stacked on my head. The top basket contained all kinds of pastries for Pharaoh, but the birds came and pecked at the food in the basket and ate it all." He looked hopefully at Joseph.

There was momentary silence. Then Joseph asserted, "This is what your dream means. The three baskets also represent three days. Three days from now Pharaoh will impale your body on a pole, and the birds will come and peck away at your flesh."

The baker slumped to the floor. "What do you know, you sorry criminal."

Three days later was Pharaoh's birthday, and he threw a grand feast for his officials and staff. He released the butler and baker from prison so they could join the celebration. At the end of the banquet, Pharaoh announced his pardon and restoration of the butler. He then read the death sentence for the baker. The next day, the baker was impaled and hung on a tree and the birds came and pecked at his body.

The reinstated butler, however, forgot all about Joseph; he never gave him another thought.

10. DREAMS AND DECEPTIONS

Joseph languished in prison. The days turned into weeks, and the weeks into months. Nearly two full years had passed when Pharaoh dreamed a dream. He summoned his magicians, priests, and counselors; they came and stood dutifully and attentively around him.

"I have had dreams and must know their meaning," he said to them. "In my visions of the night I was standing on the bank of the Nile River when I looked up and saw seven fat, healthy cows come up out of the water and begin grazing on the marshy grass. Then I saw seven more cows, scrawny and thin, come up out of the Nile and stand next to the fat cows on the riverbank. Before long, the scrawny, thin cows ate the seven healthy, fat cows.

"Then I woke up, sweating and disturbed. But soon sleep overtook me, and I dreamed again. This time I saw seven ears of grain, plump and lush, growing out of a single stalk. Then seven more ears grew up, but these were shriveled and withered by the east wind. Immediately, the thin ears devoured the full, healthy ears. Now what do these dreams mean?"

No one spoke a word. One of the men finally stammered, "We do not know, O King, what the dreams portend."

Pharaoh was distraught. "How can you not know? This is your job."

At that moment the butler appeared at the entrance to the room. "May I speak with the king? It is urgent."

Pharaoh beckoned him in. "What is it?"

The butler replied, "When I was in prison with the chief baker, we each had a dream. There was a young man there, a foreigner, whom the warden had placed in charge. He interpreted our dreams, and his words were soon fulfilled."

"What was his name?"

"Joseph."

"Send for him at once."

Joseph was taking an afternoon nap when word arrived. He arose, shaved, and was given clothes appropriate for the occasion. Several hours later he stood before the king.

"I had dreams last night," Pharaoh said, "and no one here can tell me what they mean. I've heard you can interpret visions."

"No, I cannot. But God can. He will give you an answer," Joseph said, unfazed by the king's majesty.

So Pharaoh began. "In my dream I stood on the bank of the Nile and saw seven fat, healthy cows come up out of the river and start to graze. But then I saw seven sick-looking cows, scrawny and thin, come up behind them. I have never seen such ugly cows in all the land of Egypt. These thin, scrawny cows ate the seven fat cows. But you wouldn't have known it, for they were still as thin and scrawny as before.

"Then I had a second dream in which I saw seven ears of grain, full and good, growing on a single stalk. Soon seven more ears of grain appeared, but these were shriveled and withered by the east wind. The shriveled heads swallowed the seven healthy heads. Joseph, do you know what these dreams mean?"

"Yes," he answered. "God has revealed to you what he is about to do. The dreams are one and the same. The seven healthy cows and the seven good ears of grain both represent seven years of prosperity throughout the land of Egypt. The seven thin, scrawny cows and the seven withered heads of grain represent seven years of famine which will ravage the land and erase all memories of the good years. The meaning of the dreams is sure. And the doubling of them indicates that God has decreed it to be so."

Pharaoh sat expressionless.

"May I make a suggestion?" Joseph offered. Pharaoh nodded. "I recommend appointing an intelligent and wise man to oversee the collection of one-fifth of all the crops during the seven years of abundance. Let the food be stored away—and guarded—so there will be enough to eat when the seven years of famine strike the land."

Pharaoh summoned his officials and recounted Joseph's words to them. They marveled at the elegant simplicity of the interpretation.

"It is clear," Pharaoh's voice boomed through the chamber, "that Joseph himself is to be the appointed wise man. The spirit of God rests upon him." Then turning to Joseph, he said, "I hereby put you in charge of the entire land of Egypt. All people are to take orders from you. Only I, sitting on my throne, will have a rank higher than yours."

Pharaoh removed the royal ring from his hand—the one used to sign and seal decrees—and placed it on Joseph's finger. He gave him a fine imperial robe and hung a gold chain around his neck. He also bestowed upon him a new name: Zaphenath-Paneah. The next morning, he put Joseph in the royal chariot and led him through the streets of the capital. All the people were ordered to bow down to the newly installed leader.

● ● ●

Joseph was thirty years old when he began serving under Pharaoh. As predicted, for seven years the land produced plentifully. During that time, Joseph stored up huge amounts of grain—so much that they stopped keeping records of it. During those years, too, Joseph married Asenath, the daughter of a priest, and she bore him two sons. Joseph named the first boy Manasseh, for he thought, God has made me forget all my troubles and my paternal home. The second he named Ephraim, for he said to himself, God has made me fruitful in this land of my sorrow.

Then the seven good years came to an end and the seven years of famine arrived. The drought spread beyond Egypt to the surrounding countries. As the famine wore on, Joseph gradually, judiciously, distributed food to the Egyptians. Soon people from all over came to Egypt to find something to eat. It was a severe famine indeed, and no one could recall the years of abundance.

● ● ●

Back in Canaan, life had gone on without Joseph. His brothers put their crime against him out of their minds, and his father coped with the loss of his favorite son by taking special delight in Benjamin. Jacob was also pleased to watch as God multiplied his descendants, fulfilling the promise to his grandfather Abraham. The manner in which he acquired grandchildren, and even great grandchildren, however, was not always what Jacob expected. The family of his son Judah was one such case.

Very soon after Joseph had been sold in Egypt, Judah—the fourth son of Leah—married a Canaanite girl who bore him three sons before she died. In the course of time, Judah arranged for his firstborn, Er, to marry a young woman named Tamar. But Er was a wicked man, and so God took his life.

Then Judah said to Er's brother Onan, "You must have relations with Tamar, as our law requires of the brother of the deceased, and father a child for him, so that his name will live on." But Onan was not willing because he knew the offspring would not be his own. So whenever he had intercourse with Tamar, he withdrew. Thus, Tamar did not become pregnant. God was disgusted with Onan's actions and so he killed him too.

"Er and Onan have each been with Tamar and both have died," Judah lamented to his brother Reuben one day. "I refuse to give Shelah, my youngest, to her. He'll probably end up in the grave beside his brothers."

"Just send her back to her father's home," Rueben remarked casually. "She can remain a widow there."

Judah did just that.

Sometime later, Judah happened to be in Tamar's hometown on business. When Tamar learned of it, she changed out of her widow's clothing, disguised herself as a prostitute, and sat alongside the road where she knew Judah would pass. When he saw her, he stopped and propositioned her.

"How much will you pay?" Tamar asked.

"I'll send you a young goat from my flock," Judah promised.

"But what will you give me now to guarantee you will send the goat?"

"What do you want?"

She replied, "Leave me your personal identification seal and your walking stick." So Judah gave them to her. Then he lay with her, and she became pregnant.

A few weeks after, Judah sent a servant to take the goat to the woman and to retrieve the items he had given her. But the servant could not find her.

He asked some men loitering nearby, "Where can I find the prostitute who used to sit beside the road here?"

"There's never been a prostitute," one of them chuckled. "I can tell you that for sure."

So the servant returned and told Judah, "I couldn't find her anywhere, and they said there's never been a prostitute along that road."

Judah's brow wrinkled. "Well, then, she can keep the things I gave her. I tried to uphold my end of the deal. I'd be the laughingstock of the place if I went back to look for her again."

"Yes, the laughingstock," the servant quipped.

About three months later, Judah was notified that Tamar was pregnant.

"Bring her here," Judah demanded. "And burn her to death!"

So they brought her from her father's house. But just as she was about to be tied to the stake, Tamar said, "The man who owns this seal and walking stick is the one who made me pregnant." She held them up for all to see.

Judah's lungs tightened, his face grew pale. "She is more righteous than I am," he choked, kneeling to the ground, "because I didn't give her to my son Shelah."

And thus it came to pass that Tamar lived in Judah's house, but he never had sex with her again. Soon she gave birth to twin boys, children of the covenant.

● ● ●

Tamar was thrilled to be a mother, but times were hard. They were hard for everyone, for Joseph's famine spread to Canaan and put a death grip on the land. Tamar watched as the earth slowly hardened and cracked. The crops withered and died. There was scarcely enough food for her babies.

"Please help me," Tamar cried softly to Leah one evening. "My boys and I are starving to death."

"We all are," Leah sighed, putting a wizened arm around Tamar's tiny shoulders. "I heard Jacob talking to his sons yesterday. He said there is grain in Egypt. I believe they're making preparations to travel there to buy food for us."

"Tell them to hurry," Tamar whimpered.

The following day, Leah stood beside her father Jacob and nephew Benjamin as ten men mounted gaunt mules and headed south under the burning sun. Leah turned to Benjamin, now a young man, and asked, "Are you the only one not going?"

"Yes," he replied. "Father fears something might happen to me." He paused, jabbing his foot into the dry ground. "You know, with what happened to Joseph and all."

The ten brothers soon arrived in Egypt. Like all those seeking provisions, they were required to appear before Joseph. And so one afternoon, Joseph looked up to see the next party being ushered in to bargain for food.

And it was his brothers! He knew them instantly.

His pulse raced, his hands trembled. But he kept his composure. He knew they would not recognize him. They bowed low to the ground before him. "Where are you from?" Joseph asked sharply, speaking in Egyptian through a translator.

"From Canaan," Reuben said in Hebrew. "We have come to buy food." The interpreter rendered the words to Joseph.

"You are spies," Joseph said. "You've come to scout out the land, to find our vulnerabilities."

"No, my lord!" Reuben argued. "Your servants have simply come to buy food. We're all brothers—members of the same family. We are honest men. We are not spies." Utter fear and panic shone on their faces.

"Yes, you are," Joseph persisted. "You've come to see just how much food we have left."

"Sir," Judah fell to his knees, hands clenched against his chest. "That is not true. We are ten brothers from Canaan—all sons of the same man. There are actually twelve of us. Our youngest brother is back there with our father right now, and one of our brothers is no more."

A flood of emotions overwhelmed Joseph. He remembered his boyhood dreams. But his exterior remained resolute. "This is how I will test your story. One of you must go get your brother and bring him back here. Then I will know you are telling the truth. In the meantime, I will keep the rest of you here in prison. In fact, all of you will be held for the next three days; then one of you will be released to return home."

So the ten men were handcuffed and led away to the same prison where Joseph had been confined years earlier. Joseph barely ate or slept that night.

On the third morning, he called for them. "I am a God-fearing man," he said solemnly. "And I have changed my mind somewhat. I will select one of you to remain incarcerated here. The rest of you may return home with grain for your starving families. But you must bring your youngest brother back to me. This will prove you are telling the truth. If you do not return in a timely manner, the one who remains here will be executed."

The brothers spoke to one another in Hebrew, not knowing Joseph could understand them. "Surely this is punishment for the sins of our youth, our sin against Joseph. We sold one brother to Egypt; and now we must leave one here under threat of death. We're getting what we deserve."

"I told you not to harm the boy," Reuben said. "But you wouldn't listen. Now we must give an account for his blood."

At this, Joseph turned and quickly left the room, the tears finally uncontrollable. He returned a few minutes later, unruffled.

"You will remain," Joseph said pointing at Simeon. "The rest of you will find your sacks full of grain. Go home and then return to Egypt quickly, or else this will be the last time you see your brother."

Joseph sent word to his servants to fill their sacks with grain and also to put each man's money back in his sack and to give them added provisions for their journey home. Then he called for the guards and ordered them to bind Simeon hand and foot. Simeon stood there stolidly as each brother took turns hugging him goodbye. They were sorrowful, but relieved that nine were going and only one staying—instead of the reverse.

The men loaded their mules and set off for Canaan. Judah was the first to unpack that night. "Oh, my God!" he cried. "Here is my money! We've been framed! God, no!" He fell to the ground. The others rushed over, looked into the sack, and then opened their own.

"Mine too!" Gad yelled.

"It's all here—every last bit!" bellowed Levi. "What's happening? What's God doing to us?"

Their hearts sank, and their spirits shriveled like the earth beneath them.

"We must go back to Egypt and explain the mistake," Reuben declared.

"No," Judah said. "We will return home and get Benjamin. We can explain ourselves when we get back to Egypt." The others agreed; so they continued their journey to Canaan, distraught and frightened. But with food for Tamar's baby boys and everyone else.

When they arrived, they apprised their father Jacob of everything that transpired. He sat emotionless. Then tears began to fill his eyes. "You are robbing me of my children. Joseph is gone. Simeon is gone. And now you want to take Benjamin, too. It's one bad thing after another."

His sons tried to console him, but it was futile. Reuben said to his father, "I swear I will take care of Benjamin. You may kill my two sons if I don't bring him back to you. I'll be responsible for him, and I promise he will return with us. You must let him go. If not, Simeon is sure to die."

"Benjamin will not go down with you," Jacob sobbed. "His brother Joseph is dead, and he's all I have left. If anything should happen to him, you'd send this grieving old man to his grave." The brothers scuffled off with resignation—there was no use trying to convince Jacob.

Months passed. The famine dragged on and each day the nine brothers thought of Simeon fettered in an Egyptian prison. Or was he dead now? When their grain was nearly gone, Jacob instructed his sons to return to Egypt to obtain more food.

"If you don't let Benjamin go with us, we aren't going," Judah told his father. "If we return to Egypt without him, then Simeon dies, we are proven to be spies, and we are either executed or enslaved. We would never make it back. You'd still have Benjamin, Dinah, and the women and children, but you'd have no food."

"Why did you tell the Egyptian governor you had another brother?" Jacob moaned.

Judah replied, "The man was insistent. He said we were spies. How were we to know he would tell us to bring back Benjamin? It's not our fault. You know we would not intentionally bring all this trouble on our family."

Judah fell before his father and pleaded, "Send him with us. I swear he will be safe. You may hold me responsible if I don't bring him back to you. As Reuben said, you can kill my two boys—Tamar's twins—if I fail to keep my word. Their blood will be on my hands." He paused, staring intently at his father. "Otherwise we will all die of starvation—me, you, and our little ones. We should've left a long time ago; we could've gone and returned twice by now."

Jacob said nothing. His hands covered his lined face. "So be it," he winced after a few moments. "Take some small gift, and double the money to pay for the grain last time. May God grant you mercy in that man's eyes, so Benjamin may return safely." Then he wilted to the ground. "If I must suffer, I must suffer."

Judah knelt down next to him. "You are doing the right thing. We will leave tomorrow."

11. TOGETHER AGAIN

The next day, at dawn's first light, they all set off—Benjamin riding between Reuben and Judah. When they reached Egypt and Joseph saw their names on the day's registry of those seeking food, he said to his household manager, "These men will have lunch with me today. Take them to my house, slaughter an animal, and prepare a feast."

When the brothers were informed of this, they were terrified. "He's going to accuse us of stealing the money last time," Judah said. "Then he will imprison us and make us slaves."

The men were given a comfortable place to wash up and rest before the midday meal. Reuben approached the manager. "Sir," he said, "we came to Egypt once before and purchased food. But on our way home, we discovered each man's money back in his sack. We have no idea how it got there. Here it is, all of it." He extended a bag of coins.

"Relax. Don't be afraid," the man said, refusing the sack. "Your God must've done it. I received your payment."

Rueben dropped the bag. "How can this be?" he marveled. Then he looked up and saw Simeon coming towards them. Before he could greet him, the manager ushered them into the dining hall.

When they were seated, Joseph entered. Immediately they all arose and bowed to the ground. Joseph scanned their faces. "I see you've brought your brother as promised," Joseph said, gazing at Benjamin. He was the image of their mother Rachel. Joseph's throat lumped.

"Yes, we have," Judah answered firmly. "His name is Benjamin."

"May God bless you, Benjamin," Joseph smiled. The name on his lips nearly unraveled him. Benjamin nodded. Even his movements were that of his mother.

"And your father? Is he still alive and well?" Joseph asked.

"Yes, our father, your servant, is doing fine," Judah replied.

There were several moments of silence as Joseph's eyes met each of theirs in turn. Then Joseph hurried from the room, overcome with emotion. He went into his private chambers and broke down and wept. "My God, my God! It is my brother, my own flesh and blood. It's been so many years. And, oh, my father."

After washing his face, he came back out, keeping himself under control. Then he ordered for the food to be served. They all feasted and drank freely.

As the meal concluded, Joseph announced, "Well, men of Canaan, it has been a pleasure. I bid you safe travels and health and happiness to your family back home." The men bowed again, and Joseph departed.

At daybreak the next morning, the eleven brothers arose and were soon on the road home with their loaded donkeys. "We've made it—we're all going back safely," Judah said happily to Rueben.

When they had been traveling about an hour, they turned to see the household manager running after them. "Why have you repaid kindness with such evil?" he demanded. "Why have you stolen my master's sacred silver cup? What a wicked and foolish thing you've done!"

"What are you talking about?" they all responded at once.

"We would never do such a thing," Judah insisted. "Didn't we return the money we found in our sacks last time? Why would we steal a cup from your master's house? If you find it with any one of us, let that man die. And the rest of us, my lord, will be your slaves."

"Fair enough. But only the one who stole the cup will remain here in Egypt. The rest may go home." Then the manager searched the brothers' belongings, from the oldest to the youngest.

He found the cup in Benjamin's sack.

The brothers fell to the ground and tore their clothes. They wailed and writhed and pounded the dirt. Then they trudged back to the palace.

"What have you done now?" Joseph questioned when they came in.

Judah answered, his speech cracking with anguish, "Oh, my lord, what can we say to you? How can we possibly explain this? How can we prove our innocence? God is punishing us for the sins of our youth. My lord, we will all be your slaves—not just our brother with the cup in his bag."

"No," said Joseph. "That would not be fair. Only the man who stole the cup. The rest of you may return home to your father."

Judah flinched. Then he gathered himself, exhaled, and spoke. "Please, my lord, let me say just one thing to you. Please, withhold your anger for a moment."

Joseph braced himself.

"When we came here the first time, you accused us of being spies. We said we were not and to prove the truth we brought back our youngest brother. But we almost did not return this second time—you may have noticed how long we tarried—because our father, who is very old, would not allow his youngest child to come with us. He's already lost one son from his beloved, deceased wife, and he was dearly afraid of losing the other, Benjamin."

Joseph fought off tears.

"But we had no choice," Judah continued. "Simeon's life was at stake. So I begged our father. I vowed on the life of my own sons that I would bring Benjamin safely back. So, my lord, I cannot return to my father without the boy. If I do, the old man will die, and I will be responsible for sending him to his grave. Now I plead with you, my lord, please let me stay here in place of Benjamin. Keep me, not him. I cannot bear to think of the misery it would cause my father if I returned without his youngest son."

Joseph could not control himself any longer.

He ordered his officials and attendants out of the room. Then he walked toward Judah, weeping aloud. "It is I, Joseph," he said embracing his brother. "It's me."

"Oh, my God . . . It is you . . . Joseph," Judah stuttered, returning the embrace.

The others were stunned and speechless. "Benjamin, Benjamin!" Joseph spluttered, throwing his arms around his younger brother. "I am Joseph." Benjamin squeezed him, but managed no words.

"Reuben, Reuben—I am not dead. Look at me. Levi, I am alive. Simeon, it's me, Joseph. Everything is alright. Dan, Asher, Naphtali, Issachar! I cannot believe I'm seeing you again." One after another, Joseph hugged and kissed them. They cried and laughed and held each other.

Then Joseph addressed them. "God has been in control all these many years. Don't be upset or angry with yourselves for selling me into slavery. It was God, not you, who sent me here, so that at this very moment I could save your lives from this dreadful famine. Yes, God has taken care of me, so I can now take care of you. He's the one who made me second in command over Egypt. Can you imagine that!

"Now you must return to our father—oh, how I've missed him!—and to your families in Canaan and bring everyone down here to Egypt to live with me and my family. Otherwise, you will soon starve to death. I've arranged, with Pharaoh's approval and blessing, for you to reside in the region of Goshen; it is not far from here and is the richest territory in Egypt. There you can live with your children and grandchildren, your flocks and herds, and everything you own. Oh, I cannot wait to see everybody."

The brothers spent the remainder of that day talking and marveling at one another's stories. The next morning, Joseph provided them with supplies for the journey, both leaving and returning, including the best wagons, fresh clothes, and much silver. He also sent his father a special gift: ten donkeys loaded with the finest products of Egypt, and ten additional donkeys loaded with grain, bread, and a variety of other goods. "Don't quarrel about all this stuff along the way," Joseph joked as they set off for Canaan.

● ● ●

As they drew close to home, Jacob came out to meet them. He counted eleven sons. "You've made it!" he called. Leah, Tamar, Dinah, and several small children ran up behind him shouting with joy.

"Yes, we are all here," Reuben affirmed. "And, my dear Father, it only gets better, much better!"

"What do you mean?" Jacob asked cautiously.

"Joseph. He's alive!" Reuben said. "He's alive and he's governor of Egypt."

Jacob began to tremble. "Don't do this to me."

"It's true," Judah beamed. "Not only did we bring Benjamin back, but we also found Joseph! You've got all twelve of us again."

"It cannot be," Jacob exhaled.

"He sent this as a special gift to you," Judah said, pointing to the donkeys.

"We are to load our families and possessions on these wagons and go to Egypt, where he will provide for us," Reuben interjected.

Jacob's face twisted with tears of joy as he fell to his knees. "Joseph. I'm going to see my boy again. My boy, Joseph."

That night God spoke to Jacob in a vision. "Do not be afraid to go down to Egypt, for there I will make your family into a great nation. I will protect and bless you. You will die in Egypt, but Joseph will be with you as you close your eyes in your final sweet sleep."

After a week of preparations, Jacob and his children and their families headed south. It was a large and boisterous caravan of men, women, boys, girls, infants, and livestock. As they approached the region of Goshen, Joseph came to meet them.

When he saw his father, he nearly lost his breath. He embraced him and wept, unable to speak. Jacob took Joseph's head in his hands and said, "I have missed you dearly, son. I thought you were lost forever. Now I can die in peace, since I've seen your face again."

Joseph met his sisters-in-law, nieces, and nephews for the first time. He talked at length with Dinah about their father and life in Canaan.

The following day, Joseph took his father, Benjamin, and his four oldest brothers and presented them to Pharaoh. They greeted one another affably. Then Jacob said to Pharaoh, "My life on this earth has been hard and short compared to that of my ancestors. But I am blessed to be here in your country. We thank you for the kindness you have shown to us. And now, if I may, O King, I bestow our blessings upon you."

Pharaoh replied, "May you and your family thrive and flourish in the land of Goshen."

And they did. The children of Jacob—of Israel, his God given name—were fruitful and multiplied, and their numbers grew rapidly. For seventeen years they lived securely in Goshen.

As Jacob's eyesight failed and death neared, he called Joseph to his side. "Please swear you will treat me with unfailing love by honoring my last request: Do not bury me in Egypt. When I die, please return my body to Canaan and lay me to rest with my grandfather Abraham and my father Isaac."

"I will do as you ask," Joseph said.

"Swear you will do it," Jacob insisted.

So Joseph gave his oath, and the two of them embraced. Then Joseph said, "And I have a request of you too, Father. I know God has promised to increase our descendants and to give the land of Canaan to our offspring. I want to ensure that my two sons—Manasseh and Ephraim—who were born to me here in Egypt will be part of God's covenant. Will you give them your blessing?"

"Certainly, my son. In fact, summon all your brothers. The time has come to bestow my final blessings."

The next day Jacob's entire family assembled around him. Joseph ushered Manasseh and Ephraim before his elderly father. "I never thought I would see your face again," Jacob said to Joseph. "But now God has let me see your children, too!"

Joseph positioned the firstborn Manasseh on Jacob's right hand and the younger Ephraim on the left. But Jacob crossed his arms as he reached out to lay his hands on the boys' heads, such that his right hand was on Ephraim and his left hand on Manasseh.

"No, my father. This one is the firstborn," Joseph said, grasping Jacob's wrists. "Put your right hand on his head."

"I know, my son. I know," he replied, refusing to lift his hands. "Manasseh will become a great people, but his younger brother will become even greater." Then he pronounced: "May the God of my grandfather Abraham and my father Isaac, the God who has been my shepherd all my life long to this very day, bless these boys. May they carry on the covenant given to Abraham. And may their descendants multiply greatly throughout the earth."

The two boys arose and stood beside their father. Then each of Jacob's sons, beginning with Reuben, came and knelt before him. When he finished blessing each one, Jacob addressed them all: "My days are at end. I beseech you to bury me in Canaan, our homeland."

Then he closed his eyes and said no more.

Three days later, Jacob breathed his last. His children grieved for him, and the Egyptians embalmed his body as Joseph instructed.

Shortly thereafter, Jacob's sons, along with many dignitaries from Egypt and royal chariots and horsemen, journeyed back to Canaan. It was a grand funeral procession. There they laid Jacob to rest with his ancestors and observed a seven-day period of mourning.

● ● ●

On their return trip to Egypt, Joseph's brothers began to talk among themselves.

"Now that our father is dead," Reuben fretted, "Joseph might pay us back for what we did to him. He might've been secretly holding a grudge all this time."

"Yes, that is true," Judah concurred. "He has little reason to be kind to us now. I assume he told our father how we sold him. I wonder what Dad thought about that?"

"I don't know," Reuben replied. "But remember what Joseph told us—that it was God's doing. He probably told our father the same thing."

"Well, now might be a good time to say something to Joseph," Levi added.

As they ate their evening meal at the campsite that night, Judah spoke up. "Joseph, I think you should know that one of our father's last wishes was for you to forgive us for the wrong we did to you. He desired that we live in peace and harmony with one another after his passing. Therefore, please, we ask, do not hold our past transgressions against us. We are truly regretful. Please forgive us. Or tell us what we must do to right the wrong. We will be your servants—or do whatever you say." All the brothers turned and fixed their gaze on the favored son.

Joseph's eyes watered; his jaw quivered. "I . . . I . . ." he stammered. Then he came undone. The brothers looked on in silence.

Joseph wiped his face and breathed slowly. "I forgive you. There is no need to worry. I will not seek revenge. You may have intended to harm me, but God intended it for good. He blessed me so that I could bless and save the lives of many people. No, don't be afraid. I will continue to take care of you and your families."

Tension drained from the faces of the men. Joseph looked at his brothers and spoke kind words of assurance to each of them in turn. Then they talked into the night around the glowing fire—about good times and bad, the past and the future, ancestors and heirs.

And so Joseph and his brothers and their families prospered in Egypt for many years. They held in their arms grandchildren and great grandchildren—the sons and daughters of the covenant.

When the time came for Joseph to go the way of all flesh, he assembled his progeny and said to them, "God will surely come to lead our family, our people, out of this land of Egypt. He will take us back to the land he solemnly promised to our forefather Abraham. It may not be soon, but God will fulfill his word, and when he does, you must swear to me that you will take my bones back to Canaan."

They gave their oath.

In time, Joseph and each of his brothers and Dinah died a peaceful death, old and happy, and full of years.

12. MOSES

Many, many moons passed. Generations came and went. Jacob's descendants now swarmed the land of Goshen. The children of Israel were as the stars of the sky and the sands of the sea, just as God promised.

The king of Egypt took notice. How was it that these outsiders, these strange people from Canaan, these lowly shepherds with their flocks and livestock, continued to enjoy such a peaceful and prosperous life in one of Egypt's plushest regions? The history of how it came to be lurked somewhere in the record—something about a man named Joseph and dreams and a foreign God. But what did all that matter now? It was time to deal with the Israelites for what they were: aliens who had become too influential and too powerful.

So Pharaoh summoned his counselors and said to them, "The Israelites have become far too numerous. They are eating up many of our resources and are a political and military liability. We must act now. I propose we turn them into slaves. With their forced labor we can undertake several new and much-needed construction projects." His advisors agreed.

It did not take long for the Egyptians to subjugate the Israelites. They appointed brutal masters who oppressed them with crushing tasks. They forced them to build the cities of Pithom and Rameses as supply centers for the king. But when those projects were completed, the Israelites were even more numerous and more formidable than before. Like their eponymous ancestor, they were resilient.

Pharaoh and his men increased their efforts to contain, or even eradicate, the crafty foreigners. They treated the Israelites as harshly as ever, making their lives miserable and nearly unbearable. They compelled them not only to build the buildings, but also to make the bricks. They subjected them to the most back-breaking work in the cities and fields. They were ruthless and cruel in all their demands.

When that failed to staunch the Israelites, the Egyptians turned murderous.

Pharaoh called Shiprah and Puah, the two senior Israelite midwives. "I am issuing this royal decree," he said to them. "When you and your midwives help the Israelite women give birth, you are to kill all the baby boys. Do not allow them to begin breathing, and if they do, suffocate them. You can tell the mother that the baby was stillborn. All the baby girls may live." The women listened with downcast eyes. "Do you understand?" the king asked. They nodded and were escorted from Pharaoh's presence.

Shiprah and Puah never uttered a word to each other or to their staff about Pharaoh's orders.

A year later, the king again sent for the head midwives. "Why have you completely disregarded my word?" Pharaoh barked. "My officials report no increase whatsoever in the infant mortality rate among the Israelites. I demand an explanation."

"The Israelite mothers," Shiprah answered, raising her eyebrows and shoulders, "are not like Egyptian women. They are vigorous and give birth on their own, before we can get there."

"You will regret this," Pharaoh snapped. "I will see to it these baby boys are killed. I should've known you wouldn't take the lives of your own people. But my people will. Those wretched Israelites!" Puah started to speak, but Shiprah took her by the arm and led her out.

God blessed Shiprah and Puah for their loyalty to the people of the covenant. But they were powerless in the face of Pharaoh's next decree.

"Whenever you see an Israelite baby boy," Pharaoh commanded his slave drivers, "seize it from its mother and drown it in the Nile. The river must be polluted with bloated Israelite infants!"

And so they did.

There was much mourning and weeping and wailing among the Israelites. Women prayed desperately to give birth to girls, and boys were hidden from the prowling task masters.

During this crisis, Amram, a man from among the descendants of Levi, and his wife Jochebed toiled under the heavy-handed Egyptians. They had two children, a daughter Miriam and a son Aaron. Then Jochebed conceived and gave birth to another male child. They were able to keep him stowed away quietly for three months. But when they could no longer hide him, Jochebed took a basket made of papyrus reeds and waterproofed it with tar and pitch.

She called her daughter Miriam and spoke quietly to her. "Your little brother is getting too big and noisy. He is sure to be discovered by the Egyptians. I'm putting him in this basket and placing it in the Nile. I don't know what will happen to him." She paused, her words choked by sorrow. "But what do we have to lose. Maybe God will protect him."

Miriam looked at her wide-eyed.

"About an hour before dawn tomorrow," Jochebed continued, "I will go to the river. You follow me and find a good place at a distance to watch what happens to him. It's all I can think to do." Mother and daughter held each other tightly as the little boy slept.

So Jochebed put her son in the miniature ark and carefully placed it among the reeds along the bank of the Nile. As the day's first light glimmered over the water, one of Pharaoh's daughters arrived to bathe. Miriam watched intently.

The woman took notice of the basket. Then she waded into the water and lifted the top. She jerked back. There was a baby, crying, his little fists shaking. The princess leaned over, reached in, and took the infant in her arms.

Miriam quickened from her hiding place. "What's that?" she called out to the Egyptian.

"It's a little boy. Must be one of the Israelite babies. Poor thing," she said pitifully, rocking him back and forth and patting his back.

"Would you like for me to find an Israelite woman to nurse him for you?" Miriam asked.

"Yes, yes, that would be good."

So Miriam darted off toward home. A few minutes later, she and her mother came scurrying back.

"Can you nurse this baby for me?" the princess asked Jochebed. "I want to raise him as my own son as soon as he can be weaned. I will pay you for your help in the meantime."

The boy's mother calmly reached out and took the child. "Yes, I can care for him and I will bring him to you as soon as he is ready."

"If a slave driver tries to steal him, simply present this," the princess said, handing her a royal seal.

"Oh, my God, great queen, I did not know with whom I was speaking," Jochebed blurted. Then she bowed.

"Take good care of this boy," the woman smiled.

Jochebed and Miriam bowed again, then turned and retraced their steps home. "I will have to give up my boy, again," the mother sobbed. "But he will be raised a prince of Egypt, not a slave. What more could I want?"

About a year later, after he was weaned, Jochebed sent the boy to Pharaoh's daughter, and she adopted him as her son. She named him Moses.

And so it was that Moses was reared in the palace of Pharaoh. He enjoyed all the luxuries afforded royalty—power, privilege, a good education. But he knew that by blood he was not royalty. He was a common Israelite.

● ● ●

As Moses grew older, he enjoyed taking long strolls around the capital. One day, he happened to observe some Israelites slaving under the scorching heat. As he stood squinting into the distance, he saw an Egyptian lift his rod and strike an Israelite square across the back. The slave buckled to the dust. Once more the Egyptian lifted his cane and unleashed a furious swing. He did it again and again.

Moses watched aghast. Then he dashed madly toward the Egyptian, looking to the right and left as he ran. There was no one in sight. As the slave master stood over the bruised and bloody body, Moses blind-sided him and wrestled him to the ground. He seized the rod, and with a smoky rage pummeled the man—to death!

Moses frantically dragged the body into a nearby gully and heaped dirt and sand on it. Then he fled.

The next day he returned to the scene of the crime. As he meandered near the ditch, he saw two slaves tussling with one another. "Why are you beating up your fellow Israelite?" Moses asked, trying to pull them apart.

"Who made you the judge here?" one of them said. "Are you going to kill me, just as you killed that Egyptian yesterday?"

Moses jumped back. People know, he thought. Someone must have seen me. I will be a wanted man; there will be a price on my head. Moses stood there akimbo for few moments, fighting the tears. He knew what he must do.

Moses turned and set off for the wilderness, with only a walking stick in his hand. The Egyptian skyline soon faded behind him as Moses ambled on into the night. For four days he walked, jogged, and crawled until he came to the region of Midian, which bordered Egypt on the east. There he sat down by a well in the late afternoon, fatigued and dejected. A slave by birth, royalty by fate, and now a fugitive.

Before long, shepherds came to water their flocks. Moses lay in the shade under a nearby tree. A few minutes later, shouts awakened him. He propped himself up on one elbow and peered toward the troughs. A group of female shepherds had arrived. Moses watched as a husky man shoved one of the girls to the ground. Then another man swung his staff wildly in the girls' direction, as if doing a war dance. The other men laughed.

Moses arose and approached the raucous scene. "What are you doing?" he said to the man with the rod.

"Who are you?" the shepherd sneered.

Moses ignored the query. "Let these women use the well. They have as much right to the water as you do. Now get out of here."

The men shrugged and herded away their flocks.

Moses motioned the women to the well. "Thank you," one of them said as Moses filled the troughs for them. Moses worked in silence until all the animals were satisfied. Then he went back to his shady respite.

That night, the girls returned home to their father, a priest named Jethro, and told him what happened.

"He was an Egyptian man, you say?" Jethro asked, surprised.

"I think so—I guess so," his oldest daughter Zipporah replied. "He wasn't from around here. I know that."

"Where is he now? Did you leave him at the watering hole? Why didn't you invite him home? It's the least you could've done. Go back and get him." So Zipporah and one of her sisters ran to the well and retrieved the stranger.

Moses and Jethro talked into the night, the leather tent flapping in the breeze. Moses agreed to remain with Jethro and his seven daughters. "I will be a shepherd after all," Moses said, shaking his head with a smile, "just like my ancestors."

13. A BURNING BUSH

Moses lived and worked with Jethro, the Midianite priest, and his family. In time, he married Zipporah, and she gave birth to a son. Moses named him Gershom, for he thought to himself, Who am I—but a foreigner in a foreign land. And thus he did not circumcise Gershom as an Israelite.

One day, shortly after his son's birth, Moses led his flocks in search of pasture. He ended up in a plush area at the base of Mount Sinai, several days from home. On the third afternoon there, he found himself wandering up the mountain, whiling away the hours, when he looked up and saw a peculiar bush on the hillside. The bush was on fire, but it was not burning up. Curious, Moses headed toward the strange site.

As he neared, God spoke to him from the bush. "Moses! Moses!"

"Yes?" he trembled.

"Do not come any closer. Take off your sandals, for the place where you are standing is holy ground." Moses bent over, loosened the thongs, and stepped out.

The powerful voice continued, "I am the God of your ancestors, the God of Abraham, the God of Isaac, and the God of Jacob." Moses threw his hands over his face and recoiled in raw fear.

"I have indeed seen the oppression of my people in Egypt," God thundered. "I have heard their cries of distress at the hands of the brutal slave drivers. I know their deep pain and suffering. Therefore I've come to rescue them from the power of the Egyptians. I will lead them out of that country and into their own fertile and spacious land—a land flowing with milk and honey, the land of Canaan, as I promised Abraham. Now, Moses, you must lead my people out of Egypt."

Moses' hands slid down his face. His forehead glistened, his breathing labored. "Who am I to lead the people of Israel out of Egypt? Who am I to appear before Pharaoh? And what if I am still wanted for murder?"

God answered from the bush, "Those who had a bounty on you are dead. Look, I promise I will be with you. I vow that you will lead my people out of Egypt, and you will bring them right here to this very mountain to worship me."

"What am I supposed to tell the people?" Moses questioned, lifting his eyes.

"Tell them the God of their ancestors, the Great I Am, sent you to save them. When you arrive, call together all the leaders of Israel. Tell them God appeared to you and told you he sees their afflictions and promises to rescue them and to lead them home.

"They will listen to you and believe you, Moses. Then you and the leaders must confront the king of Egypt and say to him: 'God has met with us. So please let us take a three-day journey into the wilderness to offer sacrifices to our God.'

"But I will harden the heart of the king of Egypt so that he will refuse to let my people go. Indeed, he will not free them unless a mighty hand forces him. So I will raise my hand and strike the Egyptians, performing all sorts of miracles among them. Then, and only then, will Pharaoh release my people."

Moses protested, "What if the Israelites won't believe me or listen to me? What if they say, 'God never appeared to you'?"

"What is that in your hand?" the voice from the bush asked.

"A shepherd's staff," Moses responded.

"Throw it down on the ground." Moses threw down the staff on the rocky terrain, and it turned into a snake. Moses drew back.

"Reach out and grab its tail," the deity commanded. Moses slowly stretched his hand toward the snake. As soon as he touched it, it turned back into a rod. "Perform this sign," God told him. "Then they will believe you." Moses stood there gaping at the stick.

"One more sign," the voice continued. "Put your hand inside your cloak." So Moses slid his left hand onto his chest. He waited a moment and then took it out; it was white as snow, and shriveled as if diseased. Moses trembled. "Now put your hand back into your cloak," God said. Moses obeyed, and when he removed it, it was restored.

"If they don't believe after the first miraculous sign, they will be convinced by the second sign. And if that doesn't work, then take water from the Nile River and pour it out on the ground. When you do, the water will turn into blood."

Still, Moses was reluctant. "God, I'm not very good with words. I've never been a good speaker. And even though you've assured me, I remain slow of speech. I get tongue-tied, and stutter and stammer. You know that."

"Who do you think made the human mouth? Who makes some people mute, and some deaf, some able to see, and some blind? Is it not I, God? Now go! I will be with you and I will tell you what to say."

"God, send someone else," Moses pleaded, falling to the ground.

"Alright, what about your brother Aaron?" God said, losing patience. "He speaks well. I will send him out to meet you as you approach Egypt. Aaron will be your spokesman, your mouthpiece. I will be with both of you and will instruct you what to say and do."

Then the fire extinguished. Smoke rose from the green bush. Perspiration soaked through Moses' garments. He was exhausted. How long have I been here, he wondered as he plodded down the mountain.

● ● ●

The next day Moses herded his sheep back home to his father-in-law. "Jethro," he said, looking across the evening fire, "I must return to my family and my people in Egypt. Please allow me to go—and to take my wife Zipporah and my son Gershom with me."

Jethro tossed a stick into the flames. "You may go. I wish you well."

"I will come back here to Midian—to Mount Sinai—and you will see your daughter and grandson again," Moses assured him. Jethro smiled and nodded. Moses knew he did not believe him.

So the next morning, Moses gathered his belongings, saddled three donkeys, and set off under the enormous sky for the land of Egypt. In his hand he carried the staff of God.

When night fell, they stopped and set up camp. The air was strangely cool and filled with energy as Moses pitched the tent and Zipporah warmed some meat. Something was not quite right, Moses could tell. The place felt oddly reminiscent of Mount Sinai where God had appeared to him in the bush.

Then suddenly, God appeared again. And tried to kill him! Moses yelled something. Zipporah jumped to her feet overturning the simmering pot. The camp crackled with a mysterious electricity. Panic gripped Zipporah. She seized a knife, dashed to Gershom, and circumcised him. Gershom shrieked and writhed in pain. Blood leaked from the cut.

Then everything went still.

The boy clenched in agony; his mother sat gasping in a crumpled heap; and Moses lay sprawled on the earth, motionless. God vanished. They had survived.

● ● ●

The trauma of the incident nearly muted them, and little was said for the remainder of the journey. As they approached Egypt, Aaron came running out to greet them as God had promised. The two brothers embraced and cried on one another's shoulder.

"I cannot believe you have returned," Aaron said through the tears.

"Yes, I am back, and I have much to tell you," Moses replied.

"I'm sure you do—it's been so long."

"No," Moses said somberly. "I mean we have serious business to tend to. I've journeyed back home, but now the real journey begins."

"What do you mean?"

"I will tell you tomorrow. For now, let's be on our way—I want to see Mother and Father and Miriam."

And so the four of them returned to the home of Moses' birth, where there was much hugging and laughing and sniveling. The next day, Moses told Aaron everything that happened in Midian and all God said to him. Aaron was astounded by the signs.

Two days later, Moses and Aaron called a council with the leaders of the people of Israel. They were shocked to be in the presence of Moses—

for they had heard the tales of the Israelite raised a prince of Egypt, only to flee as a criminal.

"Men of Israel," Aaron said in a melodic, baritone voice, "God has seen our misery and affliction under the heavy-handed Egyptians. And now he is about to rescue us." The council listened as Aaron spoke to them about God's encounter with his brother. "Moses' name will get us an audience with Pharaoh," Aaron explained. "We will negotiate our release from the Egyptians. Spread this word among our people. All the Israelites must know what is about to happen."

Then Moses performed the wondrous deeds. At this, the men believed, and they fell to the ground with joy and thanksgiving.

Two days later, Aaron and Moses waited at the palace entrance. Pharaoh sat on his throne in blinding splendor, magnificently adorned. "So it is Moses, the murderer from a bygone year when my father ruled the land," Pharaoh mused as the two shepherds were ushered in. "You look like a simple Israelite to me." The king stared at the two creased and sunbaked faces before him.

Aaron steeled himself for the exchange. "The God of Israel has spoken. His message to you, O King, is this: Let my people go, so they may hold a festival in my honor in the wilderness."

"Is that so?" Pharaoh snickered. "Who exactly is this God? And why should I listen to him? I only take orders from my god and father, the almighty Re."

"God has met with us," Aaron replied. "So let us take a three-day journey into the wilderness so we can offer sacrifices to our God. If we don't, he will kill us with a plague or the sword."

"That is your problem, not mine," Pharaoh retorted. Then he arose and strode out. His attendants escorted Moses and Aaron to the exit.

That same afternoon Pharaoh sent an order to the Egyptian slave drivers: "Do not supply the Israelites with any more straw for making bricks. Make them get the straw themselves. But still require the same number of bricks as before; do not reduce the quota. They are a lazy breed, and now Moses, of all people—the man raised as one of us, when the Nile should've been his grave—is trying to stir up rebellion. I will not have it!"

Without the piles of chopped straw to mix in with the mud and sand, the brick-making process slowed considerably. The slaves now had to run to the fields and scrape up dried grass. It was impossible to match the quotas. And so the task masters beat the Israelite supervisors in charge of their kinsmen. Whips cracked and rods snapped over their backs in the sight of all the work crews. With each empty cart of bricks, morale weakened.

With little to lose, the Israelite foremen asked to speak with Pharaoh. "Our people have been excellent and faithful servants for decades," they began. "But we always had straw to make the bricks. Now we are not given the straw, but still we are expected to produce the same number of bricks. And when we cannot—for it is impossible—we are thrashed. Please don't treat your servants like this. We are being beaten, but it isn't our fault. Your own task masters are to blame for not providing the necessary supplies."

"My men are to blame?" Pharaoh leaned toward the cowering group. "No. You are just lazy! A bunch of useless sloths! Now get out and get back to work!"

The foremen stumbled over one another as they hastened to leave. But their fright instantly turned to fury when they saw Moses and Aaron waiting to meet them in the palace courtyard. "Look what you've done to us! Who do you think you are? Because of you, the Egyptians now despise us and carry swords to kill us. Just leave us alone. Go back to the desert and don't speak to us again."

Moses and Aaron did not say a word, which enraged the men further. One of them had to be restrained. Moses' eyes watered as the pathetic herd shuffled out.

That night, Moses sat alone and depressed in his dark abode. "Why have you brought all this trouble on your own people, God? Why did you send me—I told you I didn't want to go? Ever since I returned, things have worsened. Pharaoh has become even more brutal to your people. And you've done nothing to rescue them. Why? Why?"

God answered steadily, "Now you will see what I am about to do to Pharaoh. When he feels the force of my strong hand, he will let my people go. In fact, he will beg them to leave his land."

"But. . ."

"I am God, and I promised my servant Abraham I would give the land of Canaan to his descendants. I've not forgotten my covenant. Therefore, Moses, give this message to the people of Israel once again: I will free you from your oppression and will rescue you from bondage in Egypt. I will bring you into the land I swore to Abraham, Isaac, and Jacob. I will give it to you as your very own possession. For I am God Almighty."

"But, God," Moses reasoned, "my own people will no longer listen to me, for their burdens have increased since I went to Pharaoh. They are discouraged and worn out. Why say anything else to them now?"

"Then go back to Pharaoh and tell him to let the Israelites go," God replied.

Moses shook his head. "But, God, if my own people won't listen to me anymore, how can I expect Pharaoh to care what I say? Besides, we know what happened last time I approached the king."

"Listen to me carefully, Moses. I will make Pharaoh's heart stubborn so that I can multiply my miraculous signs and wonders in the land of Egypt. Even when he sees the signs and experiences the wonders, Pharaoh will refuse to heed your words. So I will bring down my fist on Egypt and I will save the Israelites. Then the Egyptians will know that I am God."

Moses could resist no more. He soon fell into an exhausted sleep.

He awoke renewed. Later that day, he and Aaron stood in Pharaoh's august presence. Again Aaron repeated their demand. This time Pharaoh entertained the notion. "Show me a sign," he said tersely. So Moses immediately threw his staff on the ground, and it became a serpent. Pharaoh watched the snake for a few moments; then he summoned his own wise men. "Take your walking sticks and turn them into snakes," he ordered. Without the slightest flinch, the six magicians tossed their sticks to the earth. And instantly six more snakes appeared. Pride swelled in Pharaoh's chest.

As they watched the seven slithering creatures, Moses' snake swallowed each of the others, one by one. The wise men flushed. Pharaoh looked inquisitively at Moses and said, "Not bad, but not good enough. I will not release the Israelites." And he flicked them away.

14. PLAGUES AND PESTILENCE

At God's command, Moses and Aaron again met Pharaoh—this time on the banks of the Nile where the king routinely went each morning. Pharaoh was exasperated to see them. Before he could speak, Aaron began shouting, "God has issued an order for Pharaoh: Let my people go, so they can worship me in the wilderness. Since you have refused to obey, let this be a sign that the God of Israel reigns: I will strike the water of the Nile with this staff in my hand, and the river will turn to blood. The fish in it will perish, and the river will become foul. And all the Egyptians will have no water to drink."

Straightway Moses raised his scepter and brought it down with a snap on the face of the water. At that precise spot, the water began to bleed. Bright red swirls of blood flowed downstream. The swathes spread wider as they crept along.

Pharaoh turned to one of his magicians. "Do the same thing."

The man walked a short way up stream where the water was clear and put his rod into the Nile. It bubbled up a dark red, and soon the whole river was crimson. Pharaoh looked smugly at Moses and Aaron. Then he returned to his palace and put the whole episode out of his mind.

It took seven days for the Nile waters to become limpid again. When they did, Moses and Aaron once more went to the royal residence, ignoring the guards. Pharaoh was preparing for a public speech—he had to allay the concerns of his people, for the Nile had never bled before.

Aaron placed himself squarely in front of the throne and declared, "This is what the God of Israel says: Let my people go, so they can worship me. If you refuse, I will send a plague of frogs across your land. The Nile will swarm with them. They will come up out of the river and into your bedrooms, ovens, and cookware. The entire country will crawl with frogs."

Pharaoh was amused. The two brothers waited for a response; when they got none, they walked directly to the Nile. Moses stood on the bank and raised his staff over the waters, but this time he did not strike. As he stood with outstretched hand, frogs gurgled up from the river. They multiplied as they surfaced. Soon the waters were teeming with toads. The banks could not contain them, and before long, the wet, slimy-green creatures blanketed the land of Egypt. The croaks were deafening. Pharaoh' house was filled with them; the moist bodies dropped from the ceiling and hopped out of every nook. He could barely walk without squashing them.

Pharaoh again ordered his wise men to do the same. And they did. But this only doubled the plague. Pharaoh was furious. He summoned Aaron and Moses. "End it now! And I will let your people go, so they can offer sacrifices to your God."

"Why don't you have your magicians end it?" Aaron countered.

"They can't," the king begrudged.

"You tell me when," Aaron answered. "And I will pray to God and he will rid the land of the frogs."

"Tomorrow at daybreak."

"Alright, it will be exactly as you have spoken. Then you will know there is none like our God."

Precisely at daybreak the following morning, all the frogs, wherever they were, died. The Egyptians raked them into great heaps, and a terrible stench filled the land.

But when Pharaoh saw that relief had come, he hardened his heart and reneged on his promise, just as God predicted.

● ● ●

Now, in the houses of Egypt, people were alarmed and angry. First the bloody Nile and then mountains of frogs. What was happening? Had Pharaoh himself caused this? Or was it the workings of the two slave brothers? And who would put an end to this madness?

In the Israelite houses, there was a certain restrained optimism, mixed with confusion and uncertainty. People whispered to one another in the dark: "Moses and Aaron are doing something big, but what? Is God about to rescue us? Why are we too suffering from the plagues? We had no water for a week either, and the odor from the frogs is unbearable."

The following day, Moses and Aaron stood at a distance from the royal palace. Moses lifted his scepter and struck the earth. Instantly every fleck of dust in Egypt turned into a gnat. Swarms of gnats infested the entire country—landing on people and beasts alike, crawling up noses and into eyes and ears. The Egyptians and Israelites coughed and spit and choked up the tiny insects from their throats.

Pharaoh ordered his magicians to duplicate the plague. But they could not—their secret arts failed them. "This is the finger of God," they told the king. Pharaoh scoffed and dismissed them.

The next day Moses and Aaron intercepted Pharaoh on his ritualistic early morning walk to the Nile. Once more Aaron voiced his message. "Thus says the God of Israel: Let my people go, so they can worship me. If you refuse, I will send swarms of flies on you and your people. They will fill the air and carpet the ground. But this time I will spare the region of Goshen, where my people live; no flies will be found there. Then you will know I am not only the God of Israel, but the God over Egypt as well."

With a cold countenance, Pharaoh ignored them and continued his descent toward the water's edge. As he made his return trip to the palace, thick clouds of flies settled over the land. They crawled on the hair and faces of every Egyptian. The whole land was thrown into chaos by the infernal buzzing. But there was not one single fly in Goshen.

Pharaoh called for Moses and Aaron. "Alright! Alright! Go worship your God and offer sacrifices to him! . . . But do it here in Egypt."

"We cannot do it here," Aaron objected. "Besides, your people would detest our making sacrifices to our God, and they might kill us. No, we must take a three-day trip into the wilderness; for that is what we've been commanded to do."

"Then I will let you go into the desert," Pharaoh yielded. "But don't go too far away. And you must terminate the flies before you depart."

"I will pray to God and the swarms of flies will disappear. But I am warning you, Pharaoh, don't deceive us again," Aaron replied firmly.

So the two left Pharaoh's presence and asked God to remove the pestilence. As soon as the flies dropped dead, Pharaoh yet again hardened his heart and would not allow the Israelites to leave.

Then the hand of God struck the Egyptian livestock—donkeys, camels, cattle, sheep, and goats—with a deadly plague. They all perished in one day. But not a single Israelite animal died. Still, Pharaoh was obstinate and did not release the Israelites.

Pharaoh paced in his chambers. How could this otherwise unknown God wreak such havoc on his glorious nation? And where were his gods, the powerful deities of Egypt? Why did they not answer his prayers?

The slave masters no longer beat the Israelite foremen when they did not meet their required tally of bricks. There were no cows to haul the pallets anyway. For this, the Israelites rejoiced. "The hour of our deliverance is upon us," they sang.

Then God said to Moses and Aaron, "Take handfuls of soot and toss them into the air in the presence of Pharaoh. The ashes will spread like fine dust. When the Egyptians breathe it, festering boils will break out all over their bodies."

So, clutching fistfuls of ash, the two went to the palace courtyard. Pharaoh rushed out to meet them. Aaron and Moses said nothing. They threw the black powder into the air and walked out. The Egyptians watched as a hazy cloud settled over the land. Then their flesh began to redden, their eyes puffed, and sores exploded on their faces, hands, arms, and legs. Yellow puss oozed from the tender boils. Walking was difficult, sitting nearly impossible. Pharaoh summoned the magicians, but they were too sick to meet him. They only sent this message: "The fog did not reach the land of Goshen."

Two days later, a fresh-faced and healthy Moses and Aaron appeared again at the royal compound. They were escorted straight to Pharaoh. The body of the king was beleaguered, but his spirit unflagging.

Then God touched the lips of Moses and he spoke in a sonorous voice. "Thus says the God of Israel: If you, O Pharaoh, do not free my people, I will send still more plagues on you and your country. Then you will know there is no God like me. I could've put forth my hand and struck you and your people with such pestilence that you would've been wiped off the face of the earth. But for one purpose I have spared you: To show you my power, so that my name may be proclaimed throughout all the earth. Because you have refused to humble yourself before me, tomorrow I will send a hailstorm more devastating than any in all the history of Egypt. Anyone who does not take cover will join the livestock in the land of the dead."

Pharaoh eyed them fiercely. Then he arose and departed. Some of his officials and attendants hurried out to brace for the storm.

As Moses and Aaron left the throne room, God said to them quietly, "I have hardened Pharaoh's heart not only so I can display my miraculous signs among the Egyptians, but also so you can tell your children and grandchildren about how I made a mockery of your oppressors."

At high noon the next day, Moses raised his staff toward the heavens. Immediately dark clouds gathered and an icy wind blew. Lightening flashed and thunder cracked. Then rocks fell from the sky. The tremendous hail struck down everything that was not sheltered. People were killed, trees destroyed, crops ruined. Egypt was laid waste.

But the sun shone in Goshen.

Pharaoh thought to himself, I have sinned. God is the righteous one, and my people and I are wrong. I must let the Israelites go.

But the next day the rains ceased. And Pharaoh's tenacity returned.

As the clouds broke and the sky lightened over Egypt, Moses and Aaron once more appeared before the king. "Since you have refused to liberate my people, God says: Tomorrow I will bring a swarm of locusts on your country. They will invade the land such that you won't be able to see the ground. They will devour what little is left of your crops and trees. They will overrun your palace and the homes of everyone in Egypt. Never before has anyone seen the likes of what will happen tomorrow."

Pharaoh resisted with steadfast reticence. But several of his officials now stepped forward and fell to their knees before the king. "How long, O Great One, will you let this man plague us? Permit the Israelites to go and worship their God. Don't you realize that Egypt lies in ruins?"

Pharaoh's stern visage softened. He shifted his focus from the prostrate counselors to the audacious shepherds. "Fine, go worship your God. But who exactly will be going with you?"

"All of us," Moses said. "Every single one of us—elders and infants, sons and daughters, flocks and herds. We must all join together in the festival to our God."

"Only the men may go," Pharaoh contradicted. "Isn't that what you've been asking for this whole time? I will never let all of you go. Never! I can see through your evil plan. God help you if you think you're taking everybody!" He shook his fist at them and bellowed, "Now get out of here!"

Moses and Aaron stood firm. None of the officials or court attendants moved.

Then Moses slowly lifted his staff, waving it back and forth above his head. The officers winced and the guards held their breath bracing for the new calamity. All at once, a strong wind from the east began to blow through Egypt. It blew all that day and into the night. When morning arrived, the wind had drawn in a thick cloud of locusts. They swarmed over the whole land of Egypt, from one end to the other. A million tiny mouths devoured the plants in the field and leaves on the trees. Not one green thing was left anywhere.

The following day, God ordered a steady west wind to drive the locusts into the Red Sea. By evening, there was but a gentle breeze. Not a single beating wing remained in all Egypt.

But God hardened Pharaoh's heart, so the king still refused to emancipate the people of Israel.

That night, Moses stood in Goshen among his kin. As Pharaoh paced sleeplessly about his palace, Moses once more raised his scepter of death. When morning came, the sun did not rise in Egypt. If there were a new day, it was not visible. For a deep darkness covered the entire land. No one stirred from their houses. Panic and cries of terror filled the stillness. The utter blackness gripped Egypt for three days. Pharaoh neither ate nor drank, his mind spiraling into a rabid frenzy as the long night dragged on.

Only the land of Goshen was illuminated.

Finally, Pharaoh called for Moses and Aaron. "Go worship your God. You and all your people, everyone may go—wives, children, everybody. Only leave your flocks and herds here."

"No," Moses said. "We need the animals to make sacrifices and burnt offerings to our God. And we won't know specifically which ones to use until we get there. Thus, all our livestock must go with us; not a hoof is to be left behind."

Pharaoh leaped from his seat. "Get out of here! Get out of my sight this instant!" The king's body shivered with rage. "Don't ever appear before me again. The day you see my face, you will die!"

"It will indeed be as you say," Moses replied. "We will never see one another again."

15. THE ANGEL OF DEATH

Moses returned to Goshen. There God revealed to him the final miraculous sign, the most terrible, powerful plague of all: "At midnight tomorrow I will pass through Egypt. When I do, every firstborn male in every household will perish—from the oldest son of Pharaoh who sits on his throne, to the oldest son of the servant who mills the flour. Then a loud wail will rise throughout the land, a wail like no one has heard before or will ever hear again. But among the Israelites—if they follow my commands—it will be so peaceful that not even a dog will bark.

"Here are the instructions which my people must obey. They must take a lamb or young goat without any spot or blemish and slaughter it. They are to sop up some of the blood and smear it on the sides and top of the doorframes of their houses. Next they must roast the whole animal—including the head, legs, and organs—over a fire. Each family is to eat the meat along with bitter herbs and bread made without yeast. What they do not eat, they must burn. But they must consume it in haste, fully dressed for the escape, with sandals strapped and walking sticks in hand.

"Now, Moses, give these commands to my people. For tomorrow at the stroke of midnight I will pass through the land of Egypt and slay the firstborn son in every house. But when I see blood on a doorpost, I will pass over that house. Thus, the plague of death will not touch the Israelites. Yes, I will execute judgment against all the deities of Egypt, for I am God."

The words tingled in the ears of Moses. He summoned the multitude of Israelites, and when they heard the message from God, they cried out with joy. The moment of their salvation was at hand.

They spent all that night and the next day preparing for their dramatic flight.

At midnight the angel of death went forth. Every house wiped with blood he passed over, but every Egyptian house he attacked. And so there went up over the whole land a great and grievous wailing; for there was not a single house where someone was not dead.

Pharaoh sent a message to Moses and Aaron. "Get out. Take all your people and animals and depart from me and my land. Be gone. Go worship your God—and bless me too."

That very night the Israelites began their journey. Like a vast army, they marched quickly and methodically out of the place of their oppression and bondage. Mothers and fathers moved quietly through the darkness; little children, spellbound and frightened, scurried beside them. The sound of a thousand sandals crunching the rock and stone, the bleating of sheep, and lowing of cattle was broken only by the occasional distant whoop or holler of freedom.

As the sun streaked the eastern sky, they continued apace—hastening toward the rising light. They did not stop; they could not stop. Something seemed to be carrying them along. They were headed southeast toward Succoth, a wilderness outpost in a sparsely populated region of Egypt. The few Egyptians they encountered urged them on, lest Moses unleash another pestilence and destroy them all. A few even threw silver and gold trinkets at them, sardonically applauding their departure.

They reached Succoth on the fourth afternoon. There they camped for two nights to allow the animals and young mothers to rest. They had already been gone longer than three days and they were not coming back. Surely Pharaoh knew that, and surely he would have it no other way, for the tenth plague had been a final crushing blow to the king and his people. They were too busy digging mass graves to give the fleeing slaves any thought.

• • •

On the third morning in Succoth, Moses and the Israelites awoke to find a dense, low-lying cloud on the south side of camp. It rose straight up like a column, its edges sharply marked against the blue sky. It was the presence of God leading his people. And so they followed. At night, the pillar of white cloud became a glowing red and orange pillar of fire, lighting the way and providing protection.

From Succoth the pillar led the people due south toward Mount Sinai—the place of the burning bush and the place where they were to meet God. But between them and the sacred mountain lay the Red Sea, passable for one man, but not a mass of people.

As Moses sat in his tent contemplating their route to freedom, God spoke to him. "Order the Israelites to double back to the north and camp near Migdol. When Pharaoh gets wind of this, he will think, 'The Israelites are confused—they are going in circles. They must be trapped in the eastern wilderness.' Then once again I will harden the king's heart, and he will chase after you. In this way, I will gain glory for myself through Pharaoh and his whole army. Then the Egyptians will know that I am God."

So the pillar of cloud led the people back toward the heart of Egypt. And as God planned, the Israelites baited the Egyptians into pursuit.

"Harness the chariots and marshal the troops," Pharaoh decreed. "The slaves are confused." Instantly, six hundred of Egypt's best chariots were drawn up for battle, each with a thoroughbred and first-class driver. All the foot soldiers accompanied them. At Pharaoh's command they sped off for the wilderness, whipping the horses.

The next afternoon, an Israelite boy gathering sticks for a campfire looked up and saw a cloud of auburn dust stretching across the horizon. He stood still, watching. Then slowly the earth itself began to tremble. Horses! He dropped the twigs and ran headlong back to camp. "Egyptians! Egyptians!" he screamed. "They're coming after us!"

Panic struck the Israelites. Their freedom was gone, capture and return to servitude inevitable. Or perhaps death. Caught between sword and sea, they wailed. And they hollered at Moses, "Why did you bring us out here? We will surely die in this desert. Weren't there enough graves for us in Egypt? We knew this would happen. You should've left us alone. Better to be a slave in Egypt than a corpse in the wilderness."

Moses raised his arms, turning from side to side until the pandemonium quieted. "Do not be afraid, my brothers and sisters. Stand still and watch God's salvation. The Egyptians you see on the horizon today you will never see again. God himself will fight for you. You need do nothing. Only remain calm."

Forthwith, Moses took his staff and turned eastward toward the Red Sea. At the same instance, the pillar of cloud rose slowly over the people and sailed westward through the blue sky. It settled at the rear of the camp, forming a white wall of protection against the Egyptians.

Moses, meanwhile, stood on the shore of the sea. He stretched his staff over the waters and a strong east wind arose. It blew furiously, pushing the water into giant heaps on either side and turning the seabed into dry land. All night the wind raged.

"Hurry!" Moses called to the people. "Follow the pathway of God!"

In speechless wonder, the children of Israel rushed to break camp. From dusk till dawn, they hastened through the middle of the sea on dry ground, with walls of water on their right and left. Moses was the last to cross, reaching the opposite bank as the day's first light appeared.

Then the pillar of cloud and fire lifted, and the Egyptians saw what had happened. They mounted their chariots and rode wildly after the fleeing slaves. As they entered the riverbed, between the towers of water, God jammed their wheels, making the chariots impossible to drive. "Retreat! Retreat!" the commanders shouted. "God is fighting for them! Turn back!"

They attempted to reverse course, but Moses stood on the far side of the river and lifted his scepter. The wind abated and the waters were freed. Tidal waves collapsed over the Egyptians, swallowing them in a swirling foam. Horse and rider were drowned in the sea. They sank like a stone, like lead in the mighty waters. And so God swept away the hosts of Pharaoh.

Moses and the Israelites looked on as the bodies of men and beast washed up on the shore. Then Miriam, Moses' sister, took a tambourine and led the women in a jubilant song of victory. They danced and sang, "Oh, sing unto God, for he has triumphed gloriously. Pharaoh's chariots and army he has thrown into the sea. With your right hand, O God, you smashed the enemy, with your breath you blew and the waters covered them."

Moses watched the frenzied crowd with arms folded and a tired smile on his weathered face. He thought of his mother, his days as a prince of Egypt, his crime, the strange bush, and his wife Zipporah. They were now on their way back to her homeland—Midian and Mount Sinai.

The unmistakable voice of God shattered his reverie. "I have for one final time hardened the hearts of the Egyptians in order to display my great glory through the destruction of Pharaoh and his army. All Egypt has seen my power, and they will know I am God."

Moses returned to his tent. He looked at the box holding the bones of his ancestor Joseph. The oath made to his great predecessor was in motion—he would be buried in Canaan, alongside Abraham, Isaac, and his father Jacob. With visions of the far-off Promised Land in his head, Moses drifted off to sleep.

16. THROUGH THE WILDERNESS AND TO THE MOUNTAIN

Moses awoke with new energy. He instructed the people to gather their possessions and prepare for a journey into the wilderness of Shur, east of the Red Sea. For three days the people traveled. They found no water. On the fourth day they arrived at Marah, a small desert outpost. There was a spring and small stream. But the water was bitter.

"What are we supposed to drink out here in this blistering, God-forsaken wilderness?" the people grumbled.

God had already told Moses what to do.

Moses dragged an old tree branch toward the bubbling brook. Straining, he picked it up and tossed it into the waters. Then he wiped his brow and said, "Now you may drink."

As they gulped the cool, fresh liquid, Moses spoke to them. "If you will listen carefully to the voice of God and do what is right in his sight, obeying his commands and keeping his decrees, then God will not make you suffer any of the diseases he sent on the Egyptians; for God is the one who heals you. He is the one who turns your bitter water into sweet water."

After leaving Marah, the Israelites traveled on to the oasis of Elim which featured twelve fresh springs and seventy palm trees. They camped there for three weeks. Then it was time to press on through the wide wilderness toward Sinai.

Violent wind whipped the sand; the sun was unyielding. The people grew faint. "If only God had killed us back in Egypt," they moaned. "There we sat around boiling pots filled with meat and ate bread until we were full. But now Moses has brought us into this wilderness to starve us to death."

Moses stood next to Aaron, his hair blowing all about. "God has heard your complaints, which are complaints against him, not against Aaron and me," he said to the people. "At twilight tonight, God will rain down food from heaven for you. Yes, God will give you meat to eat in the evening and bread in the morning, for the Almighty has heard your complaints against him."

The people were skeptical. Moses continued, "Listen carefully to these instructions concerning the morning bread: Each household should gather as much as it needs for that day only. Do not collect any more than you will eat in one day—do not try to save any of it. On the sixth day of the week, you should gather enough for two days. For on the seventh day of each week, there will be no bread. The seventh day is a day of rest devoted to God, so do not go out to look for the food."

That evening a black cloud appeared on the horizon. It was a mass of low-flying quail. Soon the birds covered the campsite. People rushed about in all directions to capture the migrating birds, which were too fatigued to escape the nets and clubs of the hungry Israelites. The people feasted on fresh meat late into the night.

The next morning the area around the camp was wet with dew. When the dew evaporated, a flaky white substance blanketed the ground. "What is it?" the people puzzled.

"Why it is the promised bread. Manna, it shall be called," Moses explained. So the people came out of their tents, bags in hand, to gather the flakes before they vanished in the rising sun. "It tastes like honey wafers," they shouted gleefully.

A few people, however, disregarded the orders and stored some of the manna until the next morning. But by then it was full of maggots.

The people gathered the food morning by morning, each family according to its need. On the sixth day, they bagged twice as much as usual. On the seventh day, there was no bread, as Moses had said. So they ate the left over bread from the previous day, and this time it was good, without any infestation.

Moses said to Aaron, "Fill a container with manna—make it air-tight—so we can save it for later generations. Then they will be able to see the food God gave to us in the wilderness when he freed us from Egypt." Aaron obeyed and Moses kept the jar in his tent.

• • •

And so the Israelites ate the manna God provided each day. They were happy for a while. But, still, water was sparse in the sandy desert, and again the people grew weary and frustrated. "We need water!" they cried to Moses.

"Why are you crying out to me? Why are you testing God?" Moses asked indignantly.

"Because you are the one who brought us out of Egypt. You are the one who led us out here to make us and our children die of thirst."

Moses flashed an anguished look at Aaron and then walked briskly back to his tent. "Oh, God," Moses wailed, "what am I supposed to do with these people? They are about to stone me!"

God answered, "Go out to the people. Take your staff in your hand and call all Israel to join you. Go to the great rock at the base of Mount Sinai. Raise your staff and hit the rock, and water will come gushing out." So Moses did as God instructed, and water flowed from the boulder and the people's thirst was quenched.

Zipporah and Moses watched as the crowds scrambled to fill jugs, pitchers, and vases. She turned and said to him, "This is yet another amazing work of God I wish to tell my father about."

Moses smiled at her lovingly. "Yes, now that we are here on the outskirts of Sinai, it's time that we reunite with your father Jethro."

"And my mother and sisters," Zipporah added with a twinkle.

"Tomorrow," Moses said, "I will send an envoy with you to the other side of the great mountain to see if you can find your family." Zipporah sighed longingly and put her arm around Moses' waist.

The next day, Zipporah and her son Gershom set off. As dusk fell on the second day, they arrived in the vicinity of Jethro's home. The reunion was grand. Then Jethro gathered a few of his belongings and followed Zipporah and her caravan back to the Israelite side of the mountain.

When Moses received word, he went out to meet them. He and Jethro laughed heartily together and hugged one another tightly. As they had done years before, the two talked into the night as the campfire danced. Moses told Jethro everything that had happened—everything God did to Pharaoh and Egypt and about the hardships they experienced along the way and how God had been with them.

"Praise God," Jethro said, "for he has rescued you from the Egyptian. Now I know God is greater than all the other gods, because he saved his people from bondage under the mighty Pharaoh." He stopped to sip from his cup. "And now that God has brought you back here to the mountain, he will speak to you and your people."

The next morning, Jethro kissed Zipporah and Gershom and began the journey home. Moses watched him go. Then he turned and gazed up at the giant, jagged towering heap of rock. Sinai. The Mountain of God.

He started to climb.

As he ascended, God called to him from the mountain. "Here is what you must say to the children of Israel: 'You have seen what I did to the Egyptians. You know how I carried you—as on the wings of eagles—and brought you to myself. Now if you will obey me and keep the covenant I am about to give, then you will be my own special treasure from among all the peoples of the earth. You alone will be my holy nation.'"

Moses listened carefully. He glanced around at the scraggly shrubs, moss, and vines. Surely one of these must be the bush, he reasoned to himself.

Then the voice from the skies continued, "Go down and prepare the people, for I will appear to them three days hence. They must wash their clothing and abstain from sexual intercourse. You must mark off a boundary around the entire mountain. Warn the people sternly not to go up the mountain or even to approach the boundary. Anyone who touches the mountain will die. They must be stoned or shot to death with arrows; no hand may touch them. The same is true for any animal that crosses the line."

Moses went down and told the people.

● ● ●

At dawn on the third day, thunder roared and lightning flashed. A thick cloud descended on the mountain. There was an earsplitting trumpet blast. All the people stood at the foot of the mountain, trembling with fear; for God had come down on it in a blaze of fire. Smoke billowed into the sky and the whole mountain shook violently. Then God called Moses to the top of the mountain. So Moses began the steep, stony ascent into the black fog.

in the smoky darkness, God spoke these words to him:
God who rescued you from the land of Egypt, the place of
nd bondage. Here are your commands:
ll have no other gods besides me.

"You shall not make for yourself an idol of any kind or an image of anything in the heavens or on the earth or in the seas. You shall not bow down to them or worship them, for I am a jealous God who punishes the children for the sins of their parents to third and fourth generation of them that despise me. But I show mercy and love for a thousand generations to those who love me and obey my commands.

"You shall not take the name of God in vain, for God will not let you go unpunished if you misuse his name.

"Remember to observe the Sabbath day by keeping it holy. Six days each week you shall work, but the seventh day is a Sabbath day of rest dedicated to God. On that day no one in your household shall do any work—neither you, nor your sons and daughters, nor your male and female servants, nor your livestock, nor any foreigners living among you. For in six days I made the heavens, the earth, the sea, and everything in them; and on the seventh day I rested.

"Honor your father and mother, so that you may live a long, happy life in the land that I shall give to you.

"You shall not murder.

"You shall not commit adultery.

"You shall not steal.

"You shall not testify falsely against your neighbor.

"You shall not covet your neighbor's house. You shall not covet your neighbor's wife, male or female servant, ox or donkey, or anything else that belongs to your neighbor."

When God had spoken these ten commands, Moses walked down the mountain and stood before the whole congregation of Israel. They huddled, terrified, at its base. Moses told them what God said.

Immediately the people responded with one voice, "We will do everything God has spoken. We will obey all his commands."

So Moses built an altar at the foot of the sacred mountain. He also set up twelve pillars, one for each of the sons of Jacob, the father of the tribes of Israel. Next he instructed some of the young men to sacrifice bulls as burnt offerings to God. Moses placed a basin underneath the altar to capture the blood from the sacrificed animals. Some of the blood he splashed over the altar. The rest he sprinkled over the people themselves, declaring loudly, "With this blood, I hereby seal the covenant between you and God. He is your God and you are his people, for you, the children of Israel, have sworn to abide by the decrees of God."

Then Moses and seventy elders of Israel climbed the mountain. There they saw God. Under his feet was a surface of brilliant blue, as clear as the sky itself. The men convened a covenant meal together, eating and drinking in the presence of God. Then they returned to the base of the mountain—having beheld God, and still alive.

One week later, God again called Moses, "Come up to me on the mountain and I will write for you additional instructions and commands for the people." So Moses once more set off into the dense, fiery cloud, which was the glory of God. Moses arrived at the top of the mountain and waited. For six days, God was silent. Then on the seventh day he spoke to Moses from inside the cloud. Through forty days and forty nights, God gave Moses ordinances and statutes. God wrote them on two tablets, which he inscribed on both sides, front and back. The tablets contained the words of the covenant, written by the finger of God.

On them were moral and religious laws. He outlined civil codes of conduct, delineating punishment for various crimes. He also gave instructions for the building of the Tabernacle, a sacred, portable tent in which the people of Israel were to worship God. The Tabernacle was to house the Ark, a chest made of wood and gold. In the Ark were to be placed the stone tablets containing the laws of God. To build and furnish the holy tent, God commanded the people to bring offerings of gold and silver and other items necessary for its construction and maintenance. God also gave many commands concerning the sacrifices that were to be offered in the tent. He outlined the duties of the priests who would preside over the rituals and lead the people in appointed festivals throughout the year in honor of God.

And so God gave the laws of the covenant to Moses.

17. BROKEN TABLETS AND A GOLDEN CALF

To Aaron and the Israelites at the base of the mountain, the glory of God appeared as a raging blaze atop the grisly face of Sinai. As Moses tarried in the cloud, the people down below grew restless.

"Where is your brother?" they asked Aaron, frightened of what had become of their leader.

By the fifth week of Moses' sojourn, the people were confused and disgruntled. "What has happened to this Moses who led us out of Egypt? Where is he? Is he coming back down?"

Aaron tried to assuage their concerns. But they were unrelenting. "Has God forgotten us already? Who will lead us? Where do we go now?"

Finally, they cracked. "Let us make new gods who can lead us—gods we can see, gods who will not abandon us in the wilderness!"

"Okay," Aaron conceded. "Bring all your gold to me."

Aaron took the earrings and necklaces and melted them down and sculpted the molten gold into the shape of a calf—an image the people knew well from their days in Egypt. He set the golden calf in front of them.

"These are the gods who brought us out of the land of Egypt!" the people exclaimed jubilantly.

When Aaron saw how excited and happy they were, he decided to build an altar in front of the calf. "Bring offerings and food, and tomorrow we will have a grand feast," he proclaimed.

The next morning, the people got up early to begin the celebration. They ate and drank and bowed down and offered sacrifices to the molten calf, and there was great revelry in the camp.

God looked down and saw. Then he said to Moses, "Go down the mountain, for your people whom you brought from the land of Egypt have corrupted themselves. They have already turned away from my commands."

Moses went, one tablet of stone under each arm. As he approached the foot of Sinai, he heard a boisterous noise. He stopped and stared in horror at the site below. He was scarcely able to breathe. Flush with anger, Moses threw the stone tablets to the ground, dashing them into pieces.

He finished his descent and entered the camp; the people gradually quieted and fixed their eyes on him. Without saying a word, Moses lit the calf on fire, burning it into a fine powder. He mixed the powder with water and forced the people to drink it.

Moses confronted his brother. "What did these people do to cause you to bring such a terrible sin upon them?"

"Please calm down," Aaron stuttered. "You yourself know how evil these people can be. They asked me to make them a god who would lead them since we did not know what happened to you. So I told them to bring me their gold jewelry and I threw it into the fire, and out came this calf."

Moses turned away from Aaron and shouted to the people, "All of you who are on God's side, come here and stand with me." The descendants of Levi—Moses' own tribe—hurried to join him. No one else budged.

Moses gathered the men of Levi and spoke to them, "This is what the God of Israel says to you: Each of you must take your sword and go throughout the camp—from one end of it to the other—and kill everyone you can, even your friends and neighbors."

The Levites obeyed Moses' command. They ran madly through the settlement hacking and chopping people to death. About three thousand died that day.

When the Levites, nearly breathless, returned to Moses, he spoke to them. "Today you have ordained yourselves for the service of God, for you obeyed him, even though it meant killing your own relatives. Today you have earned a blessing. You shall be the priests of God."

● ● ●

The following day, Moses summoned the people to the edge of the camp and said to them, "You have committed a grave sin, but I will go back up to God on the mountain. Perhaps I can obtain forgiveness for your unspeakable deeds."

So once more, Moses labored up Sinai and stood in the smoldering cloud in the presence of God. God spoke first. "I have seen how stubborn and rebellious these people are—with their graven images and fake gods. Now let me be, so that my fierce anger can blaze against them. I will indeed destroy them one and all. Then I will make you, Moses, into a great nation."

Moses lifted his face and spoke softly, "Why, O God, are you so angry with your own people, the people whom you yourself brought out of Egypt with great and mighty acts of power? If you wipe them out now, the Egyptians will think you rescued them with the wicked intention of slaughtering them here in the desert. Don't do that, please, God! Turn away from your fierce anger. Change your mind and do not bring this awful disaster against your own people."

Moses paused. God said nothing. So Moses fell to his knees and continued, "Remember, mighty God, your servants Abraham, Isaac, and Jacob. Remember the binding oath you made to them. You promised you would make their descendants as numerous as the stars of heaven. You vowed to give them a place to call home forever. You cannot break your word now."

Sweat trickled down Moses' brow. Still, God was silent. Moses gathered himself and pressed on. "Yes, these people—your people, my people—have committed a terrible offense against you by making gods of gold. But please forgive them. If you won't, then kill me too. Blot out my name from your holy covenant."

Then God answered, "I have changed my mind. I will not destroy the people and break my covenant with Abraham. But . . . But these people will not go unpunished for bowing down to the golden calf. For their sin, I will inflict on them a plague of suffering; but I will not wipe out my people."

At that very instant, a painful pestilence broke out in the camp at the base of the mountain. The people were in anguish, but they did not die.

God continued speaking to Moses. "It is now time for you to lead the people to the land of promise. Go down and tell them that they are to prepare to depart. But also tell them I will not go with them, for they are a stiff-necked people. If I went with them, my wrath might consume them along the way."

"You mean I'm supposed to lead these people by myself to the Promised Land?" said Moses. "I cannot do it alone—you know that. If you don't go with us, how will we be any different from all other peoples on the earth? How can you abandon us now?"

Thunder rolled and lightening flickered. The breeze strengthened. Then the voice from the cloud spoke once more. "Because you, Moses, have found favor in my sight, I will indeed go with you. I will not forsake those I have chosen."

Moses answered unflinchingly, "Then show me your glorious presence."

"I must place you in the crevice of a rock and cover you with my hand as my glorious presence passes by, so that you do not see my face and die. Then I will remove my hand and allow you to see my back. But my face must not be seen."

The wind ceased and the mountain silenced. As Moses crouched in a nearby cleft, the glory of God began to pass, and Moses heard a voice proclaiming, "I am God. I will have mercy on whom I will have mercy, and I will have compassion on whom I will have compassion. I show unfailing love to a thousand generations. I forgive iniquity, rebellion, and sin. But yet I do not let the guilty go unpunished. I lay the sins of parents upon their children and grandchildren—even children to the third and fourth generations."

When Moses had seen the back of God, he threw himself to the ground and worshiped. "O God," he said, "yes, we can be a stubborn and rebellious people, but please forgive our iniquity. Claim us as your own special possession. And may your glorious presence be forever with us."

God answered, "For you and my people I will do wonders and perform miracles that have never been done anywhere on earth. All nations and people around you will see my awesome power. I will go ahead of you and defeat your enemies for you. But the people must obey my commands and keep the covenant with me.

"When you come to the land of promise, you are not to make a treaty with the people who live there. If you do, you will be trapped by their wicked ways. Instead, you must break down their altars, smash their sacred pillars, and cut down their poles of worship. You must be sure to follow the very first command not to worship other gods, for I, God, am deeply jealous.

"Now, Moses, you are to chisel out two stone tablets like the first ones, so that my people will always have a written record of the covenant. I will write on them the same words that were on the tablets you shattered."

So Moses obeyed, and God once again inscribed the words of the covenant on the stone tablets—front and back.

Then Moses began his decent from the mountaintop cloud for the final time. His face shined with a radiant splendor, for he had seen God. His countenance was so dazzling that as he entered the camp, Aaron and the Israelites looked away in fear.

Moses summoned the people, and they assembled at some distance from him because of his glowing face. He called them closer and explained that the plague they suffered was punishment for the golden calf. But God had forgiven their sin and promised to remain with them on their journey to the land of their ancestors. Moses showed them the new stone tablets and he reread the laws of the covenant.

The people worshipped and vowed again to remain loyal to God. Then Moses recounted the plans for the Tabernacle—the holy tent—and the people set out eagerly to build it. They also constructed the Ark of the Covenant and placed in it the stone tablets.

At the dedication of the Tabernacle, the cloud of the presence of God came down and settled upon it, and the glory of God filled the tent, so that not even Moses could enter it.

18. THE PROMISED LAND

Two months later, the cloud of God lifted from the Tabernacle. This signaled the people to gather their belongings and make ready for the journey to Canaan. The cloud of fire rose and slowly departed from the holy mountain and the wilderness of Sinai. The people followed, carrying the disassembled Tabernacle and the Ark at the head of the great procession. Three days later the cloud came to rest in the desert of Paran.

Now, from the early days of their escape from Egypt God had provided manna for the people. Every day they gathered it. They ground it, beat it, boiled it, baked it, roasted it, and sliced it every which way they could think of. But it was still manna. And now after traveling again for the first time in over a year, they were especially hungry.

"We are so tired of this same old bread," they complained. "If only we had some meat! Oh, how we remember the fresh fish we ate for free in Egypt. And we had all the cucumbers, melons, leeks, onions, and garlic we wanted. Oh, that we were back in Egypt."

When God heard their murmuring, he was angry and sent fire upon them. A few Israelites on the outskirts of camp burned to death. The people cried out to Moses, and the flames from heaven abated.

Moses was distraught. "Why, O God, are you treating me, your servant, so harshly? What have I done that you've placed the burden of leading these people on me? These are not my children. Did I give birth to them? Should I carry them like a father carries a little baby? Where am I supposed to get meat for all these people? They keep whining, saying they are tired of the manna. I can't do this by myself. The load is too heavy. If this is how it's going to be, just kill me now and spare me the misery!"

God took pity on Moses and said to him, "Gather seventy men who are recognized as elders and leaders of Israel. Bring them to the Tabernacle, and there I will take some of the spirit that is upon you, and I will put the spirit upon them also. Thus, they can share the burden of the people along with you, so you will not have to bear it alone.

"As for the people who want meat, here is what you are to tell them: God has heard your cries and he will give you meat—not just for a day or two, or for five or ten or even twenty. But for an entire month you will eat meat, until you gag and vomit it up and are sickened by the sight of it. For you have rejected God with your grumbling and complaining."

"Thousands and thousands of people are here," Moses said. "And you say you will give them meat for a whole month? Even if we butchered all our flocks and herds and caught all the fish in the sea that would not be enough for this number of people."

"Moses, Moses," God said, "I have multiplied Abraham's descendants into the tens of thousands, as I promised him. So when did I lose my power? Do you not think I can do this? Watch and see whether or not my word is fulfilled."

So Moses did as God commanded. He gathered seventy elders and led them to the Tabernacle where God bestowed on them the same spirit that was upon Moses.

That evening God sent a great wind that brought quail from the sea. Vast quantities of the fattened birds fell to the ground all around the camp, covering the desert three feet deep in meat as far as the eye could see. The people went out and collected unimaginable amounts of food. As they gorged themselves on the flesh, the anger of God stirred, and he struck them with a lethal plague. The Israelites buried many of their kindred there in the desert of Paran.

The plague sparked a fierce ire in Aaron and Miriam. The two siblings of Moses questioned his leadership and challenged his authority. "Has God spoken only through Moses? Doesn't God speak also through us and through the elders?"

When God heard this, he immediately summoned Moses, Aaron, and Miriam to the Tabernacle. God then descended in a pillar of cloud and declared, "Aaron and Miriam, listen carefully to what I am about to say. I have selected Moses to guide my people. I have granted seventy elders to assist him, but he remains the supreme leader. Sometimes I reveal myself in visions and dreams. But not with my servant Moses. With him, I speak directly, face to face, and clearly, not in riddles. He sees me and knows me. Moses trusts me and I trust him. So why are you speaking against my chosen one?"

Then the fiery cloud of God ascended, and there stood Miriam, her skin as white as snow from leprosy. Aaron stared with frozen horror. Trembling, he fell at Moses' feet. "Please, my brother, don't punish our sister for this sin she and I have so foolishly committed. Don't let her be like a stillborn baby that comes from the womb with half its flesh eaten away."

Moses looked at his ghostly sister and crumbled to the ground in tears. "Please, God, heal her now!"

God answered from the pillar of smoke, "She will be restored, but she must remain outside the camp for seven days; then she may return."

The people spent those seven days preparing for the next stage of their journey. When Miriam had been brought back into the camp, the Israelites picked up and followed the cloud of the presence of God.

● ● ●

The pillar of smoke continued its movement toward the Promised Land. Near the southern border of Canaan it stopped at a place called Kadesh. Here the tired mass of nomads unpacked and set up camp to prepare for their final march.

Moses watched as the stakes for the Tabernacle were driven into the ground. Barely were the final furnishings put into the tent when the cloud of God descended on it. "Moses," the divine voice said, "send out men to explore Canaan, the land I'm giving to the Israelites. Commission one brave soul from each of the twelve ancestral tribes." Moses kept listening, but the voice spoke no more.

So Moses chose twelve strong men and gave them these instructions: "Go north into the hill country and see what the land is like. Find out as much as you can about the people living there, whether they are strong or weak, few or many. Study the terrain, noting whether the soil is fertile or poor, and if there are many trees. Survey the towns. Do they have walls, or are they unprotected? Do your best to bring back samples of the fruit and crops you see. Gather all the information you can."

For forty days the spies explored Canaan. The Israelites waited restlessly. At dusk on the fortieth night, the band of twelve returned to the camp at Kadesh. A grand council was convened by the light of a thousand torches.

Shaphat, the scout from the tribe of Simeon, stepped forward and spoke. "Moses, Aaron, people of Israel, we have scouted out the land and we bring you this report. The land indeed is rich and beautiful. It flows with milk and honey. We saw hillsides covered with large green trees, fields ripe with crops of all sorts. Cattle and sheep grazed in well-watered pastures. The soil is fertile and the air is sweet. Here is just one sample of some of the amazing fruit we found." At that, two other spies, Joshua and Caleb, presented a massive cluster of grapes suspended on a pole between them. A rumble of excitement rolled through the crowd.

"As you can see," Shaphat continued, "the bunches of grapes were so large it took two of us to carry them." The buzz of enthusiasm grew louder. "And there are pomegranates, figs, dates, and more—some of which we had never seen," he shouted above the din.

Shaphat waited a moment and then raised his hands to hush the crowd. "But there is bad news. Very bad news." Solemn silence fell across the multitude. "The people living there are powerful, and their towns are large and fortified. The inhabitants are enormous—like giants." He extended his hand above his head to show them. "We learned that the Amalekites live in the low land, and the Hittites, Jebusites, and Amorites in the hill country. The Canaanites occupy the coast of the Mediterranean and the valley of the Jordan. And they are all strong and mighty. We cannot take this land."

The people of Israel hunched over in sorrow. The mood of the whole place was suddenly sullen and dejected. Joshua and Caleb exchanged knowing glances. Then Caleb raised his voice and said, "We can take this land! God promised to give it to us. It is a land flowing with milk and honey—and grapes like this." He and Joshua once more hoisted the enormous cluster. "We must believe!"

Shaphat interjected. "No, we cannot fight these people! They are huge. They will destroy us. We are like grasshoppers next to these beasts. Plus, they have walled cities—walls as high as the sky—and inside are well-trained warriors." The other spies nodded in agreement. "The land is good. But the people are too strong for us. If we attack, we are sure to be defeated."

"No!" Joshua said. "We must go at once and take the land, for God will be with us to protect us and fight for us!"

But it was too late. The whole community wept aloud. The crying lasted all night. In the morning, their voices rose in a great chorus of protest against Moses and Aaron. "If only we had died in Egypt, or even here in the wilderness. Why is God leading us to a country we cannot overtake? Does he want us to die in battle? Our wives and our little ones will be eaten by these giants. It would be better for us to return to Egypt. Yes, let's choose a new leader and go back to the land of Pharaoh."

Joshua and Caleb tore their clothing and cried out in anguish, "The land we explored is a wonderful land! God will give it to us. We must not rebel and be afraid of the natives. They are nothing when God is with us." At that, the whole community began to talk of stoning Joshua and Caleb.

Moses and Aaron looked on. Then Moses turned and walked to the holy tent. He knew God would be waiting for him.

"How long will these people despise and reject me?" God bellowed. "Will they never believe in me, even after all the wondrous deeds I've done among them? Now I will disown them and destroy them with a great pestilence. Then I will make you, Moses, into a nation greater and stronger than they are."

Moses objected. "What will the Egyptians think when they hear about this? They themselves witnessed your power. They know you lead your people in the pillar of cloud. They know you promised them this land. But now if you disown your people and slaughter them in a single stroke, the Egyptians—not to mention other nations that know of your great power—will say, 'See, God is strong, but he was not strong enough to bring them into the land of Canaan. So he just killed them in the wilderness.'"

God said nothing.

Moses fell on his face and made supplication. "You yourself have professed that you are a God slow to anger and filled with compassion. Thus, in accordance with your steadfast love, I beg you, O God, to pardon the sins of this people, just as you've done before. Show them mercy once more."

God said, "I will indeed pardon them as you've asked. I will not disown or destroy them. Nonetheless, not one of these people who doubted me will ever enter the Promised Land. They've seen my glorious presence and my miraculous signs both in Egypt and in the wilderness, and yet they've rejected me; thus they will never inherit the land I swore to their ancestors. Only Caleb and Joshua, who remained loyal, will enjoy the fruits of Canaan."

Moses raised his head and slowly pushed his tired body upward. Before he could get to his feet, God spoke again. "Here is what you are to tell the people: You wish you had died in the wilderness? Well that is exactly what will happen to you! Everyone who is twenty or older will perish in this barren desert. You will not enter the land of milk and honey. Only Caleb and Joshua will taste its blessings. You will wander for forty years in the wilderness—one year for each day the spies explored the land. You will wander aimlessly until every last one of you lies dead in the burning sand. Then, and only then, will I bring your children, the next generation, safely into the land, and they will see the fulfillment of my covenant with Abraham. As for this faithless generation, you will know what it's like for me to be your enemy! I, God, have spoken."

Moses was too numb to answer. As he trudged away from the Tabernacle, Aaron came running toward him, shouting, "The spies—all of them except Caleb and Joshua—have fallen over dead! Gone. Just like that!" Moses nodded woodenly. God had spoken.

● ● ●

The next morning Moses reported God's message to the Israelites. They were filled with grief. And a newly found resolve. "We were wrong not to trust God. We will obey. We will enter the land he has promised seventy elders said in one accord. "We realize we've sinned, and no are prepared to take Canaan."

"No, no, no," Moses shook his head. "It won't work. It's too late. If you go now, you will be crushed because God is not with you. God has forsaken you because you have forsaken him."

But they ignored Moses and set off toward the hill country of Canaan. Neither Moses nor the Tabernacle nor the Ark of the Covenant left the camp. Soon the Israelites returned, though not all of them; for the people who lived in the hills rushed down and attacked them and killed some; the rest they chased like a swarm of bees back into the desert.

The Israelites wept before God. But he turned a deaf ear.

The forty years had begun.

19. FORTY YEARS OF WANDERING

Defeated and despondent, the Israelites made ready for their journey into the wilderness. They turned away from the borders of Canaan and headed back south toward the sun baked dunes of Sinai. But not everyone went willingly and peacefully.

"Look here, Moses," a man named Korah said scornfully. "First you brought us out of Egypt, a land flowing with milk and honey. Then you led us through this lifeless desert to another land flowing with milk and honey. But then you don't take us in—even after we repented of our failures. And now you expect us to follow you once again into this wasteland of suffering and death, for forty years, so that we can perish there?"

Korah's rebellion was joined by Dathan and Abiram, along with two hundred fifty other prominent Israelite men. They united against Moses and Aaron. "We are not your subjects, your slaves! What right do you have to act as though you're greater than the rest of God's people?"

Moses maintained his poise. "God will hear your complaint. We will meet at the Tabernacle at this time tomorrow."

On the following afternoon, the glorious cloud of the presence of God settled above the sacred tent. Moses and Aaron stepped forward and stood next to Korah, Dathan, and Abiram, who were joined by their families. Behind them were the two hundred fifty and behind them a great multitude of Israelites. Then God spoke to the whole community from the pillar. "Moses and Aaron, get away from all these people immediately so that I may destroy them this instant!"

The two brothers looked at one another, fear scrawled across their faces. They both fell to the ground. "O God," Moses pleaded, "you are the God who gives life to all creatures. Must you be angry with your people on account of the words of one man?"

"Then at least get away from these three rebels," God commanded. "For I am about to show everyone I have commissioned you, Moses, and that these men have sinned gravely by speaking against you, for it is also speaking against me."

Panic struck the crowd. "Remember what happened to Miriam when she opposed Moses!" the people shrieked as they scrambled to escape. Moses and Aaron, too, moved quickly away from the Tabernacle where the three men stood firmly.

No one had gotten very far when the ground began to rumble. The rocks shook; the dirt shuddered. Suddenly the earth split open and swallowed Korah, Dathan, and Abiram, as well as their wives and children. They all went down alive into the grave. The earth closed over them, and they vanished forever.

When the people saw this, they fled in terror. "The earth will swallow us too!" Then fire blazed forth from the cloud of God and consumed the two hundred fifty who had participated in the rebellion.

As Israelites huddled in their tents that night, their horror over the day's events soon turned to anger. "Moses and Aaron have killed God's people," they declared. The next morning a large crowd gathered at the Tabernacle to protest.

Moses and Aaron came and stood in front of the tent. This time the voice of God from the fiery smoke was audible only to Moses. "Separate yourselves from all these people so I can destroy them now."

Moses straightway turned to Aaron. "Hurry, take some holy incense and carry it among the people to purify them. For God's anger is breaking out against them—the plague has even now begun."

Aaron did as Moses told him. The plague had indeed already begun to strike down the people. So Aaron stood between the dead and the living, holding the burning incense above his head. When he did, the plague ceased. But not before more than fourteen thousand people perished.

• • •

After this, the people did not rebel against Moses or God for a time. They journeyed dutifully from place to place in the wilderness, camping here and pitching their tents there. When the glorious cloud moved, the people followed. When it stopped, they stopped and set up the Tabernacle. And each morning, the dew turned into the bread of life—manna from God.

But water was sparse, and so on one occasion in the wilderness of Zin, the people voiced their familiar refrain of complaint: "Moses is out to kill us. Why did he make us leave Egypt and bring us here to this barren and parched desert? There are no figs, no grapes, no pomegranates. And there is no water to drink. This is torture!"

"Assemble the entire community," God instructed Moses. "As the people watch, speak to the giant rock in the center of the camp, and water will come gushing forth."

So Moses summoned the people to the huge boulder. "Listen, you rebels!" he shouted viciously. "Must I once again bring water from this rock for you?"

Then he raised his staff and struck the rock. He stood back. Nothing happened. He struck again, and water flowed out of it. So the entire community and their livestock drank until they were satisfied.

That night, in the still and crisp darkness, God spoke once again to Moses. "Because you did not follow my orders and speak to the rock, but instead struck it with your rod, because you did not trust me enough to show my power to this people, therefore you will not lead them into the land I'm giving them. You shall see it, but you will not enter it."

Moses took one last cool drink of water. Then blew out the candle and fell fast asleep.

• • •

The fresh water stimulated the people's appetites as they slept that night. So Moses was awakened the next morning by bitter cries of hunger. "We hate this horrible bread! We are sickened by the sight of it!" They kicked and stomped the white stuff on the ground. "Give us something else to eat. We are starving for some real food."

Moses did not move. He lay in his tent staring at the light sneaking in through the slits. He stayed that way until the sun was high in the cloudless sky. Then he heard shrieks of pain.

"Snakes! Snakes! Vipers are killing us!"

Moses knew: God had sent hordes of poisonous snakes among the people. They were everywhere—slithering through tents, hiding in bags, coiled up in pots, even dropping from the sky it seemed. The serpents bit and killed many.

Moses arose and went to the Tabernacle.

"We have sinned by speaking against God and against you," the leaders said to Moses. "We repent. Now pray to God on our behalf and ask him to take away the snakes." Moses scanned their faces carefully. Then he entered the tent.

There God told Moses, "Make a replica of a poisonous snake and attach it to a pole. Anyone who is bitten can look at it, and they will live."

So Moses fashioned a snake out of bronze and attached it to a pole. Then everyone who had a received a venomous bite gazed on the bronze serpent, and immediately the poison was rendered harmless.

But still, many died that day before the pole of healing had been hoisted. There were mass funerals for the next week. The faithless generation was indeed perishing in the wilderness.

● ● ●

In the thirty-sixth year of their wandering, the Israelites once again approached the Promised Land. The new generation of Israelites was tough and strong-minded, having survived the vast and dreadful desert. As they neared Canaan, they encountered various peoples living in the regions around it.

When they came to the town of Heshbon, just east of their final destination, Moses sent a message of peace to its ruler, King Sihon. "Kindly allow us to pass through your territory. We will stay on the main road and won't bother you or your people in any way. If you wish to sell us food or water, we will gladly pay for it. All we ask is permission to pass through your land."

Sihon refused, for God had made Sihon stubborn and defi- would be annihilated. Accordingly, when Sihon mobilized d declared war, God handed him over to the Israelites, who cap… . Heshbon and killed Sihon and all his people. The Israelites put every person to the sword—men, women, and children. Not a single life was spared. They took all the enemy livestock for themselves and ransacked the whole place.

The Israelites did the same to neighboring King Og of Bashan and his people. Soon, word of the Israelite's power and successes spread to surrounding areas.

When King Balak of Moab saw the Israelites camping near his territory, he first made an alliance with the king of Midian. Then he sent an urgent message to an esteemed prophet and wise man named Balaam. "A horde of people has come out from Egypt. They cover the face of the earth and have already destroyed Sihon and Og. Please, Balaam, come and curse these people because they are too powerful for me. If you curse them, perhaps I will be able to drive them from our land. For I know blessings fall on any people you bless, and curses on those you curse."

"Stay here overnight," Balaam said to the messengers when they arrived and delivered the word from King Balak. "In the morning I will tell you whatever God directs me to say."

During the night, God appeared to Balaam and said, "You are not to curse my people Israel, for they have been blessed. Furthermore, do not return with these messengers. Send them on their way."

The next morning, Balaam told Balak's officials, "You must return home. God will not allow me to speak against Israel or even to go back with you."

So the men returned home and gave the message to Balak. The king was displeased and sent a second envoy of even more distinguished officials with this message for the holy man: "I will pay you very well, if you will only come and curse these people for me."

"Even if Balak were to give me his palace filled with silver and gold," Balaam said, "I would not do anything contrary to the will and word of God. But you are welcome to stay here tonight; perhaps God will have something else to say to me."

God came to Balaam again that night and instructed him, "Since these men have come for you a second time, go back to Balak with them. But do only what I tell you to do."

The next morning, Balaam arose, saddled his donkey, and started off with the Moabite officials. But God was angry with Balaam for going, so he sent his angel to block the road. As Balaam rode along behind the diplomats, Balaam's donkey saw the angel of God standing in the road with his sword drawn. The donkey bolted into a field, but Balaam beat it and turned it back onto the path.

Then the angel stood at a place where the road narrowed between two vineyard walls. When the donkey saw the angel, it tried to squeeze by and crushed Balaam's foot against the coarse stone. So Balaam beat the donkey again.

Then the angel moved farther down the road and stood in a place too narrow for the donkey to get by at all. This time when the donkey saw the angel, it lay down. In a fit of rage, Balaam pummeled the animal with his staff.

Then God enabled the donkey to speak. "Why are you beating me? What have I done?"

"You are making me look like a fool in front of these ambassadors!" Balaam shouted. "If I had my sword, I would kill you!"

"But, Balaam, I'm the loyal donkey you've ridden all your life," the animal answered. "Have I ever done anything like this before?"

"No," Balaam admitted.

At that moment, God opened Balaam's eyes, and he saw the angel stationed in the road with a drawn sword in his hand. Balaam bowed his head.

"Why did you beat your donkey these three times?" the angel asked. "Each time the donkey saw me, it shied away. If it hadn't, I would've certainly killed you."

"I am sorry," Balaam replied. "I didn't realize you were blocking the road. Does God want me to return home?"

"No, you may go with these men, but you must say only what God tells you to say." So Balaam went on with Balak's officials.

"You have finally come," the king said happily as Balaam was ushered before him.

"Yes, I have. But I will tell you directly what I told your esteemed messengers: I have no power to say whatever I want. I will speak only the message God puts in my mouth."

The next day Balak took Balaam up a high hill where he could see the people of Israel blanketing the plain below.

The prophet said to the king, "Stay here, and I will go see if God has a message. Then I will tell you what he reveals to me." So Balaam climbed alone to the top of an adjacent hill, and God met him there.

Balak waited anxiously in the brisk afternoon breeze for a space of two hours. When Balaam returned, he declared, "I received a command from God to bless Israel. God has blessed, and I cannot reverse it. There is no misfortune in store for Israel. No curse can touch the children of Abraham; no magic has any power against them. Blessed is everyone who blesses you, O Israel, and cursed is everyone who curses you."

Balak was disgusted. "Well if you're not going to curse them, at least don't bless them!"

"I told you," Balaam replied, "I can only say what God tells me. And those were the words God gave me."

Balak took him to two different spots overlooking the Israelite camp that day. And twice more Balaam blessed and did not curse the people of Israel. This infuriated King Balak. Flailing his arms wildly, he yelled at the seer, "I called you to curse my enemies! Instead, you've blessed them three times. Now get out of here! Go back home! I promised to reward you, but not for this."

Balaam looked at him, amused. "I told your messengers that even if you gave me your palace filled with silver and gold, I would be powerless to do anything against the word of God. Now I will return home. But first let me tell you what the Israelites will do to your people in the days to come." He paused and cleared his throat. "A star will emerge from the descendants of Jacob, a scepter will rise from Israel. It will crush the forehead of Moab, and crack the skulls of Balak's people."

Then with a gentle tug on the donkey's reigns, Balaam rode down the hill. Balak watched him, and then turned to the plain. There were the Israelites who seemed to number as the sands of the sea. "I hope the contingency plan is working down there, because nothing went right here," Balak muttered as he started back toward his palace.

● ● ●

Down on the plains, the people of Israel—oblivious to what had been going on above them—began to interact with the Moabites and Midianites, who figured that one way to avoid being destroyed was to make peace with the newcomers. Or, more specifically, to make love. It was Balak's backup plan. The local girls seduced the Israelite men, and then invited them to the ritual sacrifices in honor of their gods. There the Israelites ate and drank and bowed down to the Moabite deities. So they committed both sexual and religious sins, and God was enraged.

God summoned Moses to the Tabernacle and commanded him, "Seize all the men who have slept with these foreign women and worshipped these farcical gods. Seize them and kill them in broad daylight! The plague has been unleashed, and only this will deter it."

Moses rubbed his forehead with both palms, for he knew that even at that moment death was creeping through Israel. He called the leaders of the people to the tent. A large crowd gathered there to mourn those who had already perished in the divinely appointed epidemic. Inside the Tabernacle, Moses said to the head tribesmen, "Each of you must execute publicly any of your men who have been seduced by a Moabite woman and participated in the worship of their gods."

Moses started to give further instructions, but the assembly was interrupted by a commotion. An Israelite man named Zimri was, at that very instant in the sight of everyone, bringing a Midianite woman named Cozbi into his tent. When Phineas, one of the men listening to Moses, saw this, he jumped up, grabbed his spear, and rushed into the tent. He burst through the flap, and there was Zimri lying on top of the woman. Phineas raised his weapon and thrust it into Zimri's back. The razor-sharp point sliced through him and continued into Cozbi's stomach. Zimri slumped lifelessly onto the naked body under him. The woman cried out and writhed in pain. As she took her final breath, the plague ended. But not before twenty-four thousand Israelites had perished.

The final members of the rebellious generation were dead.

The next morning, God said to Moses, "Take vengeance on the Moabites and Midianites and destroy them because they've led my people astray."

So Moses commissioned twelve thousand men to go to war. Phineas led the army with the sacred trumpet of God. As they had done before, the Israelites routed their enemy. They put every man to death with the sword, but they spared the women and children. Balaam was among the deceased.

Moses met the army as they returned triumphant. But he was furious with the captains and commanders. "Why have you let the women live? These are the very ones who caused the people of Israel to sin against God. They are the ones who triggered the deadly pestilence to break out against us. Therefore, you must kill every woman who has had intercourse with a man. You must also kill all the boys. Only spare the little girls and young women who have never known a man. You may let them live and keep them for yourselves."

So the Israelites did as Moses commanded.

They divided the spoils among themselves—cows, sheep, goats, donkeys. And young virgins, of which there were thirty-two thousand.

20. A FINAL FAREWELL

The forty years of wandering in the wilderness had come to an end. The previous generation of Israelites was dead, as God required. The life of Moses, too, was at an end. He was an old man full of years. Knowing his days were few, he bid the entire congregation to the Tabernacle. They stood solemnly around it, sensing the gravity of the moment. Moses lifted his voice and addressed them:

"I am no longer able to lead you. I cannot take you across the Jordan River and into the land God has promised. For God will not let me. But God himself will go with you. He will destroy the inhabitants of Canaan just as he destroyed Sihon and Og, Moab and Midian. And you will take possession of it."

He paused and beckoned Joshua to his side—Joshua the spy who, along with Caleb, trusted God to give the land to his people, even as the others doubted. "God has appointed this brave and wise man to be your new leader," Moses proclaimed, putting his hand on Joshua's sturdy shoulder. "He will guide you from henceforth."

Then he addressed Joshua. "Be strong and courageous. Do not be afraid, for God will be with you as you take these people into the place God promised our ancestors—Abraham, Isaac, and Jacob. God will neither fail you nor abandon you."

Moses gazed across the attentive assembly, his eyes—still keen—flashing this way and that. "People of Israel, I command you this day to love God and keep his commands, decrees, and regulations. You shall write them on your heart and bind them around your neck. You must teach them diligently to your children. Talk about them when you sit in your house, when you walk down the road, when you rest, and when you get up.

"The two stone tablets—a written record of the covenant inscribed by the finger of God—will forever remain in the Ark as a constant reminder. You must honor the covenant God made with us at Mount Sinai. It was a covenant not only with your parents and grandparents, but also with all of us here today. You know how it begins: 'I am your God who rescued you from the land of Egypt, the place of your slavery and bondage. You shall have no other gods besides me.' Thus, you shall love God with all your heart, with all your soul, and with all your strength.

"If you faithfully obey, then God will send rain on your land so that you may gather grain, new wine, and oil. Your barns will overflow. God will bless the fruit of your womb, and you will multiply, and God will open the storehouse of his bounty and bless you and the land he promised to our forefathers, the land that you yourselves are about to enter and occupy.

"But if your heart turns away from the covenant, and if you bow down and worship other gods, I declare to you this day that you will certainly be destroyed. God will send on you curses and confusion and plagues and ruin until he has wiped you from the land. God will strike you with wasting diseases and your fields with scorching heat and drought. He will turn the rain into a powdery dust until you are destroyed and your carcasses have become food for the birds of the air and the beasts of the field. And there will be no one to save you.

"Therefore, today I call heaven and earth as witnesses that I have set before you the way of life and the way of death, the way of blessings and the way of curses. Now, therefore, choose life, so that you and your children may live long in the land you are about to possess."

Then Moses raised his hands and pronounced a blessing on the whole congregation. His final words had been spoken.

At dawn the next morning, Moses walked alone to Mount Nebo in the land of Moab. His life and service would end with one final climb. His steps were short as he leaned heavily on his mighty staff.

When he reached a high precipice late in the afternoon, he raised his eyes and squinted westward into the setting sun. He scanned the fruited plains and the rich, fertile valleys. He looked to the north and to the south at the land of milk and honey stretching before him.

Then God spoke. "This is the land I am giving to the people of Israel as their own special possession. I have allowed you to see it with your own eyes, but you will not enter it, for you betrayed me at the great rock in the desert of Zin." And so Moses stood for a long time looking out across Canaan.

Then he died. No one knows where he was buried.

Never again would there be a man like Moses, whom God knew face to face.

21. TAKING THE LAND

The Israelites camped in the plains of Moab for thirty days more while they mourned the death of Moses. It was a period of sadness, rest, and reflection—and a time of eager anticipation. At dawn on the thirty-first day, God descended in the pillar of cloud and spoke to Joshua. "The time has come for you to lead the people of Israel across the Jordan River into the land I am giving them. Be strong and courageous, for I will be with you. No king or nation or people will be able to stand against you, for every place you set foot will be yours."

Joshua, a short, burly man with thick locks and an angular face, summoned his officers and commanded them, "Go through the camp and tell everyone to make ready. They are to gather up everything they have, for we are not coming back this time. In three days we will cross the Jordan and set our sights on Jericho."

Jericho. The great walled city just west of the river. It would need to be scouted. So Joshua summoned two spies and instructed them, "Get as much information as possible about the city and the area around it." As Joshua watched them sleuth off into the darkness, he thought of the tragic failure of his reconnaissance mission forty years earlier. Surely this time would be different, he prayed.

The two men stole quietly across the Jordan and slipped into Jericho. At dusk, they went to the house of a prostitute named Rahab and stayed the night.

Word of their arrival, however, made its way to the king of Jericho, who sent two messengers to Rahab. "Where are the men who came to

your house?" they asked her. "We need to know i
they're Israelite spies from across the river."

"Yes, those men were here earlier, but they left
one stays here long," she said with a wink. "I have
went. I'd guess they're on the road home, on the path leading to the shal low crossings of the river. If you hurry, maybe you can catch them." They looked at her suspiciously, started to force their way in, but then decided to follow her suggestion.

When they were safely out of sight, Rahab hustled to the roof, for there she had hidden the two spies underneath some bundles of grain. "That was them—the king's men, as I suspected," Rahab said. The two Israelites crawled out. "Are you wondering why I did not give you up?" she asked. "It is because I know your God has given you this land. We are all afraid of you. Everyone here is living in terror. For we've heard how God made a dry path through the Red Sea when you escaped from Egypt. And we know what you did to the people of Sihon and Og and Moab and Midian—how you utterly destroyed them. The hearts of those in Jericho have melted in fear. Your God must be the supreme God of heaven and earth."

The spies marveled at her.

"Now swear to me," Rahab continued, her voice unwavering, "that you will save me and my family since I have helped you. I need your word you will let me live, along with my father and mother, my brothers, sisters, and all their families."

The two men exchanged glances. Then one of them said, "If you will get us safely out of here, we hereby make a formal oath that you and your family will be spared when we take this city."

Rahab nodded. "I can do that easily. My house is in the city wall. Take this scarlet rope and let yourself down to the ground through the window. Then you will be outside the city and you can go from there. But you should be careful; the king's men will be looking for you." She pulled the rope from around the stacks of grain and handed it to the men.

"Here is what you must do," the spies informed Rahab. "We will be bound by the oath we have taken only if you follow these directions. When we attack, you must leave this red rope hanging from the window. All your ily members—everyone you want spared—must be here inside the ouse. If they go outside and are killed, their blood will not be on our hands. But anyone inside the house with the red rope will be saved."

"Agreed," the woman replied. Then she secured the cord, and the spies vanished into the cold, moonless night. They went up into the hill country surrounding Jericho. They stayed there three days, scouting the territory and waiting for the king's men to abandon their chase. Then they returned to Joshua and told him all that had happened.

At daybreak the next morning, Joshua sent word to the congregation. "When you see the priests carrying the Ark of the Covenant of God, follow it. For God is about to do a great wonder. This is the last day you will gather manna." A clamor rolled through the camp when they heard these words.

As the sun crested in the sky, Joshua ordered the priests, "Lift up the Ark of the Covenant and proceed to the Jordan. When you reach its banks, take a few steps into the river and stop there." The priests obeyed and the people followed.

Now it was the harvest season, and the Jordan overflowed its banks on its way south toward the Salt Sea. But as the priests dipped their feet into the edge of the waters, the river rolled back on each side, creating a large swath of dry ground. The priests carried the Ark into the middle of the riverbed. Joshua stood next to it and beckoned the first of the Israelites to pass to the other side. They charged across, some with shouts of joy, others in somber silence, but all in amazement. As each of the twelve tribes went by, Joshua presented its leader with one large stone taken from the dry river bottom.

When all the people were safely on the western bank, Joshua and the priests came up out of the river. As soon as their feet were on high ground, the water of the Jordan returned and overflowed its banks as before.

That night Joshua held a solemn assembly. He took the twelve stones given to the head tribesmen and set them up as an altar to God. Then he proclaimed in the hearing of all Israel: "These stones are a sacred memorial marking the spot where we crossed the Jordan. For God dried up the river, just as he did the Red Sea years ago. We have now arrived in the Promised Land."

There were cries of happiness and quiet prayers of gratitude.

● ● ●

They were indeed in the land of their forefathers, but Jericho loomed before them. Joshua knew the great city must first be defeated if the rest of Canaan were to fall. Jericho was a mighty fortress with high, thick walls—it was one of the cities that had so intimidated the spies four decades earlier.

Behind the walls, the people of Jericho had gathered all their possessions—every cow, sheep, goat, barrel, and pitchfork—into the city and barred shut its iron gates. Their harvested crops were piled in vast storehouses. Joshua could see countless warriors stationed along the top of the wall—arrows and stones in hand. "They are prepared for either a long siege or a direct attack," Joshua mumbled to himself.

That night, in the still blackness, God spoke to Joshua. "I have given Jericho, its king, and its people into your hand. Here is what you must do: March around Jericho one time each day for the next six days. Seven priests are to lead the way, each carrying a ram's horn and sounding it as they go; the Ark should follow them, and then you and all the soldiers. On the seventh day, march around the city seven times. After the final lap, the priests are to give one long, loud blast on their horns at which time all the people must shout as loudly as they can. Then the walls of Jericho will collapse, and you are to charge straight in and overtake it."

So Joshua summoned the priests and the commanders and told them of God's plan. Not a few of them looked askance at the proposed strategy. But the next day, they were all assembled in order. "Do not talk. Do not even make a sound," Joshua commanded as they prepared for the first day's march. "Not a single word from any of you." They set out, the priests leading the way blowing their horns, followed by the Ark, and the host of men with their weapons.

The people of Jericho watched the strange sight. This army of people from Egypt was marching around their city, but making no attempt to set up a siege or attack it. They stared straight ahead and marched in silence; none of them even looked at Jericho. The sound from the trumpets did not cease as they moved parallel with the wall. Rahab stared out her window, wondering and waiting. When the slow circumference had been completed, the file of Israelites went to their tents.

Likewise, on the second day the men of Israel circled the city once and returned to camp. Again, the people of Jericho looked on. So it was on the third and fourth day. On the fifth day, the king of Jericho became angry and shouted taunts and fired warning arrows into the air. But on the sixth day, he gave up worrying and laughed at the fools outside his massive brick ramparts.

On the seventh day, the Israelites arose before dawn. As they prepared for the first of seven revolutions, Joshua spoke to the men. "Today, when Jericho falls into our hands, you are to kill everyone and everything in the city as a sacrifice to God. Nothing that breathes is to remain alive. As for everything else, you are to keep none of it for yourselves. Absolutely nothing. If you do, you will bring trouble on all Israel. Everything made from silver, gold, bronze, or iron is sacred to God and must be brought to the Tabernacle. Now let's go."

When Joshua and the army finished their seventh lap late in the afternoon, the priests sounded a long, shrill blast on their horns. Then Joshua commanded the people, "Shout! For God has given the city into your hands!"

The Israelites raised a mighty cry, and suddenly the ground began to tremble. The great wall around Jericho shook, its joints cracked, its mortar split. Then it collapsed with a thunderous crash of rock and stone. The Israelites swarmed into the city and completely destroyed every living being in it with their swords—men and women, boys and girls, cattle, sheep, goats, and donkeys.

As Joshua surveyed the slaughter, a soldier came running up to him. "There it is! There it is!" he pointed excitedly at the one small portion of wall that remained upright. Through the dust, Joshua could see a red rope dangling from a window.

"We are men of honor who keep our promises. Go and rescue Rahab and her family," Joshua directed.

So the man and a comrade dashed off. They found Rahab and her relatives huddled in the doorway. "Quickly, quickly!" the two Israelites urged the prostitute and her relatives who scrambled over crumbled boulders and mounds of shattered blocks.

When Joshua received word that Rahab was safely among the Israelites, he gave orders to set fire to the rubble. Only the silver, gold, bronze, and iron were kept for the Tabernacle of God. All else was torched.

So the fame and fear of Joshua spread throughout Canaan, for God was with him.

22. TRIALS AND TRICKS

While the Israelites celebrated their dramatic victory, Joshua summoned his two spies. "Go up to the city of Ai and see what you can find. It's about fifteen miles west from here, mostly uphill. If we can take Ai, we'll have split the Promised Land in two. Then we can conquer each half separately."

The two men went and brought back their report: "The journey up was treacherous in places, but once you arrive, there isn't much to see. Taking Ai won't be a problem. It's a small, unfortified town, nothing like Jericho. It won't require more than a few thousand men to defeat it."

In accordance with their findings, Joshua sent three thousand soldiers to attack Ai. They marched on the city, planning a frontal assault. But as they approached, the men of Ai rushed out and charged down on the unsuspecting Israelites. Fear paralyzed Joshua's men, and their courage drained away. They turned and fled.

"We had to retreat," one of the generals explained to Joshua. "Thirty-six of our men were killed and the rest just gave up and ran. I don't know—something wasn't right."

Joshua listened, flabbergasted. How could this be? As word spread among the people, their spirits deflated. Joshua went to the Tabernacle, tore his clothing in dismay, and bowed before the Ark. "O God, why did you bring us across the Jordan River only to let us be defeated? What can I say to the people, now that we've lost? Plus, when the Canaanites hear what happened at Ai, they will join together and wipe our name off the face of the earth. And then what will become of your great name?"

"Get up!" God growled. "Why are you lying
Israel has sinned and broken my covenant. They st
which I designated for destruction. They took fo
to be devoted to me. So now Israel itself will suffer
longer be with you until you find and eliminate the
goods."

Joshua popped to his feet. God continued. "Here ... at you are to do. Tell the people to present themselves before me, and I myself will point out the tribe to which the guilty man belongs. That tribe must come forward with its clans, and I will point out the guilty clan. That clan will then come forward, and I will reveal the guilty family. Lastly, each member of the guilty family must come forward, and I will single out the perpetrator, who will then be burned with fire, along with everything he has, for he has violated the word of God and brought disaster on Israel."

And so it was. The next morning, after a sacrifice to sanctify the assembly, Joshua brought the tribes of Israel before God. After all the leaders of the tribes had passed before the Ark, God identified the tribe of Judah. Then the clans of Judah came forward, and God chose the clan of Zerah. Then the families of Zerah presented themselves, and God pointed to the family of Zimri. Finally, every member of Zimri's family, one by one, passed in front of the Ark. And Achan was chosen.

Joshua stood face to face with Achan. The hushed congregation circled about them. Joshua leaned in and spoke softly. "Achan, my brother, tell me what you have done. Confess. Tell the truth and don't hide anything from me."

"It is true," Achan sobbed. "I have sinned against God. When we ransacked Jericho, I saw a beautiful blue robe—the expensive kind from Babylon—two hundred silver coins, and a bar of gold. I wanted them so badly that I took them. They are buried in the ground underneath my tent; the silver is at the very bottom."

Joshua sighed and closed his eyes. "Why have you brought this trouble on us? Now God will bring trouble on you."

Joshua sent men to dig up the spoils. Then the Israelites took Achan, the robe, the silver, the bar of gold, his sons, daughters, cattle, donkeys, sheep, goats, and everything he had and brought them to a valley outside

There they stoned Achan and his family, burned their bodies, and a great heap of rocks over the charred remains.

And so God's anger abated. That night, he again spoke to the leader of his people: "Attack Ai once more. Take all your warriors and you will destroy it just as you destroyed Jericho. This time, however, you may keep the plunder and livestock for yourselves." Joshua cocked his head to one side, but spoke not a word.

The next day, Israel sent five thousand men to lie in ambush west of Ai. The remainder of the army feigned an attack from the other side of city. When the king of Ai saw the Israelites on the east drawing up for battle, he launched an all-out assault. Joshua's men turned and fled as though they were badly beaten. Then the men in ambush jumped up from their position and charged into the vacated Ai. They quickly captured it and set it ablaze.

When the soldiers of Ai turned and saw smoke filling the sky, their hearts sank. The Israelites who had fled now turned and attacked them, and the Israelites inside the town emerged and struck from the rear. The men of Ai were trapped, but they fought to the death. When it was over, not a single soldier from the tiny town survived or escaped. Only the king was taken alive.

When the Israelites finished killing all the men of Ai in the open fields, they returned to the burning town and slew everyone inside. They massacred the entire population of Ai that day—twelve thousand in all. The livestock and treasures of the town they kept as plunder for themselves, as God permitted.

Joshua took a rope, tied a brick to one end, and threw it over the limb of a tree. Then he formed a noose, tightened it around the head of Ai's king, and hoisted him high into the air. And so the king was hanged in a tree. At sunset the Israelites took down the corpse and dumped it where the city gate once stood.

God had given Israel a second mighty victory.

When the people of Gibeon heard what Joshua did to Jericho and Ai, they sent a delegation to the Israelites. They loaded their donkeys with weathered saddlebags and old, patched wineskins. They packed dry and moldy bread. They put on worn-out sandals, tattered clothes, and headed for Gilgal where the Israelites were encamped.

"We are here to see the man Joshua," they announced to several Israelites tending sheep on the outskirts of the town.

"You can find him in the center of camp, near the holy Tabernacle," one of them pointed.

Soon the Gibeonite delegation stood before Joshua and the council of elders. The leader of the Gibeonite group, a round man with short arms, spoke. "We have come from a distant land to ask you to make a peace treaty with us."

"Who are you?" Joshua inquired. "Where do you come from? How do we know you don't live nearby? For if you do, we cannot make a treaty with you."

The pudgy man answered, "We have come from a very distant country, for word of your success has quickly spread far and wide. We've heard of the great power of your God. We know what he did for you in Egypt and we know what he did to the two kings east of the Jordan—Sihon and Og. Therefore, our elders instructed us to take supplies for the long journey and to make a truce with you."

He paused and rummaged through his sack. "Look here," he said, holding up a loaf of bread. "This food was hot from the oven when we left our homes. But now, as you can see, it is dry and moldy. These wineskins were new when we filled them, but now they are old and split open. And our clothing and sandals are worn out from the very long journey."

Joshua and the Israelite leaders carefully examined the food and the clothes. But they did not consult God.

"We will make a pact of peace with you," Joshua declared. "We hereby take this solemn oath that we will not harm you, since you live beyond the land God has promised to us."

The ambassadors bowed. Then Joshua gave them provisions for their journey home.

A week later, one of the spies asked for an audience with Joshua. "Those men with whom we made a treaty do not live in a faraway land. They live right up the road. That delegation, we've learned, was from a group of four cities not far from here. The main city—and the one from which the ambassadors were sent—is Gibeon. It's just south of Ai."

"Are you sure?" Joshua asked incredulously.

"Yes, quite. I would suggest it is now our turn to send a delegation to them," the man said with a devious grin.

"We most certainly will," affirmed Joshua. "I myself will go."

They left right away.

"Why did you deceive us?" Joshua asked the council of Gibeonites. "Why did you say you live in a distant land when in reality you live right here among us? May you be cursed because of your boldfaced lie!"

The same rotund man replied, "We did it because we know your God is giving you this entire land and your God told you to destroy all the people living in it. So we feared greatly for our lives and the lives of our wives and children. That is why we've done this. But now . . . But now we are at your mercy. Do to us whatever you think is fair."

Joshua's jaw tightened. "We will not kill you, as that would violate our oath. But from now on you will be our servants—our woodcutters and our water carriers."

The men of Gibeon bowed, and then presented the Israelites with gifts.

When Joshua returned home, the people of Israel grumbled against him because of the treaty. But Joshua told them, "Since we swore an oath to God, we cannot touch them. We have no choice. But we made them our slaves. Just think—no more lifting an ax or lugging buckets of water."

At that, the people's ire was assuaged.

23. PROMISE FULFILLED, COVENANT RENEWED

Now Adoni, king of the city of Jerusalem, heard all that Joshua had done. He also learned that the Gibeonites had made peace with Israel and were now their slaves, which made Adoni and his people very nervous because Gibeon was a formidable city with strong warriors. And if they had decided to submit to the Israelites, well, then, there was not much hope for Jerusalem.

So Adoni sent messengers to kings of four nearby cities in the southern hill country of Canaan. "Let us take up arms together against Gibeon," he urged them, "for they made peace with Joshua. We might not be able to defeat Israel, but we can retaliate against Gibeon for joining them." The four kings agreed and combined their armies for a united attack. The coalition of troops soon moved into position opposite Gibeon.

When the Gibeonites saw the horde of soldiers, they frantically dispatched messengers to Joshua in Gilgal. "Come save us! All the kings who live in the hill country have joined forces against us."

Joshua hesitated. But then God spoke to him. "Go, for I will give you victory. And in this way, you will take for yourselves more of the land I have promised."

So Joshua and the entire army left Gilgal and marched through the night to Gibeon. They launched a surprise attack on the five kings just before daybreak. God threw the enemy into a terrified panic, and the Israelites attacked from all sides and slaughtered great numbers of them. As the coalition retreated south toward their homes, God hurled huge hailstones on them from the sky. The giant rocks of ice fell with a tremendous thud, squashing to death more men than the Israelites killed with the sword.

While the day wore on, Israel continued its pursuit. Joshua ordered his men, "Hurry, chase the enemy and cut them down from the rear. Don't let them get back to their towns." Then, seeing the sinking sun, Joshua cried out to God, "May the sun stand still and the moon not rise!" At that moment, the sun ceased its descent and hung suspended just above the horizon until Israel finished its slaughter. They wiped out the five armies, except for a tiny remnant that managed to reach their fortified towns.

As dusk finally came, an informant brought word to Joshua. "Adoni and the four other kings have escaped and are hiding in a cave a short distance off the main road."

"Cover the opening of the cave with large rocks, and place guards at the entrance to keep them trapped inside," Joshua instructed. And so it was done.

That night, Joshua and the Israelites celebrated their victory and then slept soundly. In the morning, Joshua addressed his men. "God is with us, for we have defeated the armies of the five main cities of the southern region of the Promised Land." The troops raised their fists and roared. "While we are here," Joshua continued, "we will finish off this half of Canaan. Then we will set our sights on the northern cities. But for now one final task remains." Turning to his high officers, Joshua said, "Remove the rocks covering the mouth of the cave where Adoni and his four comrades are hiding, and bring them here to me."

When the five rulers had been fetched, Joshua said to his commanders, "Throw them to the ground, and put your feet on their necks."

They did as they were told.

With the faces of the kings smashed into the dusty earth, Joshua made a full-throated declaration: "Don't ever be afraid or discouraged, O Israel. Be strong and courageous, for God will do this to all inhabitants of Canaan who remain, both here in the south and the north. We will stomp on their heads and crush them."

Then Joshua drew his sword and plunged it into the bowels of each king. He ordered his men to hang the corpses on five trees. The mangled bodies swayed in the stiff breeze, puddles of blood soaking the dirt beneath.

At sunset, Joshua gave instructions and the dead men were taken down and thrown into the cave. Large rocks were again piled over the opening.

And so the Israelites saved the people of Gibeon and set the stage to capture the remaining southern portion of the land.

• • •

The next day, Joshua led his army into the heart of the southern hill country. They attacked the defenseless Jerusalem and the four cities that had joined her. They smote each city with the edge of the sword, killing each and every person. There was not one survivor in any of the five towns. Then they swung back east and demolished every city they encountered. Within a few weeks, Joshua captured the entire region because God was with him. Not one Canaanite remained alive, for Joshua utterly destroyed everything that breathed, as God commanded. Then Joshua and the army returned to camp at Gilgal.

• • •

After a week of rest and rejoicing with their families, Joshua and his soldiers, full of spirit, prepared for a northern campaign. The kings there teamed up to defend their territory. But God fought for Israel. Soon Joshua and the Israelites did to all the kings of the north as they had done to those in the south. They completely annihilated the cities and towns, keeping the livestock and plunder for themselves. But all the people they slaughtered—every man, woman, and child. They spared no one.

Not one city or king made peace with Israel. For it was God himself who hardened their hearts so that they would stubbornly wage war against his people. It was God's plan to totally destroy them, exterminating without mercy. Which he did.

• • •

In this manner, the people of Israel took the land that God promised. They divided it up among the twelve tribes, and each tribe settled happily and contentedly in its allotted portion. Not long after, on a humid and overcast day, Joshua summoned all the people to the city of Shechem. First, he produced a box containing the bones of their great ancestor Joseph, and he presided over a burial ceremony to fulfill the esteemed patriarch's wish to be interred in the land of his fathers.

Then Joshua, his body now beginning to slump, ascended a small mound and addressed the congregation. "God has fought for us and given us this rich and bountiful land, a land flowing with milk and honey. Each of you—every tribe, every clan, and every family—has your rightful inheritance. God has indeed been faithful to his promise to our ancestors, Abraham, Isaac, and Jacob—and Joseph as you've seen today."

Cries of affirmation rose from the assembly.

Joshua continued: "Our God is a great God. He led us out of bondage in Egypt, rescuing us from Pharaoh's heavy hand. He brought us through the wilderness, sustaining us with manna. Now he's given us this magnificent place. God has granted you a land on which you did not toil and cities you did not build. You have livestock you did not raise and vineyards and olive groves you did not plant. Yes, God has kept his promise. For Abraham's descendants are now as the stars of heaven and the sands of the sea. You are the people of Jacob, the nation of Israel! And you are home!"

The people raised their voices in raucous praise.

Joshua lifted his hands for silence. "But dangers remain," he went on solemnly. "Foreigners are still among us, people who do not worship our God. We captured and wiped out the cities, but many natives persist in outlying areas in your territories. Moreover, there are strange peoples and gods just outside the Promised Land who remain a threat to our way of life, including the mighty Philistines on the coast of the great sea.

"We must not mix with any of these people! If you join the survivors of these nations left here among us, and intermarry with them, know assuredly that God will punish you and no longer fight for you. Rather, these nations will become a snare and a trap for you, a scourge on your backs and thorns in your eyes, until you perish from this good land God has given you. Indeed, just as all the good things God has done for you, so God will bring on you bad things, until he's destroyed you.

"Now, therefore, we must not worship these foreign gods or follow any of the strange practices of the locals. We are to remain a separate and holy people unto our God. We must serve and worship God alone. Hold fast to his commandments and statutes—they are written for you on the tablets in the Ark of the Covenant. God has chosen you to be his people. Now choose this day whom you will serve: the God of Abraham, Isaac, and Jacob, or the gods of the Canaanites."

The Israelites cried out in one voice, "We will never forsake God. We will never worship another. For our God has done great and wondrous deeds before our very eyes. We vow to honor, love, and obey God."

Joshua answered, "You cannot serve God and the gods of this land. For our God is a jealous God. He will not forgive your transgressions. If you forsake him and turn to foreign deities, he will bring disaster on you and do you harm and consume you—even after all the good he has done for you."

"No!" shouted the people in one booming exclamation. "We will worship God alone. We will bow down to no other."

"You, then, are witnesses against yourself that you have chosen to serve only our God," Joshua proclaimed.

"We are witnesses," the people echoed.

And so on that day Joshua renewed the covenant between God and the Israelites. He ordered a great stone to be set up under the large oak tree in the center of Shechem. "Behold, this rock will forever stand as testimony against us if we break the oath we have spoken to our God."

The people answered in holy unison: "It will be a testimony."

24. A FAT KING AND TWO WOMEN

The people of Israel honored God for the rest of Joshua's days. But then Joshua died, and it was not long before the Israelites forgot their sacred covenant. They forgot Moses and Joshua. They forgot the mighty things God did for them in Egypt and the wilderness and the Promised Land. And the great rock in Shechem stood as a testimony against them.

Slowly this new generation of Israelites mixed with the native inhabitants of Canaan. Young Israelite men took wives from among these foreigners, and Israelite maidens were given to them in marriage. In this way, Israel began to serve other gods.

They worshipped Baal, the god of the storm clouds. He brought rain on the rich soil of Canaan, which made the seeds grow and yielded generous harvests. Baal had a female partner, Asherah, who received his sprinkling water. The gods, after all, must be male and female in order to be fertile, life-giving. The altars of Baal and the sacred poles of Asherah were temptations to the Israelites. When the people of Canaan encouraged Israel to appease Baal and Asherah with sacrifices and other fertility rituals, they made burnt offerings and paid obeisance to these local deities.

In their desire to propitiate the gods of Canaan, the Israelites violated the first commandment to worship God alone. And so the anger of God was kindled against his people, and God sold them into the hands of their enemies, as he had threatened.

• • •

Moab lay just south and east of Israel—it was the land whose king had tried, unsuccessfully, to bribe Balaam into cursing the Israelites during their desert wanderings. Now, however, God gave King Eglon of Moab power to defeat his people as punishment for their infidelity.

Eglon attacked Israel and conquered them, and for eighteen long years he forced the Israelites to pay a large tribute from all their produce. This was a great burden on the Israelites, who barely had enough to eat after payment was made. It was as though Eglon himself ate all the food the Israelites sent to him, for he was a very, very fat man.

Then the people of Israel lifted their voices and cried to God, "Oh, God, we are suffering mightily under the hand of Eglon. Please save us from our oppression."

God heard their cries and raised up a deliverer for his people, a man named Ehud from the tribe of Benjamin.

In the eighteenth year of Moab's dominance, the people sent Ehud with the annual tribute to Eglon. Now Ehud fashioned for himself a sword with two edges, and he made a scabbard to hold it under his clothing on his right thigh, for he was left-handed.

Ehud led a group of one hundred emissaries to Moab, each of them responsible for ten donkeys loaded with wool, flax, figs, dates, olives, grapes, and barley. When they arrived, they presented the payment to Eglon, whose flesh hung over the sides of his throne like a skirt.

Then Ehud and his men began the three-day journey home. But after the first day, Ehud quietly turned back toward Moab by himself.

He came again to the royal residence and announced, "I have a message for King Eglon from the people of Israel. It is a word I must deliver privately to the king."

One of the guards went to tell the king, while another patted down Ehud in search of weapons. The man only frisked Ehud's left side where daggers were likely to be carried. Then he led the Israelite up a staircase to a shaded room atop the palace—the king's private quarters which featured a magnificent bathroom. It was surrounded by servants and counselors, cooks and bakers.

Eglon did not rise when Ehud appeared. "O King, the message I bring is a secret," Ehud said.

"Everyone depart immediately," the king ordered. Then he beckoned Ehud to join him alone in the cool room. So Ehud entered, and the door was locked behind him.

"The word is written on this parchment and is very important," Ehud said, reaching into the right side of his cloak.

King Eglon slowly raised his hand to receive it. But Ehud drew out the double-edged sword and jabbed it into the king's belly. The fat was so great that the dagger disappeared into the king—even the handle was swallowed by the flesh, such that Ehud could not withdraw the sword. The king's guts spilled to the floor.

Ehud turned and left the room, closing the door behind him. "The king may be a while," he said to the attendants outside. "The message stirred his bowels." Then Ehud was gone.

Eglon's men wrinkled their noses at the foul odor wafting from the chamber. They politely waited for the king to finish, for it was not uncommon for him to spend long stretches of time in his posh lavatory. They waited until evening. They waited until the point of embarrassment. Then they cautiously peeked in, and there lay their king, dead in a heap of filth. Already flies were gathering.

While they waited, Ehud ran as fast as he could to Israel. He ascended Mount Ephraim and sounded the trumpet of war, announcing the death of King Eglon. Soon Israel assembled its forces to attack the now leaderless Moabites.

"Follow me!" Ehud shouted. "For God has delivered our oppressors into our hands." The Israelite army first secured the fords of the Jordan, cutting off any escape routes. Then they went and struck down the foreign warriors who ruled among and over them. Not one escaped.

So Moab was subdued that day under the hand of Israel.

And the Israelites worshipped God, and the land was at peace for eighty years.

● ● ●

Then Israel began to do what was evil in God's sight, and the anger of God burned against his people. He sold them into the hands of King Jabin and his general, Sisera. Jabin and Sisera and their nine hundred iron chariots ruled ruthlessly over the land of Israel for twenty years. After two decades of cruel suffering for their misdeeds against the divine covenant, the Israelites cried out in repentance to God, and God heard them.

He raised up a savior, a woman name Deborah. Sh selor who would sit beneath the palm trees in the hill co There she served as a judge, hearing cases and resolving decisions were just, and her name was spoken with admir tribes of Israel.

The spirit of God came upon her, and she summoned a certain man of the sword, Barak by name. The warrior came and stood before her. "Barak," she announced, "God commands you to gather ten thousand men on the slopes of Mount Tabor. There you are to prepare for battle against Sisera, our terrible oppressor. God himself will lure Sisera into the valley along the Kishon River, where you are to attack his chariots. God will grant you victory. Now go."

Barak did not move. His face remained stiff.

"Now," Deborah repeated.

Barak bit his lower lip and turned his head to one side. "Sisera has chariots, you know. Nine hundred of them. Made of iron. And all we have are foot soldiers with swords."

"Yes."

"I will go," Barak stammered, his eyes dropping, "only if you will go with me. If you don't go, then I won't go."

Deborah pulled her shawl tight. "I will go with you," she answered with a steely gaze. "But because you are not willing to go alone, the glory will not be yours. The glory will go, instead, to a woman."

So Barak sent word throughout Israel and ten thousand men soon covered Mount Tabor. Deborah was there too. When Sisera's spies observed this, they sent word to him, and the general immediately called up his chariots and drove them to the Kishon River valley opposite Tabor.

Deborah perched high on the mountain, her knees pulled up close to her chin. She watched Sisera's advancing wave of solid iron. Suddenly a shrill wind whipped down the mountain and the sky darkened. Deborah arose to her feet and hurried to Barak. "Now is the time," she said pointing to the sky. "Go! For today God is giving you victory over Sisera. God himself is marching before you."

Barak obeyed. He gave the signal and ten thousand Israelites charged down the slopes of the mountain. As they went, the waters of ven broke forth. And the river below began to rise. The blinding rain sent confusion through Sisera's ranks and the mud mired every chariot wheel. The Israelite army rushed directly upon their enemy and slaughtered them, chasing them westward and cutting them down with their swords.

But Sisera himself escaped. He leapt from his chariot and fled north on foot. When he came to the region of the Kenites, he stopped running and sought safety there, for the Kenites had made an alliance with King Jabin. He approached the first tent he saw. A woman named Jael came to the entrance to meet him.

"Come in, come in," she said, looking at the drenched and breathless man. "Don't be afraid. Everything is okay here."

Sisera went in. "May I have a drink of water?" he asked, collapsing to the earth.

Jael disappeared for a moment and returned with a heavy blanket and a jug of fresh, warm milk. Sisera gave a relaxed sigh and drank until he was full. Then he lay down, and she covered him with the blanket.

"If anyone comes by and asks if anyone is here, say no," Sisera said. He closed his eyes and within moments was asleep.

Jael watched him until he started to snore. Then she picked up a tent stake and a hammer and quietly tiptoed toward Sisera. Crouching next to him, she gently rested the sharp point of the stake on Sisera's temple. He did not move. Jael raised the hammer and brought it down with full force. With one thud it drove the large nail through Sisera's skull and into the earth. A thick red line oozed across his forehead.

Jael straightened up, her heart pounding. Then she heard voices outside and rushed to the door.

"Come here. Come back," Jael called out to the men who already passed by her tent. "I will show you what you are looking for."

It was Barak and his soldiers. They turned around and ambled, without conviction, toward the tiny woman. She peeled back the tent flap, and there lay Sisera with the nail through his head.

And so on that day God subdued Jabin and Sisera.

Deborah returned to her palm trees.

The Israelites worshipped God, and the land was at peace for forty years.

25. GIDEON

Then, once again, the people of Israel did evil in God's sight, and God handed them over to the Midianites who oppressed them mightily for seven years. The Midianites descended on Israel like a swarm of starving grasshoppers. Their people and cattle—and countless camels—consumed all the crops. They ravaged the land and left nothing for the Israelites who were reduced to grinding poverty. Without homes or land or anything, the Israelites were forced to eke out a living in mountain caves and dens.

The Israelites cried out for help to God, and God sent an angel to a man named Gideon. Now Gideon was threshing his meager bundle of wheat in a hidden winepress, high in the hills to keep it from the ravenous Midianites. As he worked, crouching low so no one would notice, the angel appeared and sat beneath an oak.

"God is with you, you mighty man of valor," the angel's voice sang out in greeting.

Gideon looked up, startled. He was no man of valor and he was sure God was not with him.

"What are you talking about?" Gideon asked. "If God is with us, then why has all this happened to us? Why are the Midianites destroying us? Where are all the wonders our grandparents told us about?"

The angel stared silently. Gideon knew why God was not with Israel. It was because they were worshipping Baal and the gods of Canaan. His very own father had set up an altar to the great storm god, as well as a sacred pole in honor of Asherah.

"Go in this strength of yours," the angel intoned, "and deliver Israel from the hand of Midian. For it is God himself who is sending you."

"Me? Save my people?" Gideon mumbled doubtfully. "I'm nobody. Look at me: Gideon. My clan is the weakest in my tribe, and I'm the runt of the litter within my own family."

"I will be with you," the majestic figure pledged. "Trust me, you will defeat Midian."

Gideon swallowed. "Show me a sign your word is true."

"Bring me something to eat," said the angel.

Gideon went to his house and prepared a young goat and some bread. He put the meat in a basket and some broth in a pot and brought it to the angel.

"Place the meat and bread on this rock," the divine messenger instructed, pointing to a large stone nearby.

Gideon did so.

"Now pour the broth over them."

Gideon emptied the pot on top of the rock.

The angel reached out his staff and with the tip of it he touched the food. Instantly, fire shot from the rock and torched the meat and bread. Then the angel vanished.

Gideon fell to his knees. "I've seen the angel of God face to face! I will surely die!"

Then a voice spoke to Gideon: "Be at peace, Gideon; for no harm will come to you."

Filled with a sudden and deep tranquility, Gideon arose and built an altar to God on the blackened stone. That night, God spoke to him. "Gideon, you must destroy the altar your father built for Baal and you must cut down the pole for Asherah. In its place you are to build a proper altar to me, the God of Israel. When you've done that, take one of your father's young bulls and sacrifice it to me."

Immediately, Gideon went and, under the cover of night, did as God commanded. In the morning, the people of the town found the stones of Baal's altar scattered about and new stones laid to form another altar upon which a bull had been burnt. And the sacred wooden pole of Asherah was used for the fire. Her face had turned to dust and ashes.

"Who did this?" they buzzed. For no one knew. They asked around all morning and soon learned the truth. They surrounded Gideon's house and called to his father, Joash, "Bring out your son! He must die, for he blasphemed Baal and Asherah."

Joash stepped onto his portico and closed the door behind him. "Are you going to defend Baal?" he asked them. "If Baal is a true god, he can defend himself when someone dishonors him. Let Baal punish Gideon. You don't need to do it for him."

The people nodded their heads; then turned and left. Gideon did not go outside the rest of the day.

That evening, Gideon sat alone in his father's courtyard, his heart still restless at the task before him. A lone torch cast a gentle glow on a pile of new fleeces stacked against a stone wall. He grabbed the top fleece and threw it into the middle of the floor.

"O God, if you will deliver Israel by my hand as you have said," Gideon prayed, "then please give me a sign. Let this fleece be wet with dew in the morning, but the ground around it be dry."

And it was so. At sunrise Gideon wrung enough water from the fleece to fill a large bowl. But the earth was completely dry.

Still, Gideon wondered. That night he prayed again. "Please do not be angry with me, God. I ask you to give me one more sign with the fleece. This time make the fleece dry and the ground around it covered with dew."

That night God did so. The next morning, when Gideon picked up the fleece, the spirit of God came upon him. He sounded the trumpet of war, summoning all Israel to join him. He also sent messengers throughout the neighboring tribes calling them to arms. Soon a large contingent gathered near the spring of Harod, just south of the main Midianite stronghold.

As the troops assembled, God spoke to Gideon. "There are too many warriors here, for with this great number Israel will boast that they defeated Midian by their own strength. Therefore, tell those who are afraid that they may go home."

Gideon did as God said, and twenty-two thousand men vacated the camp. That left ten thousand with Gideon.

are still too many," God indicated. "Take them down to the I will thin them out for you there."

›n did so. As the men drank from the cool water, God said, "Put those who scoop the water and lap it from their hands on one side, and on the other side put those who kneel down to drink straight from the river."

When Gideon had done so, he counted three hundred men who drank from their hands; all the rest put their face to the waters.

"With these three hundred I will save you from the Midianites," God declared. "Tell the others to leave their jars and trumpets behind and go home now before nightfall."

Once again Gideon obeyed. Then he led his lean band of soldiers to the ridge overlooking the valley where the Midianites were camped. He could see the headquarters in the center where the two kings, Zebah and Zalmunna, and their two cruel generals, Oreb and Zeeb, were undoubtedly stationed. The Midianite tents and cattle blanketed the earth. Their red fires filled the darkness.

As Gideon stared at the glowing plain, God said, "Lead your men down into the valley and attack the Midianites, for I will give them into your hand."

Gideon's heart shook within him. How could he defeat this vast horde with only three hundred soldiers? He closed his eyes and breathed deeply for a moment. As he did, he saw a vision of a small barley loaf tumbling down the hillside and into the camp of Midian. The loaf crashed into one tent after another, overturning and destroying each one.

Gideon opened his eyes and lifted them heavenward. For he knew the meaning of the vision: He was the barley loaf.

Gideon divided his men into three companies. He gave each man a horn, an empty jar, and a torch. "Whatever I do, you also do," he told them. "When I blow the horn, you blow yours, right where you are standing. Then shatter your jars, light your torches, and shout, 'For God and for Gideon.'"

Gideon sent one company to the north, the other to the south, and one stayed with him. In this way, they surrounded the sleeping enemy in one thin, invisible line. The Midianite watchmen noticed nothing strange in the quiet rustlings of the night.

Suddenly, just as the guards took their posts for the middle watch, one shrill trumpet blast pierced the stillness. Then a loud chorus of trumpets woke the night, and empty pitchers smashed against the rocks with one great crash that echoed across the valley. A ring of flame encircled Midian as torches were lit, and a choir of voices rang out, "For God and for Gideon."

Terror and confusion gripped the Midianites. "What great army is charging down the slopes at us? We're surrounded! Fight! Fight! Or run for your lives!" They picked up their weapons and stumbled recklessly through the camp.

Gideon did not move one step, nor did any of his men. They watched as Midianites dashed this way and that, striking one another with the sword in the blind chaos. Many of them slaughtered each other. The rest fled.

Gideon and his armies pursued. They chased them all the way to the borders of the land, spearing them to death as they went. One hundred twenty thousand Midianites were killed, including Oreb and Zeeb. When Gideon's men came upon the two fallen generals, they took their swords and chopped off their heads, which they carried to Gideon.

But the two kings, Zebah and Zalmunna, along with fifteen thousand others managed to escape across the Jordan River. Gideon and his contingent of three hundred were worn out, but they continued the pursuit. When they came to the little Israelite town of Succoth late in the afternoon, Gideon said to its seventy-seven elders, "Please give my men some bread. For we are famished. We must capture the two Midianite kings, otherwise they will regroup and continue their rule over us."

The officials of Succoth replied, "How can we feed your men? We barely have enough food for us and our families. Besides, we don't see any captured kings in your hands. So what have you done for us?"

Gideon scowled at them narrowly. "When God gives these two kings into my hand, I will come back here and thrash your bare flesh with desert thorns and thistles." He then spit and strode briskly toward the edge of the town, beckoning his men to follow.

Tired but resolute, Gideon's men resumed the chase. The fifteen thousand Midianites and their two kings soon stopped for the night. When they did, the Israelites attacked and defeated them and captured Zebah and

Zalmunna. They bound the two rulers and, in the early morning light, led them back toward Succoth.

As they neared the town, Gideon saw a young man collecting wood. "Come here," Gideon called to him. The boy dropped the sticks and began to run away, but Gideon's men were faster and they caught him and ushered him to their leader.

"Tell me the names of the seventy-seven men on your town council," Gideon said.

The youth's brow wrinkled and he rubbed his hands together nervously. Gideon reached into his bag, pulled out a few crinkled pieces of parchment, and handed them to the young man. The boy glanced at the parchment, then back up at Gideon, who now extended a writing utensil. The boy took it, and then, kneeling, he smoothed out the parchment on the ground and began to write. Gideon stood over him with arms crossed.

Minutes ticked by as the boy wrote, paused to think, and then wrote again. When he finished, he handed over the paper and fled.

Gideon read through the list and directed his small army to march into Succoth. "Here are Zebah and Zalmunna, as promised," Gideon announced loudly as the two chained kings stumbled forward. The townspeople gasped. "And here are the seventy-seven naysayers who will be punished." He raised the parchment and began to call out the names of the town officials.

When all of them had been gathered, Gideon ordered his men to whip them. They lashed their flesh with ropes of thorns and thistles. Cries of anguish went up, and the townspeople covered their ears and lowered their faces.

When the last elder of Succoth had been beaten, Gideon called for Zebah and Zalmunna. They stood before him shackled, eyes cast downward.

"You have oppressed and killed our people," Gideon said to them. "So now I will kill you. You have brought death on Israel, so today death comes to you from God through my hand." Without shifting his gaze from the two kings, Gideon called his son, "Come here, Jether."

A lad, maybe twelve or thirteen, stepped forward, fear scrawled across his slender body.

Gideon said to Zebah and Zalmunna, "This is my firstborn son." Then he turned to Jether: "Kill them!"

Jether did not move.

"Kill them!" Gideon shouted again.

Jether's lips quivered and tears welled up in his eyes. The rest of him remained motionless.

"Do it yourself," Zebah gritted. "You are the warrior; he's just a boy. Lift your own hand and kill us like a real man."

Gideon immediately drew his sword and slayed Zebah in one stroke. With a second violent thrust he killed Zalmunna.

And so on that day, Gideon rescued the people of Israel from their oppressors.

● ● ●

Word of Israel's salvation spread across the land. The elders of Israel came to Gideon and said, "Rule over us. Be our king."

But Gideon answered them, "No, I will not rule. For God alone is our ruler."

Then the Israelites worshipped God, and the land was at peace for forty years.

26. BASTARD SONS

No sooner had Gideon died than the Israelites began worshipping Baal. Again. They forgot God and all he had done for them, and they prostituted themselves to the gods of Canaan. Moreover, many in Israel still wanted a king to rule over them, since Gideon had refused.

Now Gideon had many sons. Seventy of them, by multiple wives. Gideon also had a concubine—a poor slave-girl—who bore him a son named Abimelech. Despite his lowly status as the progeny of a concubine, Abimelech was ambitious. He had dreams. He wanted to be king. So he went to the elders in his hometown of Shechem and inquired, "Which would you and all Israel prefer: to have Gideon's seventy sons rule over you, or just one of his sons, me, who lives here among you in our wonderful and blessed city?"

"Are the seventy planning to set up some sort of kingship?" the council asked.

"You never know," Abimelech answered. "But should we risk a domineering rule by them? It would probably be worse than the Midianite oppression from which my father freed us."

In this way, Abimelech sowed fear into the hearts of his townspeople and persuaded them to support his bid to be king over Israel. He is one of us, they said to themselves. So they gave him a large sum of money to hire a band of military rebels, which he did.

Abimelech and his misfits journeyed to the city of Ophrah where Gideon's sons lived. There, before anyone knew what was happening, they rounded up all seventy and brought them to a boulder outside the city.

Then they systematically murdered them on the great rock. (
son, the very youngest, Jotham, escaped.

After this, Abimelech returned to Shechem, where three d
was crowned king in a grand and ceremonious coronation. Abimelech was now the ruler of the land—or at least the city of Shechem.

As the celebration wound down, a small man appeared on the hillside outside the city. He shouted, "Listen to me, citizens of Shechem. Pay attention, I have something to tell you."

Slowly the people turned from their eating and drinking and glimpsed upward.

"It's Jotham," Abimelech whispered to one of his men.

"Let's kill him now, in front of everyone," the man asserted boldly.

"No, wait. Let's hear what he has to say. He's hardly a threat anymore."

"Hear me, people of Shechem," Jotham hollered again as silence fell on the multitude. "One day the trees went out to anoint a king for themselves. They said to the olive tree, 'Be our king.' But the olive tree replied, 'Why should I give up my oil, by which both gods and humans are blessed, just so I can hold sway over the trees?'

"Next, the trees said to the fig tree, 'Come and be our king.' But the fig tree answered, 'Why should I give up my fruit, so good and sweet, just so I can hold sway over the trees?'

"Then the trees said to the vine, 'Come and rule over us.' But the vine answered, 'Why should I give up my wine, which cheers both gods and people, just to hold sway over the trees?'

"Finally the trees said to the thorn bush, 'Be our king.' The thorn bush said to the trees, 'If you really want to anoint me king over you, then come and take refuge in my shade, and I will be your king. But if you don't want me as your king, then let fire come and consume all of you.'

"Now listen to me, people of Shechem. Do you think you did a good and honorable thing when you made Abimelech—a thorn bush—your king? Look what he did to Gideon's sons, my brothers? My father fought for you, risked his own life to rescue you from Midian's tyranny. And now you've betrayed him. You massacred his sons—seventy men on a single stone! And you've crowned Abimelech, the bastard child of a worthless slave girl, as king over Shechem. If you've acted nobly, then may you and

Abimelech prosper. But if not, then let fire break forth from Abimelech and consume Shechem. And let fire break forth from Shechem and consume Abimelech."

Then Jotham turned and fled. No one chased him, and he never came back.

● ● ●

Abimelech set up his rule over Israel at Shechem. For three years he reigned as king. But God was not happy, so he sent an evil spirit—a spirit of enmity—between Abimelech and the people of Shechem. Violence marred the city day and night. Blood was shed. No one was safe. When a man named Gaal arrived, many of the people joined his movement in opposition to Abimelech. But this only increased the violence as Gaal's troops clashed with Abimelech's. In time, Abimelech retained complete control of Shechem, but not before he razed much of the city and slaughtered many of its citizens.

Soon Abimelech's brutality spilled into surrounding Israelite towns. When he attacked the neighboring city of Thebez, its inhabitants sought refuge in the fortified tower in the middle of the city. They locked themselves in and hid on the roof.

Abimelech himself led the charge toward the tower. As he approached its door, a woman at the top pushed a millstone over the side. Abimelech looked up, but it was too late. The stone cracked his skull, and he fell forward on his face.

"Kill me, kill me, so they can't say a woman killed me," Abimelech slurred. So one of his soldiers took a sword and plunged it through, and he died.

Thus, God repaid Abimelech for murdering Gideon's seventy sons—his own brothers. And God repaid the people of Shechem for making Abimelech king. Jotham's oracle had indeed been fulfilled: Shechem and the thorn bush had destroyed each other.

● ● ●

The Israelites continued to bow to Baal and pay homage to Asherah. They worshipped any and every deity except their own. Accordingly, God's anger exploded on them once more, and he sold them into the hands of the Ammonites. For eighteen years, the Ammonites crushed and shattered Israel. Then the people cried out to God, "We have sinned against you, O God! We've broken your sacred covenant by serving Baal!"

God answered, "When you were oppressed in Egypt, when the Moabites enslaved you, when the Midianites overran you, and you begged for help, did I not save you? But time and again you've forsaken me and served other gods. Time and again! So I will no longer help you. No more! Go and cry out to the gods you worship. Let them save you. Let Baal and Asherah deliver you from your troubles. I'm done!"

But the Israelites pleaded before God, "Yes, we've sinned. We are wrong and we are sorry. We will not worship foreign gods. We will serve you and only you from henceforth. Give us whatever punishment you think is best, but please, oh please, save us from the devastating hand of the Ammonites!"

Then the Israelites destroyed the altars to Baal, and they smashed and burned the sacred poles of Asherah. And they worshipped God alone.

God could no longer bear to see Israel suffer, and so he raised up a man to save them.

● ● ●

Now Jephthah was a mighty warrior. His father, too, had been a strong man of valor. But his mother was a prostitute. Like Abimelech, Jephthah was a bastard, despised by his father's legitimate children and forced to live far from them—where he had forged his own reputation by leading a band of free riders, raiders, and outlaws.

The Ammonites dominated all the land of Israel, but their oppression was particularly severe in the region of Gilead, the home of Jephthah's father from which he had been expelled on account of his mother.

One day, the leaders of Gilead sent word to Jephthah, "Come and be our general and save us from the Ammonites."

Jephthah was not impressed. He had made a good life for himself. He had a group of loyal men around him. He had a house and security. And he had one child, a daughter whom he loved very much. So he sent word back: "You have scorned and rejected me. You banished me from my family. And now you appeal to me to save you? When you're in trouble, then you call on me and expect help?"

The council in Gilead answered, "If you come deliver us now, we will appoint you as the permanent ruler of our whole region."

Jephthah was interested, but not convinced. He sent word back, "How do I know you will do this?"

"We swear to you. God is our witness," they assured him.

So Jephthah went, and the spirit of God came upon him. When he and his men arrived in Gilead, they confirmed the oath, and Jephthah was put in charge of Gilead's warriors.

As was his custom, Jephthah first attempted to make peace with the enemy. He sent a message to the Ammonites offering to negotiate. As expected, they ignored it. The sword would have to be drawn.

On the eve of the battle, Jephthah turned aside for a quiet moment with the Almighty. He knelt on one knee and prayed, "Dear God, if you give me victory over Ammon, I will give to you whatever comes out of my house to meet me when I return triumphant. I will sacrifice it as a burnt offering to you." He arose and, with a tremendous shout, led forth the army of Israel.

He attacked Ammon, and God gave them into his hand. He destroyed twenty Ammonite strongholds from one end of Israel to the other. It was a very great slaughter and a resounding victory. God had once again delivered Israel from their oppression.

In high spirits, Jephthah rode back home. His daughter, his only child, emerged from the house. She ran toward him, singing and dancing, her long robe flowing behind her, mixing with shouts of joy. Jephthah raised a waving arm. Then a pain of remembrance shot through his heart. He slumped over, hands clenched on his forehead.

He dismounted and fell to the ground. "O my most precious daughter, today you've made me the most miserable and wretched man!" he wailed.

Her celebration stopped, and she stood petrified before him.

"I've made a vow to God I cannot recant," he uttered through the tears.

She listened in horror as her father related the oath.

"Father," she swallowed, "you've given your word to God. He gave you—and Israel—a great victory. Now you must do to me what you promised."

Jephthah looked up at her.

"I only ask one thing," the girl continued. "Give me two months to wander in the mountains and to weep with my friends, for I will never marry and have children. I will never be a wife and mother."

Jephthah nodded.

She turned and went into the house. Then she was gone.

Exactly two months later the girl came back. And Jephthah did to her as he had vowed.

And so the Israelites worshipped God, and the land was at peace for six years.

27. SAMSON

Then, yet again, the Israelites broke the sacred covenant by bowing down to foreign gods, and so God sold them into the hands of the Philistines who oppressed them for forty years.

During that time, there was a certain Israelite man named Manoah who had no children because his wife was not able to conceive. One day, while the woman was alone making bread, the angel of God appeared to her and announced, "You will become pregnant and give birth to a son. Now see to it that you drink no wine or other fermented beverage. When you give birth to the boy, do not ever cut his hair. Indeed, his head is not to be touched by a razor, for that will be the sign he is dedicated to God. Your son will be the one to save Israel from the hands of the Philistines."

The woman dusted off her robe and went to the field to tell her husband. When he heard, he put his arms tightly around his wife and whispered a prayer. "O God, I beg you to let the angel come to us again, so we may know the word is true, and how to raise the boy."

A few days later the angel reappeared and repeated his message to Manoah and his wife. Manoah listened with astonishment. He said to the heavenly being, "We would like for you to stay and eat with us. We will prepare a young goat."

"I will not eat any of your food," the angel replied. "If you wish to do anything, prepare a burnt offering for God."

Manoah looked at his wife, then back to the angel. "What is your name?" he asked. "We want to honor you when the boy is born."

The angel looked at the woman, then back to Manoah. "You cannot know my name. It is beyond your understanding."

With that, Manoah turned and hurried off to get the goat. Soon he came stumbling back, holding the animal under one arm and a bag of grain under the other.

"Where should I . . ." he huffed.

His wife pointed with her thumb to a nearby rock. Manoah placed the grain on the rock; then he bound the goat and laid it on top of the grain. With a nod to the angel, he lit it all on fire as a sacrifice to God.

As the flames blazed upward from the altar, the angel ascended in the flames.

Manoah fell to the ground and cried out, "We're going to die! For we've seen God himself!"

The woman looked at her prostrate husband. "If God were going to kill us," she shook her head, "he would not have accepted this offering and he certainly wouldn't have sent us this incredible message about a baby boy."

Manoah lifted his head thoughtfully. He got to his feet, took his wife by the hand, and led her back to the house.

• • •

In time, it came to pass just as the angel said. Manoah's wife gave birth to a son. They named him Samson. The boy grew into a youth of extraordinary strength, and his thick mane was a symbol of his divine appointment. Soon the spirit of God began to stir in him.

One day Samson was in the Philistine town of Timnah. There he saw a beautiful young woman. When he returned home that evening, he said to his father and mother, "I have seen a Philistine girl. Now get her for me as my wife."

Manoah only stared at his chiseled son. After a few moments, his wife spoke up. "Samson, my son, surely you can find a nice Israelite girl to marry. Don't take a wife from among the uncircumcised Philistines. They are our enemies and oppressors."

Samson brushed the hair off his face. "I want her. Get her for me."

"But Samson," his mother griped.

"Now. Or I'll do it myself," he shot back.

They both turned to Manoah, who shifted from one foot to the other, rubbing the back of his head.

Early the next morning, Samson set off again for Timnah. As he approached the vineyards surrounding the city, a young lion roared against him. The spirit of God came upon him and he tore the lion apart, breaking its joints in two as if it were a baby lamb. He left it lying dead on the road and continued on.

He spent the day with the Philistine maiden, and she made him very happy. So he determined to marry her. With persistence and passion—and compromise—he secured his parents' blessing. "I will take her as my wife, but she will continue to live in her father's house," Samson conceded. "That way, you won't have to deal with a Philistine daughter-in-law, but I will visit her whenever I want."

A short time later, Samson traveled to Timnah for the wedding ceremony. On his way, he noticed the carcass of the lion. Bees swarmed around it, and upon closer inspection, he saw a hive in the hollowed out beast. Samson carefully scooped out some honey and ate it.

The wedding ceremony was a grand feast—seven days of wine, food, dance, and merriment. As was customary, the groom, Samson, was accompanied by thirty men who helped him celebrate the occasion.

On the first day, Samson said to the men, "Let me tell you a riddle. If you can give me the answer by week's end, I will give each of you a fine linen garment. If, however, you can't tell me the answer, then you must each give me a linen garment of the highest quality. Thirty for thirty."

"Alright," they answered heartily. "It's a deal. Now let's hear the riddle."

Samson smiled and, looking around at all of them, said, "Out of the eater, something to eat; out of the strong, something sweet."

"Oh, clever," the men laughed and returned to their wine. They discussed the riddle amongst themselves in hushed tones for three days. But none of them could decipher its meaning.

On the fourth day, they took Samson's bride aside. "Coax your husband into explaining the riddle to you. Or else we will burn you and everyone in your family to death."

The girl shook with fear. "But I . . . I . . ." she stammered. The group of angry men turned and left.

That night she threw herself on Samson, sobbing, "You don't love me. How could you keep secrets from me, your own wife?"

"What are you talking about?" Samson asked.

"You know. The riddle. You've not told me the answer."

"I haven't told anyone."

"But now you have a wife." She wept loudly, clinging to him. She did not stop crying the rest of the night, or the next day, or the day after that.

On the morning of the seventh day, he finally told her the meaning of the riddle, for her tears and sorrow made him sad.

As the sun set that night, and the week of celebration came to a close, the thirty men gathered around Samson, wry grins everywhere. Then one of them spoke up. "We know the answer, Samson."

Samson's stomach churned, for he knew what had happened.

Then, in one mighty voice, the thirty men cried out, "What is sweeter than honey? What is stronger than a lion?"

Samson growled in a low, icy voice, "If you hadn't plowed with my heifer, you would not have solved my riddle. Nonetheless, I will pay what I owe."

Samson dashed madly from the house, and the spirit of God came powerfully upon him. He went and killed thirty Philistine men, stripped them of everything, and gave their linen garments to those who had explained the riddle.

Then, burning with anger, he returned to the home of his parents.

Not long thereafter, at the beginning of the wheat harvest, Samson's heart again longed for his Philistine wife. So he took a gift for her father and journeyed to Timnah.

When he arrived, Samson announced to his father-in-law, "I am here to see my bride."

The man ran his hand through his wispy gray hair and stared at the floor. "She's not here."

"When will she return?" Samson asked.

Lifting his eyes timidly, the Timnite replied, "Look, Samson, I did not think you were coming back, with the way the feast ended. I thought you hated her for what she did. So I . . . I . . . gave her to one of your thirty men. She is his wife now."

Samson's face twisted and his chest swelled with rage.

"Please, Samson, just take her younger sister as a wife. She is more beautiful anyway."

Samson gathered his long thick locks and tied them back from his face. "This time," he grunted, "when I destroy the Philistines, I will be justified."

Then he stormed out and went to a nearby forest. He caught three hundred wild foxes and tied their tales together two by two. He fastened a torch to each pair of tails. That night, he lit the torches and set the foxes loose in the tall, ripe fields of the Philistines. With great howls of agony, the foxes ran through the crops, setting ablaze the sheaves of harvested grain, the stalks of corn, the vineyards, and olive groves.

The smoke and light awoke the slumbering Philistines. "What's happening? Who's done this?" they cried out.

The word went among them: "Samson the Israelite did this; for his wife was given to another man."

The next morning, the Philistines assembled at Timnah. They seized Samson's bride and her father and set them on fire.

● ● ●

Then the Philistines summoned a one-thousand-soldier garrison and set out for the Israelite region of Judah, where Samson was thought to be hiding out.

"Why are you drawing up to fight us?" the people of Judah said in terror. "What have we done to you?"

"You are harboring a fugitive, Samson, who has ruined our land. We've come to bind him and do to him as he's done to us."

Hearing this, the people of Judah sent men to search the clefts and caves within their borders. When they found Samson, they said to him, "What have you done? Don't you realize the Philistines rule over us? Why are you bringing this trouble on Israel?"

"I've simply done to them what they did to me," he answered.

"We don't care what they did to you—one man in all Israel! We are arresting you and handing you over to them. Now give yourself up."

"Promise me one thing," Samson said. "Promise me that you yourselves will not kill me."

"We swear," they answered.

So he came forward willingly, and they bound him with two new ropes and led him from the cave.

When his enemies saw him tied up like an animal, they raised a shout of triumph. At that instant, the spirit of God rushed powerfully on Samson. The thick cords on his arms became as a thread and fell to the ground. Seeing a sun-dried jawbone of a dead donkey, he grabbed it and, with that as his weapon, he rushed upon his would-be captors. Again and again he struck furious blows with the sharp edge of the bone, until all the Philistines lay dead on the earth around him.

Then, turning to the men of Judah, who stood like statues, Samson said, "With a donkey's jawbone, I've made donkeys of them. With a donkey's jawbone, I've killed a thousand men."

After this, Samson's fame spread throughout Israel. And the Philistines feared him.

Samson fell in love with another Philistine woman named Delilah. When the five chief warlords of the Philistines learned of it, they sent word to her: "Use your womanly wiles to find out the source of his great strength so we may know how to capture him. If you do, we will each give you eleven hundred pieces of silver."

It was a very large sum of money, and so Delilah agreed.

The next time Samson came to visit, she cuddled close to him, her fingers stroking his massive chest, and said, "Tell me, Samson, what is it that makes you so wonderfully strong, and what could possibly tame your marvelous muscles."

Samson smiled and caressed her head. "If I were to be bound with seven fresh bowstrings, brand new and never used, then I would be as weak as any other man."

She laid her head on him and closed her eyes. Soon they were both asleep.

The next day, Delilah passed the word on to the Philistines, who provided her with the bowstrings, and then hid themselves outside her house. As Samson slept that night, Delilah bound him, wrist and ankle, with the bowstrings.

Then she shook him. "Samson, the Philistines are here! Quick, get out!"

Samson awoke and easily snapped the strings. Delilah watched in shock. "You lied to me," she sobbed. "Please tell me the secret of your mighty power. I deserve to know."

Samson sat down and leaned back. "Alright," he breathed, "if I am bound with new ropes, strong and sturdy, then I will be as weak as any other man."

"Are you telling me the truth," she said softly, her hand taking his.

"I am."

So the next night, when he had fallen asleep, she took new ropes and bound him, legs and arms, foot and hand. Again, the Philistine soldiers crouched outside the door.

Then she called out, "Samson, Samson, you are being attacked. Hurry, get up!"

He again arose and shredded the ropes in two. And again Delilah wept piteously. "Why do you deceive me? Why won't you confide in me?"

"If you weave my hair into the fabric you are weaving on your loom and tighten it with the pin, I'll become as weak as any other man."

Delilah looked at him scornfully and walked out. But that night she separated his long hair into seven thick strands and wove each one into the cloth on her weaving frame, securing it tightly with a pin. When she awakened him, he got up and walked away, pulling behind him the large frame and the web of cloth in which his hair was sewn.

At this, Delilah came at Samson, swinging her arms wildly and screaming, "How can you say you love me when your heart is not with me? You've made a fool of me three times. Three times you've lied to me about your strength. Will you ever tell me the truth?"

Samson said nothing. But Delilah would not give in. Day after day she pleaded with him, night after night she pressed him for the answer. Finally, worn out, he told her. "A razor has never touched my head, not once since my birth. If I am shaved, then my strength will depart, and I will become as any other man."

Delilah knew this was the truth, so she sent, once more, for the Philistine lords. They hurried secretly to her house, bringing the bags of silver with them. That night, Samson fell asleep on Delilah's lap. When his breathing was slow and steady, she called one of the Philistines to bring a razor. "Shave him," she ordered.

The man quickly cut through the dense tangle of hair. One by one, the locks dropped quietly to the floor. Then Delilah shook Samson. "The Philistines are upon you."

Samson awoke from his sleep and began to arise as before. He did not know his hair was shorn and God had left him. As the Philistines emerged from their hiding places and surrounded him, Samson lunged to strike. But he was powerless.

The Philistines quickly subdued him. They bound him and plunged a spear into each eye, blinding him forever. Then they led him in a boisterous procession to the city of Gaza where they threw him in prison. There they made Samson their slave, forcing him to do a woman's work—grinding grain.

• • •

Samson toiled day after day. All the while, the hair on his head began to grow back. Then came the day when the Philistines gathered to offer a great sacrifice to their god, Dagon, and rejoice in their capture of Samson. "Our god has saved us from our enemy!" they sang. "The one who laid waste our land has now fallen into our hand."

At the height of their celebration, one of the Philistine lords shouted, "Bring out Samson to entertain us!" Others picked up the cry, and soon a young lad led Samson in his rags and chains into the magnificent house of Dagon. The boy brought him to the center of the temple, between its two great pillars, where all three thousand people could see and cast their taunts at the blind, helpless giant.

Samson heard the roars and felt the jeering. He put out his hands until he found the two pillars. Then he lifted his face and prayed, "God, remember me one more time and strengthen me just this once, so I may take revenge on my enemies for my two eyes."

Bracing himself against the stone columns, his right hand on the one and his left hand on the other, Samson cried out, "Let me die with the Philistines!" Then he bowed with all his might, and the temple crashed down in a thunderous ruin.

So it was that in his death Samson slew more Philistines than he had slain during his life. And the power of the Philistines was broken with the temple.

28. RAPE AND CIVIL WAR

Free from Philistine oppression, the Israelites again enjoyed the bounty of the land of milk and honey. The Philistines, however, represented an ever present danger, a constant source of trouble for the Israelites even when they were faithful to God. Thus, some in Israel continued secretly to wish for a king who would fight their battles and protect them from their enemies. They wanted a strong centralized government to unify the twelve tribes, eliminate the squabbles among them, and bring a sense of common order, decency, and justice.

But of course there was no king in Israel, and so everyone did what was right in their own eyes.

Now a certain man from the tribe of Levi took a concubine from the town of Bethlehem in the territory of Judah, the same tribe that had once given up Samson to the Philistines. One day the concubine became angry with the Levite and ran away to her father's house. After she had been there three or four months, the Levite took his servant, saddled two donkeys, and went after her to bring her home.

When the girl's father saw him coming, he came out to welcome him and invited him to stay. For three days, the Levite ate and drank and lodged there. By the third evening, he had persuaded his concubine to return with him. So on the fourth morning, they arose and prepared to leave. But the father said to his son-in-law, "Why don't you stay and have breakfast and then you can depart."

The Levite agreed, and they ate and drank and talked and laughed together. Soon the sun was high in the sky, and the father-in-law said, "Look, it's too late to leave now. Why don't you stay and spend one more night. Then you can get up early in the morning and go."

The Levite consented and at dawn the next day he was ready to depart. But again, the girl's father pressed him, saying, "Have something to eat first." The Levite reluctantly agreed. When they had finished eating, the father said, "It's a little too late to start back now. Stay just one more night and get a fresh start tomorrow."

But the Levite had made up his mind. He saddled his donkeys and left Bethlehem, traveling north with his concubine and servant.

When the day was nearly gone, they came to the city of Jerusalem. The servant suggested, "Let's stop and spend the night here."

"This place is mostly foreigners—Jebusites, I think," the Levite answered. "Let's keep going until we reach Gibeah. We don't want to lodge here with strangers."

So they journeyed on, and as the sun vanished they arrived at Gibeah in the tribe of Benjamin. They entered and sat down in the town square, hoping someone would offer them a place to stay for the night. But no one did.

Finally, an old man came trudging in from the fields. "Where are you headed?" he asked.

"Back home to the hill country of Ephraim," the Levite said.

"Is that right," the old man remarked. "That's where I'm from originally. Been here in Gibeah awhile now."

The Levite smiled at his good fortune. "We just need a place to stay for tonight. We have straw and fodder for our donkeys and plenty of food for ourselves—me, the woman, and the servant here."

"You are welcome at my house," the old man said. "I'll be happy to give you whatever you need. Only don't spend the night here in the square." So he led them to his home, gave them provender for the donkeys, and hurried to prepare a meal.

While they were eating and drinking and sharing stories of life in Ephraim, the men of Gibeah surrounded the house and began to beat on the door. "Hey, old man," they shouted, "bring out the guy who came to your house so we can have sex with him!"

The Levite's blood ran cold. The servant jerked back. Panic surged through the girl.

The elderly host got up and went outside. "Look, fellows, what are you doing?" he said, feigning calmness. "Don't be so crude and vile. This man is my guest. I've promised to take care of him tonight. Leave us alone."

But the crowd became louder and more insistent.

The old man's throat tightened. "Alright, how about I hand over my virgin daughter and the man's concubine. You can take the two girls and do whatever you wish with them. Use them however you want. But, please, don't do this outrageous thing to the man."

"You don't have a virgin daughter!" the mob roared. They raised their fists and brandished knives.

At that moment, the door of the house swung open, and the Levite shoved his concubine outside. Then he pulled in the old man, slammed the door, and threw his body against it. He did not move until the voices outside faded into the night.

The men of Gibeah took the concubine and brutally raped her all night long. At dawn, they let her go.

In the early morning light, the girl stumbled and crawled back to the house. She collapsed on the doorstep.

The Levite arose in the morning and opened the door to continue the journey home. There was his concubine lying on the ground, her hands nearly on the threshold.

"Get up. It's time to go," he said.

But there was no answer.

He bent down, scooped her up, and laid her on the back of one of the donkeys. Then he set off.

When he arrived home, he took a knife and cut up his concubine, limb by limb, into twelve pieces. He sent the severed chunks of flesh throughout the territories of Israel with this message: "Such a thing has never happened from the day that we came up from the land of Egypt. Ponder this. What should we do?"

● ● ●

All the people of Israel gathered together. The leaders of the tribes took their places and said to the Levite, "Now tell us exactly what happened."

The Levite stepped forward and spoke. "I and my concubine were traveling from Judah to Ephraim. On the way, we stopped to spend the night in Gibeah in the land of Benjamin. While we were eating and resting with our host, the men of the town surrounded the house. They intended to kill me. They raped my concubine, and she died. I took her, cut her into pieces, and sent them out so every ear would hear of this lewd and outrageous act. Now, people of Israel, tell me: What ought we to do about this?"

The council members answered, "We have two declarations, two oaths to take before God. First, we swear none of us will return home until we make Gibeah of Benjamin pay for this heinous and vile crime which they have perpetrated against all Israel. Second, we vow that no man among us will ever give his daughter to a Benjaminite in marriage."

They sent a message to the tribe of Benjamin: "Hand over the wicked men of Gibeah, so that we may put them to death and purge this evil from Israel."

But the Benjaminites would not listen to their Israelite brothers. Instead, they mustered an army of twenty-six thousand from among their cities and readied for battle against the rest of Israel. Among them were seven hundred left-handed troops who could sling a stone at a hair without missing.

The Israelite coalition was distraught. Civil war seemed inevitable; but justice had to be served. So they gathered four hundred thousand soldiers and prepared to fight the Benjaminites. They turned to God for guidance. Standing before the Ark of the Covenant, they asked, "Which tribe shall lead us in battle against Benjamin?"

"Judah shall go up first," God answered.

The next morning, the Israelites took up their positions, with Judah at the head. But when they attacked, the army of Benjamin beat them back, killing them as they fled. By nightfall, twenty-two thousand Israelites lay dead on the field.

Under a full moon, the people of Israel wept before the Ark. "What happened today, God? Should we again attack our Benjaminite brothers?"

"Yes, go up against them."

The Israelites took courage and once more drew up for battle. Again, the army of Benjamin broke forth from Gibeah and struck down the men of Israel. Eighteen thousand more perished by day's end.

All Israel assembled at the Ark. They fasted and offered sacrifices. And they prayed: "O God, should we attack or should we retreat and make peace?"

"Attack," God answered, "for tomorrow I will give them into your hands."

On the third day, Israel set an ambush behind the city of Gibeah. Then they made a frontal assault as they had on the two previous days. The entire army of Benjamin rushed forth from the city. As before, Israel retreated and Benjamin pursued. But this time the men in ambush emerged and charged into the evacuated Gibeah. They set it ablaze and struck down everyone in the city with the edge of the sword. When the retreating Israelites saw the smoke billowing into the sky, they turned to attack the Benjaminites, who tried to escape. But the Israelites cut them off at every road, lane, byway, and pass.

The slaughter was very great that day. Only six hundred men from Benjamin survived. The Israelites went throughout the territory of Benjamin and torched every city, town, village, and outpost. Benjamin was all but destroyed.

Although they were victorious, the assembly of Israel grieved. "Why has this happened? Why have we nearly wiped out one whole tribe of our brethren?"

Soon they focused their thoughts on how to keep the inheritance alive for the Benjaminite survivors, how to prevent an entire tribe from extinction. "In what way can we find wives for the six hundred men who remain," they asked themselves, "since we have sworn by God not to give any of our daughters to them in marriage?"

They examined their records to see who had not supported the coalition against Benjamin. It was discovered that not one man from the city of Jabesh had joined them. So the congregation of Israelites sent twelve thousand of their best soldiers to Jabesh with this command: "Kill everyone, including women and children. But spare the young women who are virgins and bring them back here. We will give them as a peace offering to the men of Benjamin."

So in the middle of the night, the Israelite army attacked the unsuspecting city. They entered each house and hacked to death husbands and wives, boys and girls. But any young woman who had not slept with a man they bound and took as a prisoner of war, four hundred in all.

The Israelites sent word to the six hundred Benjaminites who were holed up in remote caves. "Please come out and make peace with us, for we are your brothers." Cautiously, the men emerged. They were welcomed with a grand celebration and a mass wedding of the four hundred virgins from Jabesh.

But two hundred of the Benjaminite men had no girl to marry. So the council of Israel convened. One man stepped forward and spoke, "As you know, one of the annual festivals in honor of God will be held next week in Shiloh at the central sanctuary, where the Ark of the Covenant is housed in the Tabernacle and where the old man Eli is the priest. As you also know, one of the customary activities at this festival is the Dance-of-the-Daughters. Why don't we tell the men of Benjamin to hide in the vineyards and when the young women come out for the dance, each man can rush out and seize a girl to be his wife. Thus, they will obtain wives, but we will not be guilty of breaking our oath, since we won't be *giving* our daughters to them. They are being *taken* from us."

"But what about the fathers of the girls?" another elder asked. "What will we say to them?"

The first man answered, "We will simply ask them to do us this favor. It is in fact a favor for all the people of Israel, so that one tribe is not lost."

The council approved the plan.

While the young women were talking and laughing with one another on the way to the dance, each of the two hundred Benjaminite men jumped from the bushes, snatched a girl, and carried her off to be his wife.

No one intervened.

Then the six hundred men of Benjamin returned to their land, rebuilt their towns and lived in them with their wives and children.

In those days there was no king in Israel, and everyone did what was right in their own eyes. And this was manifestly leading to violence and chaos. Israel needed a leader—a prophet, a priest, a king, a general. Somebody. Somebody to save them from the Philistines and, more urgently, from themselves.

29. SAMUEL

Just down the road from the Levite's house in the hill country of Ephraim, there lived a man named Elkanah. Elkanah had two wives, one called Hannah and the other Peninnah. Now Peninnah had children, but Hannah did not, for God had closed her womb.

Elkanah and his family traveled each year to Shiloh to celebrate the festivals of God, which the ancient priest Eli officiated. During the last such celebration, the Benjaminites had taken wives for themselves, and Elkanah was happy he did not have any daughters.

It was the case that Elkanah loved Hannah more than Peninnah, even though Hannah had not borne him any offspring. So Peninnah would taunt Hannah because God had kept her from having children. It was the same thing year after year—Peninnah would mock Hannah whenever they went to offer sacrifices at Shiloh. Each time, Hannah would be reduced to tears and refuse to take her meals.

And each time, Elkanah would ask, "Why are you crying, Hannah? Why aren't you eating? Don't be so depressed. You have me—isn't that better than having ten sons?" But his soft words and gentle touches did little to soothe her pain.

Once when they finished partaking of a sacrificial meal, Hannah got up and went to pray, weeping bitterly. "O God, if you will look upon my misery and answer my prayer and give me a son, then I will give him back to you. He will be yours for his whole lifetime. No razor will come on his head—his hair will never be shorn—and he will be dedicated to God from birth. Like our mighty ancestor Samson."

As she was praying, Eli sat in his usual spot watching her. Her lips moved but she made no sound.

"Have you been drinking?" he demanded. "Put away your wine, woman!"

"Oh, no!" she replied. "I haven't been drinking at all. I am pouring out my heart to the Almighty, beseeching him to help me. Please don't think I'm a wicked woman! For I am in great anguish and sorrow."

Eli peered into her heart. "Well, then, go in peace. And may the God of Israel grant your petition."

Hannah arose and left, her spirits raised.

The next morning, Elkanah and his family returned home. It was not long afterwards that Hannah conceived. When she told her husband, the two of them rejoiced together. Peninnah said nothing.

In due time, Hannah gave birth to a son and named him Samuel. The baby boy was a great comfort and pleasure to his mother, especially since she knew her days with him were numbered. When the child was weaned, Hannah and Elkanah took him to the Tabernacle in Shiloh. After sacrificing a bull to God, they presented the boy Samuel to Eli.

"Do you remember me?" Hannah asked the priest. "I am the woman who stood here praying to God to give me a son. You thought I was drunk." She smiled and looked down at the boy clinging to her leg. "God has granted my request, and now I'm here to keep my word: I dedicate my boy Samuel to God. He will belong to him his whole life, serving here in the Tabernacle under your care."

Eli bent over to greet the child. "Samuel," he uttered pensively, as the boy tightened his grip on his mother.

Hannah reached down, picked up her son, and went to the precise spot where she had prayed before. She fell to her knees and let forth a song of thanksgiving and gratitude. Then, with one last tearful kiss, Hannah handed Samuel to Eli.

• • •

Now Eli had two sons of his own, Hophni and Phineas, who were priests with him. But they were wicked. They greedily took excessive portions of the meat from the sacrifices the people brought, and they engaged in sexual relations with the women who served at the Tabernacle.

In the course of time, Eli confronted them. "I know the evil things you do. I've heard the reports about your wicked ways. Why must you keep sinning? You must stop now! If someone sins against another person, that is one thing. But if someone sins against God as you've done, well, that is something altogether different. Repent before it is too late."

But Eli's sons would not listen to their father, for God was already planning to put them to death. God sent a messenger to Eli with this word: "Thus says the God of Israel: Why do you give your sons more honor than you give me? Why do you scorn my sacrifices and the holiness of my Tabernacle? You should know I honor those who honor me, and I scorn those who scorn me.

"Therefore, Eli, the honor of serving as priest of my Tabernacle will be taken from your family and given to another. All your descendants will die an early death. None will reach old age. They will watch with envy as I pour out blessings on others. But none of them will live a long and happy life. As a sign that this will come to pass, I will cause your two sons, Hophni and Phinehas, to die on the very same day."

Before Eli could speak, the messenger turned and departed.

● ● ●

Meanwhile, the boy Samuel grew and served God in the Tabernacle under Eli. One night, when all was quiet and only a lone candle flickered in the sanctuary, a voice called out, "Samuel!"

"Here I am," Samuel replied. And he got up and ran to Eli. "You called me?"

"I didn't call you," Eli said. "Go back to bed." So he did.

A short while later, the voice called out again, "Samuel!"

Again Samuel got up and went to Eli. "Here I am. Did you call me?"

"I didn't call you, my son," Eli said. "Go back and lie down."

The voice called a third time, and once more Samuel arose and went to Eli. "You called? Here I am."

Then Eli realized it was the voice of God. "Go and lie down, and if you hear the voice again, say, 'Speak, God, for your servant is listening.'"

Once more the voice called out, "Samuel! Samuel!"

"Speak, God, for your servant is listening," Samuel answered dutifully.

God said to Samuel, "I am about to do a shocking thing in Israel—something that will astound all who hear and see it. I am going to carry out my threats against Eli and his family because of the sins of Hophni and Phineas. He knew what they were doing and yet he did not punish them. Therefore, I have vowed that the sins of Eli and the sins of his sons will never be forgiven. Never."

Samuel lay rigid in bed until morning; he did not sleep. At daybreak he got up and opened the doors of the Tabernacle as he always did. But he did not seek out Eli, for he was afraid to tell the old man what God had revealed.

Eli waited for Samuel, but when he did not come, he summoned him. "Samuel, my son."

"Here I am," Samuel replied.

"What did God say to you last night? Tell me everything."

Samuel balked; his shoulders drooped.

"May God strike you severely if you hide anything from me," Eli warned.

At that, Samuel reported everything; he kept nothing back.

Eli lowered his head. "It is God's will. Let him do whatever seems good to him." After a moment, he raised his eyes and motioned Samuel toward his morning work.

● ● ●

The time for the completion of the divine word had not yet come, and thus Samuel grew to manhood in the Tabernacle in Shiloh under the priesthood of Eli. But as Samuel grew, so did the wickedness of Israel, for the people once again broke their holy covenant and worshipped other gods. Also growing in strength since the days of Samson were the Philistines. And so, as he had done before, God sold his people into the hands of their enemies.

The Philistines gathered and attacked Israel, killing four thousand. The Israelites asked one another, "Why did God allow us to be defeated by the Philistines? Who will deliver us this time? Should we search for a king?"

After a while, someone suggested, "Let's bring the Ark of the Covenant from Shiloh and take it with us into battle. Remember how it led our ancestors safely through the wilderness and how it went before us in the great victory over Jericho. If we carry it with us against the Philistines, it will surely bring victory."

They sent men to Shiloh to fetch Hophni and Phinehas and the Ark. Samuel stood at the entrance of the Tabernacle and watched as the sacred chest departed. When the Israelite soldiers saw it coming down the road, they raised a great shout—so loud was the noise that it made the ground shake.

The Philistines heard the uproar and soon received word of the Ark. "We must fight like men!" they said to one another. "For their God is advancing with them. We must be strong and courageous and fight to the death."

The next morning, trumpets sounded, and Hophni and Phineas carried the Ark ahead of the Israelite regiments. But the Philistines fought desperately, and they again defeated Israel. The slaughter was great: Thirty thousand Israelite soldiers did not return. The few remaining ones fled. The Ark of God was captured. Hophni and Phinehas were also killed. On the same day at the same time. Just as God promised.

A soldier from the tribe of Benjamin ran from the battlefield and arrived at Shiloh later that afternoon. Eli perched on a stool near the Tabernacle waiting to hear news of the war. Samuel stood anxiously next to him. When the people in Shiloh saw the messenger approaching, they cried out in anguish, for they knew the tidings were bad since the man had torn his clothes.

"What's all the noise about?" Eli asked. He was now nearly blind.

The messenger rushed straight to the priest. "I've just come from the fighting—I was there this very day."

"What happened? What happened?" Eli asked, hands folded against his chest.

"We've been defeated by the Philistines," the man replied. "The army was slaughtered, your two sons are dead, and the Ark of God captured."

When Eli heard these words, he fell backward from his seat, broke his neck, and died; for he was old and heavy. Samuel turned and went into the Tabernacle and stared forlornly at the empty space where the Ark had rested ever since he could remember.

30. TUMORS

As Shiloh and all Israel mourned, the Philistines transported the Ark to the temple of their god Dagon in the great city of Ashdod—the temple they rebuilt after the blind Samson pushed it down. With much fanfare, they placed it next to the statue of Dagon.

When the citizens of Ashdod went to see it the next morning, Dagon had fallen with his face to the ground in front of the Ark. They took Dagon and put him back in his place. But the following morning the same thing happened. This time his head and hands were broken off; only the torso remained intact.

Moreover, God struck the people of Ashdod and the nearby villages with a plague of rats and tumors. Infected fleas from the rodents bit the Philistines causing their armpits and groins to swell with black lumps. Gangrene attacked fingers and toes. Within days, many died. When the people realized what was happening, they cried out, "We can't keep the Ark of the God of Israel any longer! He's against us. We'll all be destroyed along with Dagon."

So they sent the Ark to Gath, a neighboring Philistine town. When the Ark arrived there, God also struck its inhabitants—both young and old—with an outbreak of rats and tumors.

The people of Gath dispatched the Ark to the town of Ekron, but when the people of Ekron saw it coming, a terrible fear gripped them. "The Ark of Israel is on its way to kill us. Look, the plague has already started! We don't want it here. Send it back home."

The Philistines called in their priests and asked them, "What should we do about this Ark? Tell us how to return it to its own country."

The priests answered, "Send it back to Israel with a gift, an offering, so the plague will cease."

"What sort of offering?" they asked.

The priests replied, "Make gold models of the rats and tumors that have ravaged the land. Perhaps then this God of Israel will stop afflicting us. Do as we have instructed. We must not harden our hearts as Pharaoh and the Egyptians did, for look what happened to them: The God of Israel nearly wiped them out.

"Also, build a new cart and find two cows that have just given birth to calves and that have never been yoked to a cart. Hitch the cows to the cart, but take away the calves and pen them up. Put the Ark on the cart, and beside it place a chest containing the gold tumors. Then let the cows go wherever they want. If they cross the border and go straight toward the Israelite town of Beth-shemesh, then we'll know it was God who brought this disaster upon us. If they don't, then it was nothing more than chance."

The Philistines did accordingly. And sure enough, without veering off the road to the right or the left, the cows went directly eastward to Beth-shemesh, lowing as they went.

Now on that day, the people of Beth-shemesh were harvesting wheat in the valley. They looked up, squinting into the midafternoon glare.

And behold, the Ark!

They watched and cheered as the cart rumbled slowly along. It finally came to rest beside a mossy boulder in a field, and the people rushed upon it in jubilation. They broke up the wood of the cart for a fire, killed the cows, and sacrificed them to God. Several men lifted the Ark and the box of gold tumors and placed them on the large rock. Then the people of Beth-shemesh offered many sacrifices and burnt offerings to God.

One of the men raised the lid of the sacred shrine and peeked inside. There were the stone tablets of the covenant. He waved over several friends who also glanced into the box. Then others tiptoed by and leaned down to see. Seventy men in all looked into the Ark.

God struck all seventy dead.

And so the occasion of celebration turned into mourning because of the blow God dealt them. "Who is able to stand in the presence of this holy God?" they cried out. "Where can we send the Ark?"

Presently, they sent word to the people at Kiriath-jearim. "The Philistines have returned the Ark of God. Come and get it, and it can remain with you."

So the men of Kiriath-jearim took the Ark back to their town where it remained nearly forgotten for a long time—twenty years in all.

The Ark had been in Philistine territory for seven months. Each and every one of those days Samuel waited and prayed. When it finally returned to the land of Israel, he used the occasion to rally the people. He summoned the assembly to Mizpah and said to them, "Even though the Philistines have suffered destruction because they stole the Ark of God, you know we still labor under their hand. And we all know why: God is punishing us for our infidelity, for serving other gods.

"Hear, then, O Israel. If you are ready with all your heart to return to God and God alone, then rid yourselves of foreign idols and decide—simply decide—to worship and obey only the God of Israel. Then he will rescue you from the Philistines."

The people listened to the words of Samuel, and in a great ceremony, they confessed their sins before God. And they fasted.

When the Philistine rulers heard Israel had gathered at Mizpah, they mobilized their army and advanced. The Israelites were badly frightened and confronted Samuel. "Do something to save us! Do something like Ehud or Gideon or Jephthah or Samson who saved us from our oppressors."

"I am not like them," Samuel answered. "I am a priest of God."

"Well, then, plead with God to save us from the Philistines!" they begged.

So Samuel took a young lamb and sacrificed it to God. As the meat roasted on the altar and the smoke ascended into the heavens, the Philistines launched their assault.

At that moment, a cloud rolled over the sun and God spoke with a terrible voice of thunder from the skies. The air trembled and the ground shook. The Philistines were thrown into panic and confusion, and they turned and fled. Samuel lifted a sword and the men of Israel pursued the Philistines, hewing them down as they ran.

So God subdued the Philistines that day, and the land was at peace throughout the remainder of Samuel's life.

31. SAUL, THE FIRST KING

When Samuel had grown old, the elders of the twelve tribes convened a meeting with him. "Samuel," the chief counselor said, "you have served Israel well, and for that we are thankful. But now you are old, and your sons are not good men. Like Eli's boys, they are wicked and greedy and not fit to be your successor. Thus, we ask that you appoint a king to govern us like all the nations around us."

Samuel shrank, his lips pressed together, for he was displeased with their request. He stood to his feet and studied the face of each man in the room. Then he strode out and sought the counsel of God.

"Do what they have asked of you," God said to the prostrate priest, "for they are not rejecting you; rather they are rejecting me. Indeed, they've had a king—me!—all these many years. Now they don't want me to reign over them any longer. Ever since I saved them from bondage in Egypt and brought them into this land of milk and honey they have continually forsaken me and bowed down to other gods. So, do as they ask. But solemnly warn them about the way of a king."

Samuel returned to the elders and said, "You will have a king, O Israel. But you don't know what you're asking for. This is how a king will reign over you: He will take your sons and compel them to drive his chariots; he will make them plow his fields and harvest his crops, and some will make his weapons of war. He will take your daughters from you and force them to cook and bake and make perfumes for him. He will take away the best of your fields, vineyards, and olive groves and give them to his own officials. He will take your grain and your grape harvest for himself. He will take your male and female servants and the best of your cattle and he will put them to his work, not yours. You will be his slaves! Then you will cry out for relief from this king you are demanding, but God will not help you."

The elders of Israel would not be dissuaded. "Even so, we want a king like the nations around us. We want a king to govern us, to unify us, to lead us into battle. We have one God and one common history, and so we need one king to rule us. Right now we are twelve separate tribes, and we are vulnerable in the face of the Philistines and other oppressors. We need a centralized government to unite us. Now appoint for us a monarch."

Once more Samuel left the room and repeated to God the words of the elders. And again God replied, "Do as they say, and anoint for them a king."

Samuel returned and told everyone to go back home.

A short time later, Samuel called all the people of Israel to meet at Mizpah. He stood on a mound and addressed the multitude. "This is what the God of Israel has declared: I rescued you from the Egyptians and from many people who have oppressed you since then. Though I have repeatedly saved you from misery and distress, you have rejected me and insisted on a king. So a king you will get. Now, therefore, present yourselves before me tribe by tribe and family by family, and you will cast lots to determine who will be your ruler."

Samuel brought all the tribes of Israel before God, one by one, and the tribe of Benjamin was chosen by lot. Then he brought forward each family of the tribe of Benjamin, and the family of Matri was chosen. And from the family of Matri, Saul son of Kish was singled out to be king. But when they looked for him, he was not to be found.

"Well, where is he, God?" the people asked.

God replied, "He is hiding among the baggage." So they went and found him, brought him out, and stood him next to Samuel in front of the great assembly. He was a handsome man, and tall, a full head higher than anyone else.

Then Samuel proclaimed, "This is the man God has selected as your king. King Saul. There is no one in all Israel like him." Saul bowed uncomfortably as the crowd roared. Then Samuel directed Saul to kneel, and he took a flask of oil and poured it on Saul's head. "I hereby anoint you the king of Israel."

All the people chanted in unison, "Long live the king! Long live the king!" As the noise rang through the valley, Saul leaned in close to Samuel and said, "I am from the tribe of Benjamin, the smallest of the tribes—we were nearly wiped out a generation ago. And my family is the least of the families within Benjamin. That makes me the least of the least. Are you sure this is right?"

Samuel only smiled and nodded. When the hoopla subsided, Samuel spoke to the congregation, explaining to them the rights and duties of a king. Then, after one more affirmation of Saul, the people returned home, as did Saul to his house in Gibeah, not too far from the house where the Levite's concubine suffered her terrible fate.

● ● ●

It was not long before the newly anointed king encountered his first challenge. King Nahash the Ammonite attacked and besieged the Israelite city of Jabesh. Nahash had a ruthless reputation, and so the frightened townspeople of Jabesh said to him, "Make a treaty with us, and we will be subject to you."

But Nahash replied, "I will make a treaty only on the condition that I gouge out the right eye of every one of you."

Terrified by the threat, the elders of Jabesh sent word back to Nahash, "Give us seven days so we can send messengers throughout Israel. If none of our people comes to rescue us, then we will submit to your demands."

"Sure," Nahash sneered haughtily. "Go beg your brothers to help you. Let the mighty Israelites come. It will only be more eyes for me to gouge."

So the people of the town sent four able-bodied young men to appeal to King Saul.

When they arrived in Gibeah, Saul was returning from his work in the fields.

"What is wrong?" Saul asked the breathless messengers.

"Nahash is threatening to blind every one of us. He's that crazy king of Ammon—you've heard of him—who humiliates his defeated enemies by plucking the right eye. We've come to you to save us."

It was then that the spirit of God came powerfully upon Saul, and his eyes blazed a black fire. He drew his sword, swung it over his head, and slew a pair of his oxen. Then he cut their decapitated carcasses into huge chunks of meat and bone. He called his servants and handed a bloody hunk to each, saying, "Take these throughout Israel and declare: This is what will be done to the oxen of anyone who does not heed this call to arms to defend our bothers in Jabesh."

Within two days, Saul mustered an army of thousands, each with his armor and spear.

Saul summoned the messengers from Jabesh. "See what a king can do," he said, sweeping his hand over the sea of soldiers. "Go back home and tell your townspeople what you've seen. And tell them that before the sun sets tomorrow, you will be rescued."

The men dashed off and ran through the night. The council of elders in Jabesh listened joyfully to their report. Then they sent word to Nahash, "Tomorrow we will surrender to you, and you can do to us whatever you like."

By that time, Saul had divided his army into three companies and begun the march to Jabesh. As Nahash and his officers gloated in their tents in anticipation of the next day's eye-gouging, Saul's soldiers crept quietly around them on all sides. Then Saul shouted, and the three companies swarmed into the Ammonite camp from every direction. Swords and spearheads flashed and slashed. Saul and the Israelites slaughtered the Ammonites through the heat of the afternoon, pursuing them until the sun vanished. The few Ammonites who survived were so scattered that no two of them were left together.

So Saul and his army returned victorious, and all Israel celebrated together in thankfulness for their new king.

32. ROYAL TROUBLE

After the victory over Nahash, Saul surveyed his army. He kept two thousand warriors with him and assigned one thousand to his son Jonathan. The rest he sent back to their home territories under the leadership of local captains.

Now it was Saul's plan to build his army deliberately, one piece at a time. It would require patience to construct a well-trained and organized military; for Israel had never had one.

But Jonathan had other ideas, and he himself was a man to be reckoned with. Tall, broad-shouldered, and winsome, like his father, Jonathan took his division of soldiers and attacked the small Philistine outpost at Geba. His raid was a success, and at once Israel was at war. Even as Jonathan celebrated his triumph, a message was on its way to the Philistine generals who reacted without delay. They summoned three thousand chariots, six thousand charioteers, and soldiers beyond measure.

When Saul heard of their mighty approach, he sent word to Samuel, "Come and reveal to me the oracle of God concerning this matter. Offer sacrifices and intercede with God on my behalf."

But there was no response from Samuel. Saul waited seven days, and still there was no sign of the holy man. Saul's garrison of two thousand men began to lose heart and scatter. His forces slowly dwindled.

"Kings can't wait a week for the proper sacrifices to be made," Saul grumbled to his chief officer. "This is war! Bring me an animal, and I will do the sacrifice myself."

A heifer was brought and Saul made the burnt offering. Just as he finished, Samuel arrived.

"What have you done?" asked Samuel, looking at the scorched altar.

Saul finished washing his hands and replied, "My men were growing weary with the delay, and I had no idea where you were. What was I supposed to do? I didn't want to proceed without first seeking the will of God, so I made the offering myself."

"You have done a foolish thing," Samuel said. "You are not to sacrifice. God will punish you for this misdeed."

"But . . ." Saul grimaced.

Samuel turned and walked off. Saul stood there, hands clasped on the back of his head, bewildered. He sighed and said to his servant, "How many men do we have left."

There were only six hundred.

In the meantime, Jonathan was again doing his own thing. For about the time Saul offered up the sacrifice, Jonathan spoke to his young servant. "Come on, let's go over—just you and me—and take a closer look at this Philistine hoard who has drawn up against us. Maybe God will work with us. Why wouldn't God save us as he has many times before?"

"I am the one who carries your armor, and I carry it wherever you want to go," the lad grinned.

"Good," Jonathan said, patting him on the back, "Here's the plan. We're going to the pass between Geba and Micmash. We will descend the near side of the gorge, so the Philistines can see us. If they mock and yell out, 'Come on up, you Israelites,' then that's exactly what we will do, for that will be the sign God has given them into our hands."

The young man gathered ropes and weapons, and at dawn the next day the two of them set out into the thicket that surrounded the canyon. After rappelling down the rock, they stood together between the crags. As the morning mist blew away, they moved out into the open. Philistine faces peered over the edge of the towering rock.

"Look!" they laughed. "The Israelites are crawling out of the holes they were hiding in. Behold, the mighty army of Israel—two boys standing on a rock!" They mocked and pointed and playfully punched at one another. "Come on up to us and we'll teach you a lesson."

Jonathan put his arm around the boy. "You heard them. Follow me up. God has given them to us."

Jonathan clawed his way to the top with his armor-bearer right behind. Then they attacked in tandem and killed twenty of the enemy in the blink of an eye.

Straightway, panic struck the entire Philistine army—those in the camp and in the fields, those at the outposts and at their stations. It seemed to them that whole earth was shaking. For it was a panic sent by God.

News of the tumult surging through the Philistine army soon reached Saul. "Who started the war this time?" he asked.

"Jonathan," came the answer.

"Well, let's finish it!" Saul hollered. "Today the Philistines will be destroyed! Cursed be anyone who eats food before sundown, before I have avenged myself on my enemies."

King Saul summoned his six hundred soldiers and sent word throughout Israel. Then he mounted his horse and headed toward Micmash. As he galloped through the countryside, he saw shepherds and farmers emerging from their homes, swords and arrows in hand; for they heard that the Philistine army was melting away in all directions, and that Saul's army was swelling again.

When Saul and his men came upon the enemy, they found them in complete confusion, striking one another mortally. King Saul ordered an all-out attack, and the Israelites rushed into the fray. Soon Philistine blood flowed from the battlefields.

As Jonathan hunted the escaping foe, he came upon some beehives. He stopped, reached out his dagger, dipped it into a honeycomb, and ate. His strength was renewed and he finished the battle that he and his armor-bearer had begun. By day's end, Jonathan had slayed twenty times twenty. The carnage was massive.

So on that day God saved Israel.

● ● ●

When darkness descended, the Israelite troops pounced on the plunder. They seized sheep, cattle, and calves, which they butchered and devoured.

Saul raised his voice and proclaimed, "Let us pursue the Philistines by night and pillage them 'til dawn—'til not one of them remains alive."

His troops just kept on eating. So Saul bade them to finish. "You will need it!" he yelled. Then he turned aside, genuflected, and asked God, "Shall we chase the Philistines? Will you give them into Israel's hand?"

But God did not answer him.

Again, Saul sought the Almighty.

Still nothing.

The divine silence distressed the king, so he summoned his commanders. "God is not revealing himself to me. Perhaps it's because of the sacrifice I offered, instead of waiting on Samuel. But I don't think so. I think it's something else. So tell me: What sin has been committed today?" He gazed sternly at the hushed circle. But none of them said a word. "God is silent and now you are too?" Saul continued. "I must discover the reason. Know this: Whoever has sinned will perish—even if the guilt lies with my son Jonathan."

The men shifted their armor and stared at the ground.

"Alright," Saul bellowed. "You all stand over there, and Jonathan and I will stand here."

When the division had been made, Saul prayed in the hearing of the assembly, "O God, why have you not answered your servant today? Please show me the answer by the casting of these lots."

They cast lots and it fell to Jonathan and Saul. "Maybe God is indeed punishing me for the sacrifice," Saul wondered aloud. "Now cast the lot between Jonathan and me."

They did, and Jonathan was signaled.

Saul stood in front of his son with one hand on each shoulder. "Tell me what you've done, Jonathan."

"I ate some honey today," he replied unwaveringly. "But I didn't know you had forbid it until I'd already eaten. Why did you utter this oath? How much better it would've been if the men had eaten during the battle. How much greater the slaughter of the Philistines if we had our full strength."

Saul winced. "I have made a vow to God. To keep my word, you must die."

At this, one of the commanders stepped forward. "Why should Jonathan die? He's the one who brought this great victory? No way will we let him perish! Not a hair of his head will fall to the ground, for he did this today with God's help."

Saul collapsed. "Then he shall not die."

Jonathan knelt on the ground next to his father, and they cried together.

Then all the Israelites withdrew to their hometowns.

• • •

Sometime later, Samuel, now hoary and wrinkled, went to see Saul. The two talked over cups of wine.

"You recall that God instructed me to anoint you as king of his people," Samuel remarked knowingly.

"Yes."

"Then listen to the words of God who made you king: The Amalekites have been a long-time enemy of my people. Their day of reckoning has come. You, King Saul, are to attack and completely destroy the entire Amalekite people. Everyone and everything must die—men, women, children, babies, cattle, sheep, goats, camels, and donkeys. Nothing is to be spared."

Saul's countenance fell. "God has not demanded this since the days of Joshua. So why now?"

Samuel looked up at the king. "This is the word from God."

"Okay," Saul acquiesced. But his mind was unsettled. He had done his best to subdue the Philistines, and now he was being asked to pick a fight with an old enemy who had not caused any trouble recently.

Be that as it may, once more Saul lit the dark flame in his eye and summoned Israel to gather at Telaim near the home of the Amalekites. He issued this order to his troops: "As in the days when our ancestors took this great land, we are to kill everything that breathes—man, woman, child, and animal. Nothing is to be left alive. Nothing."

Then Saul mounted his horse and led the way. The Israelites surrounded Amalek in the early morning hours, and at sunrise they attacked and slaughtered them.

They went through houses, huts, tents, and foxholes, putting to death every single person. Every person but one: Agag, the king. Plus, some of the soldiers kept the best of the sheep and goats, the cattle, the fat calves, and the lambs.

In a dimly lit house somewhere in the Israelite countryside, the word of God came to Samuel, "I regret that I ever made Saul king, for he has not been loyal to me and has refused to obey my command."

Samuel was so deeply distraught when he heard this that he wept before God all night.

Early the next morning Samuel went to see Saul in Gilgal where the king was offering thanksgiving sacrifices to God.

"May God bless you," Saul said to Samuel with a wide grin. "I've carried out God's command. Amalek has been avenged."

"Then what is the bleating of sheep that I hear?" Samuel asked.

Saul looked at him, still smiling.

"And the lowing of cattle in my ear?" Samuel said, louder.

"Oh," Saul replied casually, "the people brought back some of the best sheep, goats, and cattle to sacrifice to God. We've destroyed everything else. All the rest—"

"Stop."

"The rest of the animals and people," Saul continued, "we put to the sword."

"Stop!" Samuel shouted. "Do you want to know what God told me last night?"

Saul drew a deep breath. "What did he tell you?"

Samuel answered, "You are the leader of the tribes of Israel. God has anointed you king. God sent you on a mission to utterly destroy the Amalekites, until they were wiped out. Completely. Why haven't you obeyed God?"

"But I did obey," Saul insisted. "I did what God sent me to do. I only brought back King Agag. I destroyed everyone else. My troops saved the best of the sheep, goats, cattle, and plunder for a grand sacrifice to God here in Gilgal."

Samuel wagged his head. "What is more pleasing to God: your burnt offerings and sacrifices or your obedience to his word?" He paused, his eyes flashing. "To obey is better than sacrifice, and to heed is better than offering the fatted calf. So because you have rejected God's command, God has rejected you as king."

Saul's shoulders sagged. "I have sinned," he admitted. "I have transgressed. But now, Samuel, please intervene before God and pardon my wrong-doing. Surely the Almighty will forgive me like any other man."

Samuel was unyielding. "I will not. For God has rejected you as king of Israel."

The old man turned to go.

"Wait!" Saul called out. "Don't leave."

Samuel kept walking away, but Saul reached out and took hold of the elderly man's robe, and it tore. He quickly let go and fell to his knees. Samuel turned and looked at his garment. He held the rip in both hands in front of Saul's pale face. "Just as you have torn my robe," Samuel gritted, "so God has torn the kingdom of Israel from you today and given it to someone else—someone who is better than you."

Samuel dropped the garment; Saul's head sank. "And God does not change his mind like people do," Samuel added. "God has rejected you. Period."

"No, please, no," Saul cried.

"But since I'm still here," Samuel continued in a dark tone, "bring Agag to me."

Saul gestured for his servants to obey, and Agag was led to Samuel.

Samuel eyed the shackled king standing before him and said, "As your sword has killed the sons of many mothers, now your mother will be childless." Then Samuel took Saul's sword and hacked Agag to pieces. With the final Amalekite slain, he flipped the weapon to the side and departed for home.

Samuel would never again see Saul in this life.

God was sorry he had appointed Saul to be the ruler of his people.

33. A SHEPHERD BOY AND A GIANT

Samuel was depressed. He felt pity and sorrow for Saul. He mourned what had become of Israel's first ruler. But the words, "Someone who is better than you," echoed in his head. They had rolled off his tongue in his bitter frustration. But were they right? Had God already decided who would be the next king after Saul's death? And if so, who was it?

The answer came to him one afternoon as he strolled through the byways near his home in Ramah.

"You have mourned long enough for Saul," God said. "I have rejected him as king of Israel, so fill your flask with oil and go to Bethlehem. Find a man named Jesse who lives there, for I've selected one of his sons to be my next king."

"How can I do that? Saul is still king," Samuel replied. "I cannot anoint another man, unless perhaps it were Saul's own son, Jonathan. If Saul hears I've appointed another, he will kill me."

"Do it in private, not like you did with Saul. And do it now," God answered.

Immediately, Samuel set out for Bethlehem, carrying the sacred flask under his robe, its tear flapping in the breeze. When he arrived, he sought out the man named Jesse.

Now Jesse was a farmer and his sons were shepherds. After learning the reason for Samuel's visit, Jesse eagerly summoned his boys from the fields. Within a short time, seven youths lined up before Samuel. When the oldest, Eliab, stepped forward, Samuel was sure he was God's anointed. For he was a towering, sharp-eyed, well-built young man.

But God said to Samuel, "Don't judge by his appearance or height. For I, God, don't see as people see. People judge by outward appearance, but God looks at the heart. I have not chosen him."

Then Jesse beckoned forward his second son, Abinadab. He likewise was strong and impressive. But God said nothing, so Samuel shook his head. Next Jesse summoned Shammah, but he was not the chosen one either.

It was the same result for each of the remaining young men. Then Samuel asked Jesse, "Are these all the sons you have?"

"There is one more, the youngest," Jesse replied doubtfully. "He's out in the fields watching over the sheep."

"And probably playing his harp," Eliab added mockingly. "Little music boy."

"Or practicing with his sling shot," Abinadab chimed.

"Send for him at once," Samuel instructed.

When Samuel saw the boy leaping down the hillside and running swiftly toward him, Samuel knew in his heart the search was over. David was vigorous and handsome and pleasant to behold. He had beautiful eyes and a tanned body. He stopped in front of Samuel and greeted the old man courteously.

"This is the one," God spoke to Samuel. "Anoint him."

As David stood there among his brothers, Samuel took the flask and poured it slowly on David's head. The oil trickled down his hair and face and shoulders. Samuel leaned in close and whispered in David's ear. At that moment, the spirit of God came powerfully upon David, and the lad knew he would one day rule Israel.

But neither Jesse nor any of his sons said anything to anyone about what took place that day. For Samuel swore them to secrecy until the appropriate time. That time had not yet come, for Saul was still king.

● ● ●

Meanwhile, Saul too had been wondering about those words: "One who is better than you." The thought of them ate away at his soul. Why had he been rejected? How could God have already chosen another?

About the same time the spirit of God came upon David, it left Saul, and an evil spirit from God tormented him. Saul began to have nightmares;

he would wake up in a running sweat. During the long, hot afternoons, he sometimes broke into a nearly uncontrollable rage. A tremendous noise racked his brain and he could barely keep it from issuing forth in howls of anguish.

Saul's attendants observed his black despair and they knew it was from God. Perhaps war would cure Saul, they thought. So when the Philistines once again gathered to attack, they secretly wished it were a blessing in disguise for their haggard king.

The enemy, with their mighty weapons of war, marched boldly into the territory of Judah and pitched their tents on a mountainside at Socoh. Saul hastily marshaled the men of Israel on the slopes directly opposite the Philistines. Between the two encampments lay the valley of Elah—its rocks, trees, and streams waiting for war to break forth upon it.

After three days of anticipation, neither side had made a move. This only worsened Saul's bouts of depression. On the fourth morning, a lone man emerged from the Philistine camp and stood in the middle of the valley. He was a giant—tall, much taller than Saul. He wore a great brass helmet on his head and he was sheathed in a heavy coat of armor, the likes of which no one in Israel had ever seen. Huge plates of brass covered his arms and legs. The shaft of his spear was as heavy and thick as the beam of a house, and it was tipped with an iron head. His name was Goliath.

"Why aren't you attacking us?" Goliath called scornfully. "Choose one man to come down here and fight me. If he kills me, then we will surrender. But if I kill him, you will surrender and be our slaves." He paused to let the echo fade. Then he laughed loudly, "Today I defy the armies of Israel! Send a man to fight me!"

Saul and his army were crestfallen. That night Saul's fits of anxiety were almost unbearable.

Twice a day—morning and evening—for an entire month Goliath came forth and shouted his challenge. Every day he mocked Saul and the Israelites. And every night Saul could not eat or think or talk or sleep. Sometimes he could scarcely breathe.

"Music," Saul whispered one night, "I need some music to soothe me."

So word was sent through the troops to find a musician for the king. When Eliab heard the request, he sent a message to Saul. "I have a younger brother back home who is quite skilled with the harp. He wanted to come to war with me and my other brothers, but our father Jesse wouldn't let him. His name is David."

Saul sent word to Jesse who loaded up a donkey with provisions and dispatched his youngest son to the battle site. That night as Saul paced and tossed and turned, David played sweet melodies. Then the evil spirit from God departed from Saul, and the king closed his eyes and rested peacefully for the first time in a long while. He could not have imagined the young man with the harp would one day succeed him as king of Israel.

● ● ●

Early the next morning, David sought his brothers among the troops. As he talked with them, Goliath stepped into the valley and shouted his usual taunts.

"Who is that?" David asked.

"Goliath," Eliab replied. "He's been doing that every day for weeks now. The king has offered a lot of money to the man who kills him. Plus, he will be given the king's daughter in marriage and will be exempt from taxes."

David turned to the other men. "Is this true?"

They nodded.

David peered down into the valley. "Who is this uncircumcised Philistine that he should defy the armies of the living God?"

"And who are you?" Eliab smirked. "You came here to play music for the king, not to fight. Leave fighting to the real men. Maybe you should go back to your sheep. I know how conceited you are and how wicked your heart is."

"What've I done?" David fired back. "Can't I even speak?"

"You can speak—and sing—but that's about it."

David ignored him. "Nobody disrespects Saul and the soldiers of God and gets away with it," David snorted, and then walked away with purpose.

That afternoon, as rumors swirled in the Israelite camp that someone was going to fight the giant, David approached Saul in front of the royal tent. He went straight to the point. "Why is everyone afraid of this Goliath fellow? I will go fight him."

Saul laughed. "You are only a youth—and a shepherd at that. He is a giant, and has been a warrior ever since his boyhood."

David stared straight into the king's eyes, not in the least bit intimidated. "Yes, I am a shepherd. And also a warrior. A slayer of beasts bigger than Goliath."

Saul eyed David dubiously.

"When lions or bears snatch sheep from my flocks, I go after them, strike them with my club, and rescue the lambs right out of their mouths. If the beasts attack me, I seize them with my bare hands and kill them. I've slayed many lions and bears; and this uncircumcised Philistine will be just like one of them. Yes, O King, God has many times saved me from the paw of the lion and the claw of the bear. He will surely deliver me from the hand of this giant."

Saul gauged the fine-looking youth who glowed with vigor and health. Hope flickered in Saul's heart, but his speech remained cautious. "None of my mighty warriors are willing to face him, so how could I possibly send you? Besides, if you die, then who will play music to keep the evil spirits away?"

"It is exactly as you say," David replied. "No one else is willing to go. So what other option do you have?"

Saul smiled. "And it is as exactly you say: Go, and may God be with you. Now wait here a moment."

Saul ducked into his tent and returned carrying his full coat of armor. He put it on David, but the boy staggered under its weight and could barely see out from under the helmet.

"I cannot use these," he said to Saul, grunting to lift off the heavy equipment. "Then what will you use?"

"This." David reached into his pocket and produced a long leather sling.

"That?"

"Yes, with stones, of course."

"Go, and may God be with you."

So David departed and went to a nearby stream where he carefully chose five smooth stones and placed them in his shepherd's pouch. He then descended the slope toward the valley of Elah. It was late afternoon, about the time of day the giant would emerge for a second time to call forth his challenge.

Saul stood watching. He saw the giant saunter to his place, throw back his great head, and roar, "I defy the armies of Israel to send out a man to fight me!"

Saul earnestly scanned the valley floor. There was David. Goliath saw the young man too.

"What! Am I a dog that you send out a boy to me?" The giant took off his helmet and threw it to the ground in disgust, muttering curses in the name of his gods. "Come here! And I'll give your flesh to the birds and the beasts!"

David never slowed his easy pace. His voice rang out, "You come against me with sword and spear and javelin, but I come against you in the name of God Almighty, the God of Israel, the God you've defied. Today God will give you into my hands, and I will strike you down and cut off your head. This very day I will give the carcasses of the Philistine army to the birds and the beasts, and the whole world will know there is a God in Israel."

At that, Goliath charged toward David. The young Israelite pulled a rock from his bag and placed it in the sling. As Goliath lumbered furiously toward him, David whirled the sling above his head. Then, with a snap, he let it fly. The stone streaked through the air and struck the Philistine square in the forehead. It seemed to sink into his skull. The giant swayed and fell face down on the ground.

David quickened his steps toward the flattened Philistine. He seized the huge sword from the giant's hand, lifted it high, and brought it down with all his might. The blade sliced through flesh and bone and into the earth. Goliath's head rolled free.

When the Philistines saw their hero was dead, they picked up their tents and took flight. With a shout of triumph the Israelite army gave chase. Before darkness, the Philistine dead were strewn along the road for miles. Saul's men took the daggers and armor of each slain soldier. David, for his part, took Goliath's weapons and kept them in his own tent—along with the giant's head.

So David defeated the Philistines with a sling and a stone; without a sword in his hand, he struck down the giant and killed him.

When the Israelite army returned home, women danced in the streets and sang their songs of praise. "Saul has slain his thousands. And David his ten thousands."

David, the youngest son of Jesse, the shepherd boy and harpist for King Saul, was now a hero in Israel.

34. DAVID IN THE PALACE OF SAUL

Israel rejoiced, for Saul did just as the people hoped a king would do, save them from their enemies. And now there was David. Everyone talked of the giant-slayer, who remained with Saul instead of returning home with the other soldiers.

Jonathan also had great admiration for a warrior as bold and beautiful and youthful as David—and such a talented musician besides. And it happened as David lived in his father's palace that Jonathan came to love David. And David, Jonathan.

"Let us make a covenant, you and me," the prince said to David. "Let God be our witness that we will forever be as one."

"It is a pact," the king-to-be said. "We shall be as one." The two embraced.

To mark their bond, Jonathan took off his robe and gave it to David, along with his tunic, and even his sword, his bow, and his belt.

Saul himself was pleased with David and entrusted to him important military matters. David did whatever the king of Israel commanded. He successfully fended off the Philistines and other enemies. He was a champion. Everybody loved him; everybody praised him.

It was good for Saul to have such a wise and brave man to lead the armies of Israel. But every time David was victorious, the same refrain rang throughout the land: "Saul has slain his thousands, and David his ten thousands." Outwardly, Saul's countenance was bright. But on the inside, a fire of jealousy flickered and his spirits fell. *They think David is ten times better than me—they want him to be king,* he brooded to himself.

One night, the evil spirit from God returned violently on Saul. He awoke in a smoldering fury. He twitched and jerked; his arms flailed as if he were throwing things wildly across the room. His attendants called for David, who rushed in with harp in hand. Soon a soft melody filled the king's chambers. But this time, David's songs only served to remind the king of the songs of the women. And his dark mood only became darker. He grabbed a pitcher of water and smashed it on the floor. Then he seized a spear and flung it at David, screaming, "I will pin you to the wall!"

David ducked. The spear stuck in a crack in the stone behind him. Saul's chest heaved; his face warped with hatred. David remained crouched on the floor. Then Saul grabbed a dagger and hurled it at his personal musician. David rolled to one side. The iron tip narrowly missed his ear. Finally, Saul collapsed and began to sob as David stumbled from the room.

The next morning when Saul came to and saw the spear sticking out from the wall, a great fear swept over him. For he knew God was with David; but he did not know what David would do. Would he tell others what happened? Would there be an uprising? Was his own life in danger?

In a moment of fresh clarity, Saul determined this was the time to fulfill his promise to give David his oldest daughter in marriage as a reward for slaying Goliath. When he told his officers of his intentions to offer Merab, they pointed out it was Michal, his younger daughter, who was in love with David and would make for a better wife. Saul took their advice, for it made no difference to him. He had other plans in mind: "I cannot kill David myself," Saul ruminated, "for he is too well-liked among the people. No, I will not raise my hand against him. I will let the Philistines do it."

Saul sent a message to David, "I hope you can forget my past actions. Now it's time for me to remember my past words. You saved Israel from the hand of the Philistine giant, and so, to keep my oath, I am pleased to give Michal to you as a wife. She loves you and is ready to marry."

David sent word back, "It is no small matter to become the king's son-in-law. At heart, I'm just a poor man, a shepherd boy from a lowly family in a lowly tribe."

"So he's feigning humility," Saul huffed. "How clever."

"Your humility is admirable," he replied to David, "But we both know Israel delights in you. And I truly would like nothing better than for you to be my son-in-law. If you are worried about a sizable dowry, I ask for nothing other than proof that one hundred Philistines have perished. Are you valiant enough to pay with one hundred Philistine foreskins?"

Saul figured David would not be able to resist the gruesome challenge. He will surely be killed by the Philistines, and then he will no longer be a threat to my throne, Saul thought. And besides, if he produces the bride price, then I have sent more terror among my enemies, and David will simply be family. I cannot go wrong either way.

Though he felt sure of his plan, something made him uneasy. Saul paced back and forth as he waited for David's reply.

In the evening, his servants came and reported, "David has accepted the offer and he's already left for Philistine territory."

"Very good," Saul said, without much conviction.

Two days later, David entered the king's residence. He had a bloody burlap bag in his hands. "O King Saul, I have killed not one hundred, but two hundred Philistines. Here are their foreskins," he boasted, placing the sack on a low table.

Saul pulled the string and peered into the bag. A foul odor met him, and he recoiled. It was indeed as David had said.

And so Saul gave Michal to David to be his wife. Michal loved David; but Saul loathed him. And then there were those words, "Someone who is better than you," which forever rattled painfully in Saul's head. God had chosen someone else to be king. Saul was now sure David was that man. This was more than he could bear, and his festering jealousy and fear of David turned again to thoughts of murder.

● ● ●

Once more war broke out, and Saul and David fought the Philistines. When they returned home victorious, the women came out singing songs of adulation and dancing. Their chorus was the same: "Saul has killed his thousands, and David his ten thousands."

As before, Saul smiled and waved, but his heart seethed with envy. A few nights later, the evil spirit from God returned. It tormented him miserably, and the king's attendants sent for David and his music. David hesitated, but Michal encouraged him to go; so he did. As soon as he began to play, Saul sat back and rested, his eyes closed, his breathing rhythmic. He remained that way for nearly an hour. But then, in a flash, he awoke, reached for his sword and rushed toward David. At the last moment, David nimbly stepped aside and the sharp weapon bit into the wall. It hung there quivering while Saul raged and David slipped into the darkness.

The king-in-waiting ran back home to Michal. "He tried to kill me! Again!"

Michal grabbed him by the coat. "What? What do you mean he tried to kill you? And what do you mean 'again'"?

"He tried to spear me. He's tried twice before."

Michal was terrified; she went blank as she struggled to digest the news—her father had attempted to murder her husband. "If you don't escape tonight, you'll be dead by morning," she cried. "He may already have his men on the way here." She hurried David to the window on the rear of the house. With his head in her hands, she kissed him. "Send for me," she implored, and then she threw open the shade.

When David had vanished into the cold night air, Michal drew the curtain and set to work. She fluffed some pillows under his bed sheets and placed a cushion of goat hair at the head of the bed. It was not long before the king's guardsmen knocked on the door.

"He's sick and cannot get out of bed," Michal told them.

"Well, then, we'll have to take the whole bed," the captain chortled. But when he pulled back the blankets, the cushion of goat hair fell to the ground, and there were the pillows.

When Saul received the message, he dashed to the house. "Michal, my daughter, how could you betray me? How could you help my enemy escape?"

"I had no choice," she cringed. "He threatened to kill me if I did not help him."

Saul covered the top of his head with both hands and doubled over. "How could you?"

● ● ●

David remained in hiding for a few days. Then he sent word for Jonathan to meet him at nightfall on the outskirts of the nearby city of Ramah.

"What have I done? What is my crime?" David asked him wearily. "How have I wronged your father that he is trying to take my life?"

Jonathan grasped David's shoulders. "You will not die. I won't let that happen. My father tells me everything; he won't be able to hide his plans about you from me."

David shook his head. "Your father knows we're friends. He won't apprise you of anything. I'm telling you, Jonathan, there's but a step between me and death."

"What do you want me to do? You know I will do anything for you."

"Tomorrow is the New Moon feast," David replied. "I've always eaten with the king on this occasion. But this time, obviously, I will not be there. Instead, I will be hiding by the great stone pile." He pointed over Jonathan's shoulder. "When your father notices I'm not at the feast, say I went home to celebrate it with my own family. If he says that's fine, that will be the sign the evil spirit has departed from him, and I can return home safely—at least for now. But if he becomes enraged, then we will know he's still bent on destroying me. In that case, Jonathan, you must keep your sworn friendship with me. Please." He gazed intently into Jonathan's eyes. "Look, if I am guilty, slay me yourself. But don't betray me into the hands of your father."

"Oh, David!" Jonathan burst forth. "How could I ever hurt you? Don't say such a thing. If I had the least inkling my father was planning you harm, I would tell you."

David asked, "Who will inform me how your father responds tomorrow?"

"I will."

"How? Your father will keep a close eye on you."

"The pile of stones," Jonathan nodded over his shoulder, "you will be hiding among them. On the third day of the festival, when things are winding down, I will come back here with my bow and arrows. I'll have a boy with me to gather the arrows I shoot. My father will not suspect a thing—I go out to practice all the time. But just in case I'm being followed, here's what I will do. I will call loudly to the boy. If I say to him, 'The arrows are near you,' that is the signal my father is not angry and you may return. But if I yell, 'The arrows are far beyond you,' then you will know he answered madly, and you must flee."

The men hugged and went their separate ways.

The next evening, Saul sat down to the feast in his usual place, with Jonathan opposite him. Abner, the top general, sat next to Saul. David's place was empty. They ate the meal with typical conversation. Saul said nothing about David.

But David's seat was empty the second night too.

Saul mused out loud, "I wonder where David could be. We could use a little music."

Jonathan answered, "I believe he's in Bethlehem celebrating with his family. His brothers told him to come home."

"Let me tell you something, Jonathan," Saul said, standing up and facing his son. "You're a stupid bastard! Do you think I don't know that you and David have sworn an oath of friendship? Don't you understand? As long as the son of Jesse lives, you will never succeed me as king. He will! Don't you get that, you dumb son of a whore! Is that what you want—David to be king in your place, shaming you and your mother? Now bring him to me, so I can kill him myself!"

Jonathan shot from his chair. "What has he done? Why should he be put to death? He's not wronged you. No! He's saved you and your kingdom. He killed the Philistine giant, and he's been a great warrior ever since. Why would you murder an innocent man for no reason? Why are you so bitter?"

Saul exploded. He drew his spear and hurled it at Jonathan. It barely missed his left arm. Then the king crumpled to the floor, and his son dashed out.

Early the next morning, Jonathan stood not far from the rough heap of stones outside Ramah. Beside him was a boy.

"I'll shoot three at a time. Then you run and get them, like we always do," he said to the youth. Jonathan notched the first arrow, drew the shaft to his ear, and released. As the third one sailed through the air, the boy took off.

"They are beyond you! Beyond you!" Jonathan shouted a few moments later.

The lad glanced back and ran on.

Jonathan turned toward the heap of rocks. He saw no movement, but he knew his friend was there. He also knew it was not wise to risk seeing David—perhaps his father's men were watching even now. But how could he let David go without saying goodbye.

A moment later Jonathan and David were face to face. "You heard me, right? You know what you must do," Jonathan said.

David nodded.

Then they embraced, kissed each other, and wept together. David cried harder.

"David," Jonathan encouraged, "go in peace. May God be with you. And may there be peace and kindness between our descendants forever. God is our witness."

And so Jonathan and David reaffirmed their covenant of loyalty, and Jonathan loved David as himself.

35. RENEGADE

As the sun rose, David set out for the town of Nob. He was now the prey and Saul the hunter. When he came to Nob, he went to the see the priest of the village, Ahimelech, a hunched and bearded man. Ahimelech shuddered when he recognized David. "Why are you alone? Why is no one with you? Great men in Israel don't travel by themselves. Something is amiss."

"The king has sent me on a secret mission," David said. "He told me not to tell anyone why I'm here. I've instructed my men where to meet me later."

Ahimelech looked sideways at him.

"My warriors and I need some food," David continued. "Give me loaves of bread or anything else you have."

"We don't have any regular bread," replied the priest. "Only the holy bread, which you can have—if you and your soldiers are holy, which means you've not slept with any women recently."

"Don't worry," David chuckled. "I never allow my men to be with women when we're on a campaign."

Ahimelech lowered his eyes and told his servant Doeg to bring the sacred bread. As Doeg placed the loaves in a bag, David studied him, for he recognized him as one of Saul's servants—the one-time head shepherd, David thought, but he wasn't sure.

From Nob, David went to the Philistine city of Gath. He needed a few days to think and make plans, and he was confident Saul would never search for him among the Philistines. But certain men in Gath identified him. "Isn't that David, the great Israelite warrior," they whispered to one another. Before David realized that they knew, they arrested him. He was chained and led to the palace, to King Achish. On the way, David began to act like a mad man. He howled and drooled. He twitched and stumbled.

When they reached the king, David clawed madly at the pillars. "Who in the world is this?" Achish asked, mystified.

"It's David, the great Israelite warrior," the Philistines answered.

Achish ignored them. "Look at this man. He's insane. Why are you bringing him to me? Don't we already have enough mad men around here?"

And so they let David go.

He went back toward his hometown in Israel and hid in a cave. But once again he did not escape notice.

● ● ●

In the meantime, Doeg sent word to Saul that David had been in Nob. Immediately the king and his men set out for the little town. When they arrived, Saul commanded the villagers to gather around their priest Ahimelech.

Saul, spear in hand, raised his voice and said, "Listen to me, all of you. Has David promised you fields and vineyards? Will he make you commanders of his army? Is that why you've conspired against me?" Then, glancing around at his men, he went on. "And no one tells me when my son makes a covenant with the son of Jesse. None of you is concerned about me or informs me of anything. David is my servant. *My* servant. And he is now lying in wait for me, and no one does a thing to help me."

Everyone fidgeted.

Saul fixed his eyes on Ahimelech. "Why have you plotted against me? Why have you helped David by giving him bread? Why didn't you tell me he'd been here?"

"O King, I've plotted against no one. David is your most loyal servant; he leads your army into battle; he is even your own son-in-law. He said he was on a secret mission from you, and I believed him. I had no reason to doubt. Please do not accuse me of any wrong doing. I know nothing about this whole affair."

Saul did not flinch. "You will surely die, Ahimelech. You and your whole family."

"But . . ." Ahimelech quivered.

Saul turned to his guards and ordered, "Kill him and everyone who belongs to him. For they've sided with David. They knew he was fleeing, yet they did not tell me."

Not one of Saul's men moved; for they were unwilling to raise a hand against a priest of God.

Saul's face tensed. He strengthened the hold on his spear. "Doeg, kill them!"

Doeg stepped forward, drew his sword, and ran it through Ahimelech. A cry went up from the crowd. Then Doeg stormed through the helpless pack of villagers, striking down men, women, children, and animals. Blood spewed and bodies collapsed. Saul watched blankly. Only one descendent of Ahimelech's survived: Abiathar.

Abiathar hurried through the night to a cave near Bethlehem. There he found David with a group of men who had joined him, some four hundred in all. They were men in distress, men in debt, men discontented with their lot. Bandits and outlaws. Abiathar told David what had happened in Nob.

"Doeg," David said, shaking his head. "I knew he was one of Saul's men. I knew he would tell the king I'd been there." David put his arm around Abiathar. "I am responsible for the death of your whole family. I'm sorry. Stay here with me and you will be safe. For the man who is seeking your life is seeking mine also."

● ● ●

Rumors went through the land of Israel. The great David was now a renegade. People might either befriend him or betray him. He never knew. And then there were the Philistines to contend with. Presently, the vaunted enemy attacked the city of Keilah. David guessed Saul would do nothing, so he asked his new-found confidant and priest Abiathar to inquire of God about whether he should intervene.

"Attack the Philistines, for God has given them into your hand," Abiathar advised.

David and his warriors went directly and saved the inhabitants of Keilah. He was certain word of the victory and his whereabouts would quickly reach Saul, so he turned again to Abiathar. "Ask God if Saul will come here to attack me. And ask him if the citizens of Keilah will protect me or hand me over."

Abiathar sought God and returned with the word: "Yes, Saul is on his way, and the people of this place will surrender you to him."

David's head dropped. "Even after I saved them?"

David fled, this time south to the region of Ziph. When Saul was informed, he gave chase. For several months he pursued David and his men through the desert sands and rocky hills, but God did not give David into the king's hands. Then the Philistines renewed their raids on Israel, and Saul was forced to turn back and defend his kingdom.

• • •

While Saul rallied Israel against their perpetual nemesis, David and his crew slipped off eastward to the wilderness of En-gedi on the Salt Sea. As soon as Saul put the Philistines to flight, he turned his attention once more to David, choosing three thousand elite troops for the search.

One hot afternoon, Saul went into a cave alone to rest and relieve himself. As it were, David and several of his men were napping farther back in that very cave. Saul took off his outer garment, tossed it aside, and lay down in the damp cavern.

David crouched motionless in the dark.

"God has given your enemy into your hand," one of David's soldiers whispered.

David put his finger on his lips and watched in silence until Saul was breathing deeply. Then he inched forward and cut off a piece of the hem of Saul's robe which was draped over a large rock. Then he stole back to his spot deep in the cave.

His comrades stared in disbelief.

"God forbid I should kill God's anointed king. No, I will not lift a hand against him," David said.

"Then I will do it," one of them proposed.

"No, no one will," David insisted. So each man sheathed his sword and slumped back on the cold floor.

A few moments later, Saul arose and left the cave. David followed him out.

"My lord the king!" David called.

Saul spun around, and David bowed low.

"It is your servant David," he shouted. Saul stood perplexed.

David cried out, "Why do you listen to the people who say I'm trying to harm you? Today you can see with your own eyes it isn't true. Look at what is in my hand. It is a piece of your robe." He held it up for Saul to see. "I cut it off as you slept, when I could've killed you. God placed you at my mercy, and some of my men urged me to kill you, but I didn't. I spared you. For I will never harm the king—he is God's anointed one. I harbor no ill will toward you, nor have I done anything wrong that you are hunting me like a criminal."

Saul's staff fell from his hand. His legs wobbled.

"May God avenge you for what you're trying to do to me," David continued. "As the old saying goes, 'From evildoers come evil deeds.' But you can rest assured I will never, ever harm you. Who are you trying to catch anyway? I'm as worthless as a dead dog or even a flea on that dog. May God rescue me from your power."

Saul called back, "Is it really you, my son David?" Then he bent over and began to weep. "You are a more righteous man than I, for you've been kind to me, even though I've been searching to slay you. When God put me in your power in the cave, you spared my life. Who else would let his enemy get away? May God indeed reward the kindness you've shown me today."

The king was too far away for David to peer into his soul.

Saul straightened up and slowly retrieved his staff, keeping his focus on David. Then he turned and left. David watched until he disappeared around a bend.

● ● ●

David sensed Saul would be after him again. So he and his small army of bandits moved down to the territory of Maon. A very wealthy man owned

much of the land in this region where he pastured his cou
goats. His name was Nabal, and he was surly and mean in
His wife was Abigail, and quite the opposite. She was an i
cious, and beautiful woman.

It was spring, a time of celebration in Israel, and David's men were eager to honor their customs. David sent ten of his young men with this message for Nabal: "Peace and prosperity to you, your family, and all that is yours. We and your shepherds have gotten along quite well. We've never harmed them or stolen from them. Ask your own men, and they will tell you this is true. So now we request a favor from you. Since it is the time of annual feasting, please kindly share with us any provisions you might have on hand."

Nabal sneered at David's messengers. "Who is this fellow David? Who does he think he is? There are renegades running all over the place. Should I take my bread and my water and my meat and give it to a band of outlaws from who-knows-where?"

David's men returned and told him what Nabal said. "Get your swords!" David barked as he strapped on his own. "A lot of good it did to help this fellow. I saw to it that his flocks were safe in the wilderness. And now he's repaid me evil for good. I swear not one person in his household will be alive tomorrow morning." Then David led his men in a spirited march toward Nabal's estate.

Meanwhile, one of Nabal's servants said to Abigail, "David sent messengers from the wilderness to greet our master, but he insulted them. These men have never bothered us. In fact, they've been very good to us. Please figure out what to do, for there will be big trouble now. Forgive me for saying so, but your husband is so ill-tempered that no one can reason with him."

Abigail lost no time. She gathered two hundred loaves of bread, two large jugs of wine, the perfectly cooked meat of five sheep, a bushel of roasted grain, one hundred clusters of raisins, and two hundred fig cakes. She loaded them on donkeys and set off for David's camp without informing her husband.

As Abigail rode through a mountain ravine, she looked up and saw David and his men approaching. She quickly dismounted and bowed. David motioned for his men to halt while he went ahead to meet the woman.

She fell at his feet. "Please listen to me, my lord. I did not know you sent messengers to Nabal, my husband. He is a wicked and mean man; he's an utter fool. Please ignore his response and accept mine instead. Here are gifts for you and your men." She gestured at the loaded donkeys behind her.

"Please forgive me if I've offended you in any way," Abigail went on. "I know you are a warrior for God, and God will bless you. I know men are seeking your life, but God will protect you. May God hurl away the lives of your enemies like stones shot from a sling. May God make you the leader of Israel. And when he does, you don't want the murder of Nabal and his household on your conscience. You don't want to bear the burden of needless bloodshed and vengeance." She paused, then added, "When God raises you up, please don't forget about me, your servant."

David spread his arms in happy disbelief. "Praise God for sending you to meet me today. And thank God for your good sense. For you've kept me from shedding blood with my own hands. Indeed, I swear if you hadn't stopped me, Nabal and his men would've been dead by this time tomorrow."

David turned and ordered his troops to take the presents. "We accept your offering," he said to Abigail, who remained kneeling in front of him. "Return home in peace."

When Abigail arrived home, she found Nabal feasting like royalty. He was in high spirits and very drunk, so she retired quietly to her quarters. In the morning when Nabal was sober, she told him about her meeting with David. He said nothing. As soon as Abigail left the room, Nabal clutched his chest and fell to the floor. He lay paralyzed like a stone. For God had struck Nabal dead.

When David heard of it, he said, "Praise be to God, for he has avenged the insult I received from that fool and he's kept me from having to do it myself. Nabal got what was coming to him."

Then David sent men to ask Abigail to become his wife.

"I would be honored and delighted to marry David," she responded, prostrating herself before David's messengers. "I am ready to serve him and his warriors." She quickly called five attendants, mounted her donkey, and went to David. And so Abigail became his wife.

36. AMONG THE PHILISTINES

"It's time to leave Maon," David said to Abigail late one evening. "Now that the spring celebration is over, Saul will once again turn his attention to stalking me."

She lifted her head from his shoulder. "Where are we going?"

"Back to the region of Ziph," replied David. "He couldn't catch me the last time we were there; and plus, it's possible he won't anticipate us returning to a place we've already been."

So David and his adventurers—and Abigail—set out for the district of Ziph. But the people there reported their arrival to the king, and soon Saul was on his way, accompanied by his chief military officer, Abner, and an elite regiment of soldiers.

Now David had given quite a bit of thought to his fortuitous encounter with Saul in the cave. He had proven he was not out to assassinate the king, and even though this had not deterred Saul's pursuit of him, maybe, David thought, a second such instance would take hold in the king's heart.

One cloudy and windy afternoon, David said to one of his men, Abishai, "Will you go down to Saul's camp with me tonight?"

Abishai stopped sharpening his sword and looked up. "Go to Saul?" he asked with scrunched eyebrows.

"Yes, I have a plan that might save us all."

"You know I will do whatever you ask," Abishai replied, turning again to the blade.

"Good, we will set out secretly, just after dark," David confirmed.

That night, David and Abishai crept toward Saul's men. They snuffed out their torches and emerged from the thicket just after midnight. There was Saul, lying asleep in the middle of camp with his spear stuck in the ground by his head. Abner and the other soldiers slept soundly around him. Except for their breathing, they were as dead men, for God had put them into a deep sleep.

"Let me do it," Abishai mouthed as they tiptoed around the sleeping warriors. "Let me pin him to the ground with one thrust of my spear; it won't take two."

David wagged his head. "We are not here to slay him; for whoever lays a hand on God's anointed is guilty. No, God himself will strike Saul dead, or he will perish in some battle with the Philistines, or who knows, maybe he will just grow old and die. But God forbid I should do it myself. Now get his spear and water jug and let's go."

But Abishai just stood there, so David jerked the spear from the ground and carefully picked up the jar. Then the two hurried quietly out of the camp. No one saw them or heard them, nor did anyone stir.

David and Abishai crossed over a ravine and stood atop a hill some distance away. David took a deep breath and shouted, "Abner, Abner, answer me!" His voice shattered the stillness. Saul and his men jolted upright.

Abner peered into the blackness and cried out in terror, "Who are you? And where are you?"

"I thought you were a man, Abner! I thought you were the king's trusted captain," David boomed back. "Why didn't you guard your master? You deserve to die for not protecting God's anointed. Take a look and tell me if you see the king's spear and water jug."

Saul recognized David's voice. "Is that you, David?"

"Yes it is, my lord the king. I have your spear and water. Now you see for a second time that God delivered you into my hands, but yet I didn't slay you, for you are the anointed one. So tell me, why are you still pursuing me? Why are you driving me from my home and my people? I'm telling you again, I'm nobody. You are looking for a flea—as one hunts a partridge in the mountains. As surely as I valued your life today, so may God value my life and deliver me from all trouble and allow me and my men to return home."

Saul cried out, "I have sinned against you David, my son. Please come back home. You have once more proved your loyalty by preserving my life, so I will no longer seek to harm you. I've been a fool. I am wrong. Please forgive me." His words echoed through the ravine between them.

Then there was silence.

Saul shouted once more, "May you be blessed, my son David. I know you will do great things. Yes, I know one day you will be the king of Israel. Now swear to me when that happens, you will not kill my family and destroy my descendants."

"I swear," David answered. "You have my word." Then he raised the spear and thrust it into the ground. "Let one of your young men come get your sword."

"David, are you coming home?" Saul called.

But there was no answer, for David had melted into the night.

● ● ●

David was growing weary of his life on the run. If he were not going to kill Saul, and if Saul did not cease his pursuit, then it could only end badly for David. One night he talked things over with Joab, one of his most skilled warriors and smartest strategists.

"One of these days, you and I and our people will be destroyed by the king," David said to the gruff man sitting across from him.

"What about Philistine territory?" Joab said. "Saul has always fought a defensive war against them. He's never invaded their land. So what if we went there, where he's never ventured? Maybe then Saul would give up."

"That has crossed my mind before," David replied, thinking back to his earlier excursion to the Philistine city of Gath when he first fled from Saul, alone. That trip would have been fatal, were it not for his pretending insanity. Neither Joab nor anyone else knew the story. "I think that's a good idea," David continued. "Better than you realize. We can deceive Saul by escaping to the Philistines, and we can deceive the Philistines by acting as if we've joined them. It shouldn't be difficult to convince King Achish of Gath that we've defected."

"Gath," Joab smiled. "So I see you've given this some thought already." David returned the grin.

It would be a large group heading west across the border, for David and his men and their wives and children now numbered six hundred. And they were all fugitives.

When they arrived in Gath, David requested a meeting with the king. On his way, David could barely suppress laughter as he thought of the last time he had seen the Philistine ruler.

"I am David, son of Jesse the Israelite," David said, bowing low before Achish. "As you know, I am a sworn enemy of King Saul of Israel. I come to you seeking an alliance. Let me and my band of warriors side with you against Israel. Your enemy is my enemy."

Achish was pleased by the idea. "Very well. I will give the small outpost at Ziklag to you and your bandits. From there you are to be a menace to the southern border regions of Israel."

So David and Abigail and all their company journeyed south to their new home.

"Saul won't ever think to look for us here," David said, cuddling his wife. Then he added, "And I have a plan." She rolled her eyes and poked him playfully in the ribs, though she was sure it would involve danger for all of them.

She was right. From Ziklag, David led his men on raids against a number of people in the desert region south of Israel. He never set foot one place within Israel. Whenever he attacked, David ordered his soldiers to leave no one alive, but to take the animals, clothes, gold, and silver. Then he would send reports to Achish, "I am chipping away at the southern boundary of Israel. I am wreaking havoc on Saul's kingdom. May King Achish of Gath be blessed."

At the same time, David would take the spoils of his wars and send them as gifts to the cities throughout the southern part of Israel. In this way, David bound their hearts to his own. He was thus not only safely hidden from Saul, but was also strengthening his position within Israel.

• • •

Soon, King Achish mustered his forces to the north near Shunem for a major assault on Israel. David's band of men joined the Philistines at the back of the formation.

"You are about to see for yourself what I can do," David sa

But the night before the attack, Achish's commanders their king. "What are these Israelites doing here with us?"

"It is David," he answered. "Yes, he was once one of Saul's greatest soldiers. And yes, this is the same David who killed Goliath. But it's different now. He defected to us about a year ago and he's been a faithful soldier down at Ziklag ever since."

But the Philistine generals refused to fight alongside the mercenaries. "Then send him back to Ziklag. Otherwise, he will turn on us in battle. What better way for him to regain Saul's favor than by taking the heads of our own warriors? Just like he took Goliath's. After all, this is the guy about whom the women in Israel once sang songs of praise. You are too trusting, O King."

Achish called David. "You've been faithful to me and the Philistines. I've found no fault in you from the day you arrived, and I would be pleased to have you fight for us. But my generals don't approve. Thus I have no choice but to send you back in peace. I cannot afford to alienate my own military."

"What have I done?" David threw up his arms in exasperation. "What do you have against me? Why can't I go fight the enemies of my lord the king?"

Achish's eyes fell. "I know, David," he lamented. "You've been like an angel to me. But my commanders object. So please take your men and return to Ziklag at daybreak tomorrow."

At the first streak of light, David and his men set out for home. As they neared the place, a cry of anguish arose. Ziklag had been torched. The outpost was a black heap, and all their wives and sons and daughters were gone. The mighty men of war fell to the ground in agony. They wept until they could weep no more. So broken were they that they spoke of stoning David.

David mourned bitterly for Abigail. He called the priest Abiathar and said, "Ask God what I should do now."

Abiathar sought the divine and returned to David. "Pursue the bandits who destroyed your home and take back your wives and children, for they are not dead."

Quickened by this message, David and his six hundred men set out in the direction of the marauders. On the way, two hundred of the soldiers became exhausted and, unable to cross a ravine, ceased the chase. Four hundred pressed on and soon came upon a man lying under a tree beside the road. He was dark-skinned and nearly dead. They gave him water to drink and two fig cakes to eat.

"Who are you and where are you from?" David asked the man when he had revived.

"I am an Egyptian, a slave. My master abandoned me here three days ago when I became ill. We were on our way home from burning and plundering Ziklag in retaliation for their raids on us."

"Can you take me to your master?" asked David.

"Swear to me," the dusty man answered, "that you won't kill me or hand me over to him, and I will do it."

"You have my word."

So the man chugged more water and then led the way. A few hours later, as the sun waned, David looked down from atop a small hill. And there they were, scattered over the countryside, eating and drinking and reveling in the spoils. Immediately, David gave the signal and his men rushed down and slaughtered them throughout the night and all the next day. Only a few of the raiders escaped on camels. David's soldiers recovered everything. Nothing was missing—sheep or goat, necklace or bracelet, boy or girl, nor any wife. They were all rescued.

David and the four hundred gathered everyone and everything and headed back toward the charred remains of their home. "This is David's plunder!" they shouted happily as they went.

When they came to their two hundred comrades who had stayed behind, some of the troublemakers raised a stir. "These guys can have their wives and children, but that's it," they huffed. "They didn't fight with us, so they get none of the loot."

"No, no, my brothers," David said breaking up the argument. "We cannot act this way with what God has given us. God protected us and helped us. Please don't talk like this. We share and share alike—regardless of who went to battle."

At this, the bickering stopped, and they all made their way back, full of heart.

When they arrived home, David sent some of the booty as a token of good will to the tribe of Judah in Israel.

37. SUICIDE

While all this was taking place, Saul summoned his forces to Gilboa, opposite Shunem, to battle King Achish and the Philistines. But the militia was slow to assemble and listless in their drills. Israel was tired. Saul's kingship was slipping from him. Samuel, the man who had long ago anointed him king, was now dead, and it seemed to Saul that he and his people would soon perish too.

Saul rode in the darkness to survey the enemy. He observed a plain burning. He saw myriads of Philistine fires, with tens of thousands of troops talking and laughing around the flames. Saul's knees buckled and he became frantic with fear. He cried out, "O God, what should I do? How can I possibly defeat this multitude? Please help me."

But God refused to answer him.

Saul returned to camp, called his priests, and told them to seek an answer from God.

But God did not respond.

Saul then said to his advisers, "Find a woman who is a medium, so I can ask her what to do."

They said, "There's a medium in the village of Endor just a few miles north."

Saul took off his royal robes and disguised himself by wearing the rough leather skins of an ordinary man. He pulled a hood over his head and went in the shadows of night to Endor. He came to a tiny wooden house and tapped on the door. It cracked open and a woman's voice said, "What do you want?"

"I need you to call up a spirit for me," Saul explained. "Can you bring up the person I want to speak with?"

"What? Are you trying to kill me?" the woman demanded. "You know King Saul outlawed all mediums and wizards. Is this a trap?"

"I swear to God you will not be punished for doing this."

She reached out and pulled him inside. "Whose spirit do you want me to call up?"

Saul swallowed. "Call up Samuel."

The woman turned and sat in the corner by a flickering candle. She bowed her head and pressed her fingers into her temples. In a gentle voice, she chanted, "Samuel, Samuel." She paused for a few moments and then repeated, "Samuel, Samuel." The room was still. Saul drew a sharp breath. A third time, she called out, "Samuel, Samuel."

Suddenly the woman screamed, "You've deceived me! You are King Saul!"

"Don't be afraid!" Saul exhaled, throwing off his hood. "What do you see?"

The woman began to tremble. "I see a spirit—a god—coming up out of the earth."

"What does he look like?" whispered Saul.

"Like an old man. A bony old man wrapped in a robe—a torn robe."

Saul knew at once that it was Samuel, and he knelt to the ground. Then he heard Samuel's voice, "Why have you disturbed me? Why have you called me up?"

"Because I am in great distress," Saul replied. "The Philistines are planning an attack, and God has turned from me. He won't answer. So I've called for you to advise me."

Samuel's voice answered, "What good is it to ask me, since God has abandoned you and become your enemy? God has done just as he said he would. He has torn the kingdom from you and given it to someone who is better than you: David. This is God's punishment for failing to utterly destroy the Amalekites, all the animals and people. You remember. The sheep and King Agag."

Saul nodded. "But what about the Philistines? What can I do to save Israel? Just tell me and I will do it."

"Nothing," said the voice. "God is delivering you and the ar Israel into the hands of the Philistines. By this time tomorrow you will be with me."

Saul fell full length on the ground, paralyzed with fright. His strength was gone, for he had eaten nothing all that day and night.

The woman came and knelt beside him. "I'm sorry, my lord," she said putting a hand on his back. "I did everything I could, at the risk of my life. Now let me give you a little something to eat."

The king did not move, so she arose and brought him a small piece of meat and bread. Saul got to his feet, took the food, and went out into the night.

● ● ●

The next day, the battle was fierce. Many Israelites were slaughtered on the slopes; others fled pell-mell down the mountains. Saul's son Jonathan was among the dead.

Saul himself entered the battle on Mount Gilboa. A Philistine archer spotted him, drew his bow, and sent an arrow whizzing toward the king. It found a crease in his armor. Saul lurched to the ground, the arrow protruding from his shoulder. "Take your sword and kill me," he moaned to his armor-bearer, "before the Philistines find me and torture me."

But the young man was petrified and would not do it. So Saul took his own sword and fell on it—the sharp blade slicing through his abdomen. When the servant saw this, he threw himself on his own spear and died beside the king. And so Saul and Jonathan and all the army of Israel were destroyed that day, just as Samuel foretold.

The next morning, the Philistines went out to strip the dead. They cut off Saul's head and sent it throughout their cities proclaiming victory. Then they took Saul's decapitated body and fastened it to the wall of the Israelite city of Beth-shan.

When the people of the town of Jabesh heard about this, they gathered and said to one another, "King Saul saved us and our children from Nahash, lo those many years ago. If it were not for him, our eyes would be gouged out. We must not forget what he did for us." So they sent their mighty warriors to Beth-shan, and they took down Saul's corpse and brought it back to Jabesh. There they burned the body and buried the bones.

Israel's first king was dead.

• • •

Word of Saul's demise and Israel's defeat soon reached David in Ziklag. A man came riding in at breakneck speed, waving his arms and crying out, "A message for my lord David!" He jumped down and ran to him, bowing again and again. There was dust in his hair—the dust of mourning.

"What is your news?" David asked,

"Just yesterday I escaped from the Israelite camp," the man said.

"And what happened? Tell me."

"The men of Israel fled from the Philistines. Many perished. King Saul and his son Jonathan are dead."

David turned aside, his face scrunched with emotion. "How do you know?"

The messenger seemed suddenly pleased. "I just happened to be on Mount Gilboa, and I saw the king lying wounded, with Philistine chariots and horsemen closing in on him. He looked up and yelled to me, 'Please come kill me, for I'm in great pain.' Then his eyes rolled and he collapsed to the ground. I knew he could not survive, so I went over and ran my dagger through him. Then I took the crown from his head and the band from his arm and have brought them here to you, my lord David."

David hunched over and wept. After a few moments, he tried to gather himself, but could not. He dropped to one knee and shed more tears. Behind him, his men stood with heads bowed. The messenger squirmed uneasily.

Finally, David straightened and said, "How is it that you were not afraid to lift your hand against God's anointed one?"

"I . . . I . . ." the man faltered, his chin dropping to his chest.

"Your own testimony has condemned you," David cried. Then he beckoned one of his warriors and nodded toward the messenger. In an instant, the soldier's spear flashed from its sheath. The messenger never saw death descending on the back of his neck.

David turned away and sunk to the earth. "Saul and Jonathan! Oh, how the mighty have fallen!" he sang faintly through the tears. "Saul and Jonathan—in life they were loved and gracious, and in death they were not divided. Oh, how they were swifter than eagles and stronger than lions. Daughters of Israel, weep for Saul, for he clothed and protected you. Sons of Israel, mourn, for he led us into battle against our enemies." David's men looked on in solemn silence as David continued. "Jonathan, Jonathan—I am sick with sorrow! O my brother, how I loved you. Your love for me was wonderful, more wonderful than the love of women. Oh, how the mighty have fallen!"

38. CIVIL WAR, AGAIN

When a month had passed, David summoned his top men. There was Joab the appointed general of his army; Joab's two brothers, Abishai and Asahel; and the priest Abiathar who had escaped from Nob. They sat in a circle, each knowing the reason for the meeting: to determine their next move, now that Saul was dead and Ziklag remained in ruins.

Joab spoke up. "I have good information that Abner remains in command of Saul's army—what's left of it. He's planning to install Saul's son Ishbosheth as the new king of Israel. Ishbosheth, as you know, is the only living son of Saul. Abner knows we were in Gath with the Philistines and he knows we've sent gifts to the people in the tribe of Judah. I believe we should arrange a meeting with Abner."

They all turned to David. "I have asked God what we should do," David said, as if Joab had not spoken. "I asked if we should stay here or return to Israel. God said to return. Then I asked where, and God told me the city of Hebron in the tribe of Judah."

"That is good," Abishai affirmed. "For the leaders of Judah are expecting us. In fact, they're expecting you to be their leader."

"Leader?" David asked.

"Yes . . . their king," Abishai said.

No one spoke.

Then David turned to Joab. "Let's meet with Abner and his men—after we move to the tribe of Judah."

So David and Abigail and all David's warriors, along with their wives and children, and all their possessions came to the land of Judah and settled in Hebron. The elders of the place welcomed David and anoir their king. The people of Judah shouted, "Long live King Davic God's anointed." They danced and rejoiced and sang.

There were now two kings in the land: Ishbosheth and David. And they each had an army and a general: Abner and Joab. Civil war lurked on the horizon.

● ● ●

Joab and a group of David's men journeyed to the pools and springs outside the city of Gibeon to meet Abner and Saul's men. Abner and his contingent sat down on one side of the central reservoir and Joab and his soldiers on the other. The two generals met in the middle at one end of the waters. Neither had a sharp plan.

"Why don't we do this," Abner said grimly. "Why don't we simply have our men fight each other right here, hand-to-hand, in front of us? Whichever side prevails, that army will rule the land with their king."

Joab eyed him menacingly. "You choose your best twelve fighters, and I will do the same."

Soon, two lines of a dozen warriors stood facing each other, with Joab and Abner positioned behind the row of their combatants. At the signal, each man rushed at the soldier opposite him. They lunged with daggers and punched with fists. Blades flashed and helmets rolled. It was a bloody melee.

Suddenly Asahel broke through and charged directly at Abner. Saul's general bolted to his left and began racing away across the adjacent field. But Asahel was as fleet-footed as a wild gazelle and he soon closed in on Abner.

"Is that you, Asahel?" Abner called, glancing back and gripping his spear.

"Yes, it is," the young man shouted.

"Stop pursuing me now! Turn back and fight one of the twelve chosen men."

Asahel kept on coming.

Abner stopped and faced him. "I am warning you again. Stop chasing me. Don't make me kill you. How could I look your brother Joab in the face?"

But Asahel refused to stop. So Abner drew his spear and turned it backward, hoping not to inflict a mortal wound. But the speedy warrior came upon him with such force that the butt of the spear pierced him through the stomach and came out the small of his back. Asahel writhed in the dust as Abner dashed away.

Joab and Abishai came running upon the scene. The sight of their brother impaled on the shaft of a sword sent both men into shock. As they stood their numb, other soldiers arrived, and they too fell into a horrified daze. Then they all set off after Abner.

As night approached, Abner appeared on a hill. "Must the sword devour forever?" he called to Joab. "You know this will end bitterly."

Joab stared up the hill. Then he shook his head and beckoned his men to turn back. On their way, they retrieved the body of Asahel. Then Joab and his men marched through the night and arrived at Hebron. There they buried Asahel.

● ● ●

So civil war broke out between the house of Saul and the house of David. In the course of time, David grew stronger and stronger, and the house of Saul weaker and weaker.

Now Ishbosheth was not a strong man, in any way. He was not cut out to be a king. Abner had all the power, and that was no secret. He was a brilliant general and fought valiantly against David and his army. Slowly, his relationship with Ishbosheth deteriorated. When Abner took for himself one of Saul's concubines, a woman named Rizpah, Ishbosheth suspected it was a conspiracy to seize the throne: Whoever took the king's women took the king's crown as well. Though he knew he could do little about it, Ishbosheth confronted Abner. "Why did you go into my father's concubine? We both know what you're doing."

Abner was indignant. "Am I some dog? After all I've done for your father and for you, this is how you thank me? This is my reward for not handing you over to David? You're going to accuse me of some wrongdoing with this woman?" He shook an angry finger at Ishbosheth's and stormed off.

The next day, Abner gathered his most trusted men and sent them to David in Hebron with a message: "Make a covenant with me, and I will

deliver all Israel into your hand. I have conferred witl
land, and we are prepared to install you as the king of a u

David replied, "I will gladly make a covenant with you
one thing: When you come, you must bring Michal, my wife
for with one hundred Philistine foreskins and whom I've n ... ince
she helped me escape from her father Saul."

Abner was pleased by David's answer. So he sent men to retrieve Michal who had since been given in marriage to a man named Palti. When Abner's soldiers arrived, Palti pleaded with them not to take Michal. But it was of no use. As they led her away, Michal's husband followed them on foot, weeping for his wife. When they came to Abner, the general said to Palti, "Go back home. There's nothing you can do. Michal is David's wife again."

Palti turned away. His heart was broken.

Abner and twenty of his best men took Michal and went to David. A grand feast welcomed them. Michal sat stone-faced through the festivities as David and Abner celebrated the end of the civil war.

"I will go throughout Israel and spread the news," Abner said to David. "All the tribes from north to south and east to west will be gathered under your throne. We will anoint you as king, and you will rule over us." Then he left.

As it happened, though, Joab was not present for the grand occasion, for he was leading a band of raiders against the Philistines. When he returned and learned what had taken place, he was irate. "What have you done?" he said to David. "How could you let Abner go in peace? You should've known better than that! Abner is our enemy. He is the man we risk our lives to fight. And yet you let him walk away? Abner is cunning and deceitful. He duped you into thinking he wants to end the war—that he's surrendering. It's nothing but a ruse!" Joab stomped away before David could reply.

Joab immediately sent messengers after Abner, summoning him back to Hebron. Joab went out to the edge of the city to wait for his nemesis. There Joab greeted him warmly and took him aside as though to speak with him privately. But Joab never said a word. Instead, he drew his sword and stabbed Abner in the stomach. "That's for my brother sahel," Joab hissed, as Abner twisted in the throes of death." He shoved the spear through Abner a second time, pinning him to the ground. Then he walked off.

When David heard of Abner's death, he sent word throughout the city saying, "I swear to God that I and my kingdom are forever innocent of this crime against Abner. Joab is the guilty one. May the family of Joab be cursed in every generation with a man who has sores all over his body, or hobbles on crutches, or begs for food, or dies by the sword."

The next day, David said to Joab and his men, "Tear your clothes and put on sackcloth and mourn for Abner." In the funeral procession, David walked behind the bier all the way to the grave, lamenting in a loud voice, "Should Abner have died as the lawless die? Your hands were not bound; your feet were not fettered. No, you were murdered—the victim of a wicked plot."

They buried Abner in Hebron, and David and the people fasted and wept at his graveside—except Joab, who stood and watched, cold and indifferent. At the gathering, David spoke about the deceased. "A great commander has fallen today in Israel. Yes, a brilliant general has perished. And even though I am the anointed king, Joab and his brother Abishai are too strong for me to control. So may God himself repay the evildoer for his evil deed."

In this way, all the people knew David had no part in the death of Abner. This pleased them very much. But they did not say a word against Joab.

● ● ●

When Ishbosheth heard of Abner's death, he lost all fortitude. On a steamy afternoon a few weeks later, Recab and Baanah, two captains of Saul's old army, went to the despairing king's house. The guard was sleeping. They entered and found Ishbosheth dozing in his bed. Without making a sound, they speared him to death and cut off his head. Then, carrying the head with them, they raced through the night to Hebron and came before David. "Look!" they exclaimed. "Here is the head of Ishbosheth, the son of your enemy Saul who tried to take your life. Today God has given my lord the king revenge on Saul and his offspring."

David looked at the lifeless face of Ishbosheth. Then he said to the two men, "Someone once told me, 'Saul is dead,' thinking he was bringing good news. But I seized him and killed him. That was his rew then should I reward you who have killed an innocent man in house, on his own bed? . . . Shouldn't I hold you responsible for his blood and rid the earth of you?"

Recab and Baanah dropped the head of Ishbosheth and fell to their knees. "No, no," they pleaded.

David turned and said to his bodyguard, "Execute them." The man did. Then he cut off their hands and feet and hung their bodies beside the pool in Hebron.

The head of Ishbosheth they buried in Abner's tomb.

● ● ●

As word of Ishbosheth's death spread throughout the land, the people of Israel came to David in Hebron and said, "We are your own flesh and blood. Even in times past, when Saul was king, you were the one who led us in war. Indeed, we know God has said to you, 'You will shepherd my people Israel, and you will be their king.' So now we ask you to become our ruler."

That day David made a covenant with the people, and they anointed him king of Israel. He was thirty years old. Abraham's descendants were once again united under a single monarch.

39. THE CITY OF DAVID

The city of Hebron was too small and vulnerable to serve as the center of David's kingdom. He needed a bigger and stronger place. And a more neutral place—one not located in the tribe of Judah, which would no doubt be a constant reminder of the days of civil war with Saul. Israel needed a fresh start and a glorious new capital. The city of Jerusalem would be perfect, only David did not control it. For after Joshua's conquest of Canaan three hundred years before, Jerusalem had recovered and grown into a mighty fortress—a fortress inhabited by foreigners.

"The Jebusites in Jerusalem have been there long enough," David declared to his advisors. "We must attack it and take it as our own, and there we will set up our administration."

So Joab and the army marched on Jerusalem. As they approached, a messenger came out to them. "The king says you have no chance to defeat our city. You might as well go home. Our walls are so high that even the lame and blind could fend you off."

Joab flashed a wicked grin. "It's been a long time since Israel has had a united army. In fact, it has never been as united as it is today under our new king David. You and your people might want to think again."

Then he turned to the troops and shouted, "Let's destroy this city of blind and lame fools!" He blew the ram's horn, and Israel's soldiers charged. Arrows rained on them from the walls, but Joab and his men were too numerous and too inspired to be defeated. They took the city in one day.

On the next, David rode triumphantly into his new capital. "This is the City of David," he proclaimed to the cheers and roars of the crowd.

David quickly and efficiently set up his government in Jerusalem. He first built a grand palace on the highest ridge in the city. Its walls and beams were made of cedar, and magnificent gardens covered the roof. Besides Abigail and Michal, the king took more wives and concubines, and each of them enjoyed their own splendid sanctuary in the palace. David's children ran happily through the halls as he carried on business from his ornately decorated office. David knew God had blessed him and raised him to be the king over his people Israel.

In his gratitude, David remembered the Ark of God, the powerful, sacred chest that represented the deity's presence. It had remained with a man named Abinadab in the town of Kiriath-jearim for nearly two decades, forgotten, after it had wreaked havoc on the Philistines—and the seventy Israelites who looked into it.

So King David gathered a group of elders from the twelve tribes and journeyed to the hilltop house of Abinadab. Once there, they loaded the Ark ceremoniously on a new cart and set off for Jerusalem with Uzzah and Ahio, the two sons of Abinadab, guiding the cart. Ahio went in front and Uzzah behind. On the way, David and his entourage broke into song and dance. They played lyres and harps and tambourines and castanets and cymbals. It was a boisterous and festive procession.

But then the oxen stumbled, and Uzzah reached out his hand to steady the Ark. At that, God's anger was aroused against Uzzah, and God struck him, and Uzzah died right there beside the holy chest.

The color drained from David's face. "If God has burst forth against Uzzah," he cried, "how can I ever bring the Ark into my care?" So David commanded them to take the Ark to a nearby house belonging to Obed-edom. He and the elders returned somberly to Jerusalem, empty-handed.

Three months later a report was brought to David. "God has richly blessed Obed-edom's household and everything he owns because of the Ark." So David again gathered his people and went to bring the Ark to Jerusalem. This time, the priests carried it with poles on their shoulders, as they had done in the wilderness. When they had taken just six steps, David ordered them to stop and he sacrificed a bull and a fattened calf.

Then they proceeded toward the capital with whoops of joy and clapping of hands. David himself led the dancing. In his revelry, his outer royal robe fell off, leaving only his white linen undergarments blowing free in the wind. As the Ark entered Jerusalem, people lined the streets and roared with delight; they looked down from their windows and cheered. Michal, too, peered out from her palace balcony. When she saw her husband leaping and gyrating, half naked, she despised him in her heart.

They brought the Ark to the special tent David had prepared for it. There the king sacrificed burnt offerings and peace offerings to the Almighty. When he finished, he blessed the people in the name of God and distributed a loaf of bread, a cake of dates, and a cake of raisins to every man and woman in the crowd. Then they all returned home.

When David arrived back at the palace, Michal came out to meet him.

"What a great day in Israel!" David exclaimed. "Why did you stay home? Were you ill?"

Michal glared at him. "How distinguished the king of Israel looked today, shamelessly exposing himself to the servant girls like any vulgar man might do."

"So I see you *are* ill," David replied sardonically. "I was dancing before God, not you or anyone else. I was praising the God who chose me over your father as the prince of Israel. In fact, I'm willing to look even more foolish than this. I'm willing to be humiliated for the honor of God. And speaking of honor," he paused, a twinkle in his eye, "those servant girls you mentioned, they will indeed hold me in honor."

Michal whirled and departed.

She remained childless to the day of her death.

• • •

A few nights later, David sat in the dark on his rooftop. Most of the torches in the city below had been extinguished. A cold wind blew. David lifted his eyes and prayed, "O God, I am living in a beautiful cedar palace, while the Ark of God remains in a tent. Let me build a house for you, a temple where you and the Ark may dwell."

God answered, "I have not lived in a house from the day I brought Israel out of Egypt until this very day. I have always used a tent as my dwelling place. So, no, David, do not build me a house. Instead, I will build a house for you—a dynasty of kings. I took you from tending sheep in the pasture and chose you to be the leader of my people. I have been with you wherever you've gone, destroying your enemies before you, and I will always be with you.

"When you die, I will raise up one of your descendants, your own offspring, and I will make his kingdom strong. I will establish his throne forever. He is the one who will build a house—a temple—for my name. I will be a father to him, and he will be my son. When he does wrong, I will punish him with the rod, as any father would. But I will never take away my love from him as I took it from Saul, whom I removed from my presence. Your house, David, and your kingdom will endure forever. Your throne will be secure for eternity."

David bowed his head. "Who am I, O God, and what is my family, that you have brought me this far? And now, as if this were not enough, you speak of giving your servant an everlasting dynasty. How great you are, O God! There is no one like you. What other nation on earth is like Israel? What other nation have you redeemed from slavery to be your own people? You have indeed made a great name for yourself by performing awesome wonders and miracles and driving out peoples and their gods from the land you've given to us.

"And now, O God, please do as you've promised concerning me and my family. Confirm it as a solemn oath that will last forever—like the promise you made to our great ancestor Abraham. May the house of your servant David continue before you to eternity."

"It is confirmed," God answered.

● ● ●

Encouraged by this promise and with the Ark in Jerusalem, David went forth boldly to battle the enemies of Israel. Not only were the Philistines a continual hazard, but the Moabites and Ammonites and other surrounding kingdoms and peoples also rose up to challenge Israel, the budding new power in the region.

Once, when the Philistines marched against Israel, God instructed David to circle the enemy and to hide among the mulberry trees. "Then," God commanded, "when you hear the sound of marching in the tops of trees, strike quickly, for that is the sign I am with you." David did as God commanded and he crushed the Philistines.

On another occasion, the Moabites attacked, and David defeated them. He made them lie down on the ground and measured them off with a length of rope. Every two lengths of them he put to death, and the third length he spared. The survivors became his servants and brought him tribute.

The people of Aram rose up and fought with the Israelites. David conquered them and captured a thousand chariots. He hamstrung their horses by severing the tendons and muscles in their legs, rending them useless.

One time, David sent a delegation to King Hanun of the Ammonites to express his sympathies for the death of Hanun's father. But the Ammonites thought the delegates were spies, and they seized them and humiliated them by shaving off half their beards and cutting off their robes at the waist, exposing their genitals. David was incensed and routed the Ammonites in retaliation.

And so David's kingdom, founded on the promises of God, grew in length and breadth and power.

40. ADULTERY AND MURDER, RAPE AND INCEST

David himself typically went with Joab and the army on military campaigns. After all, he was a warrior. One spring, however, David remained in Jerusalem while Joab laid siege to the Ammonite city of Rabbah. Late one pleasant afternoon during that spring, the king took a stroll in the gardens on his palace rooftop. The flowers and fruits and smells invigorated him. He picked a few fresh greens and crunched them in his teeth as he surveyed his rich and prosperous capital. Then something caught his eye in one of the courtyards below. He looked more closely and saw a woman bathing in a pool, alone. She was very beautiful, with long slender arms and flowing brown locks. David could not take his eyes from her.

He watched until she stepped from the water, covered herself in a red robe, and went back inside. David hurried downstairs and called the secretary on duty. He described the house where he had seen the woman and named the street opposite it. "Who lives there?" he asked.

"Uriah, the Hittite," the man answered. "He is one of your soldiers; he's at Rabbah with the rest of the army."

"Uriah," David repeated thoughtfully. "What's his wife's name?"

The man looked down at the scroll. "Bathsheba."

David stood silently for a few moments, then said, "Send for her. Tell her the king needs to see her."

The secretary dispatched a messenger to Uriah's house, while David went to his quarters and sat down on a couch. It was nearly dark when Bathsheba entered, her face strained with anxiety as she stood between the lamp flames.

"Bathsheba," David whispered, beckoning her.

She came toward him haltingly.

He reached out and drew her in. Then he had sex with her. When it was over, she got up and returned home.

● ● ●

David did not see her again for some time. Her courtyard was always empty.

About eight weeks later, Bathsheba sent a message to the king. "I am pregnant."

David did not sleep a wink that night. At dawn he sent a message to Joab: "Send Uriah the Hittite to me."

Two days hence, Uriah arrived with the dirt and grime of war and in full armor.

"How are Joab and the men?" David greeted him.

"Well, my lord," he responded with a cautious grin. "I think victory will soon be ours once again."

"You think so?" the king said flippantly. "You never know with Joab."

"Yes, my lord, you never know," Uriah echoed uneasily.

"Listen, Uriah," David said, "I want you to go home and rest and relax and be with your wife. You've served with distinction and deserve a respite."

Uriah bowed and left.

David managed some sleep that night. But in the morning when he arose, his chief bodyguard apprised him that Uriah had not gone home, but had instead slept at the palace with the king's attendants.

"Why did you not go to your own house?" David asked the Hittite.

"All my comrades are sleeping in the open field," Uriah said solemnly. "How then could I go home and eat and drink and sleep with my wife when they have no comforts at all?"

"You are a loyal soldier," David conceded with a thoughtful frown. "How about you stay here with me for a day, and then you may return to the war."

The king commanded the best food and wine be brought out for Uriah. The two men ate and drank together, and David saw to it that Uriah got drunk.

As the afternoon faded, David said, "Go home, Uriah. Go home to the woman who is waiting for you."

Uriah laughed and stumbled from the room.

Before dawn the next morning, David tiptoed from his bedroom and peered into the palace courtyard. There was Uriah sleeping soundly among the king's servants. David returned to his quarters and in his own hand wrote a note to Joab: "Put Uriah in the forefront where the fighting is fiercest. Then draw back from him so that he may be struck down and killed."

David sealed the letter and gave it to Uriah, saying, "Return to Rabbah and deliver this to Joab."

Uriah obeyed. And so did Joab.

A few weeks later, a messenger arrived at the palace and said to the king, "Joab sent me to give you this update on the war: The men of Rabbah came out of the city and attacked us. We successfully drove them back inside the walls. But then their expert archers shot arrows at us, and we had to retreat. Some of our men died."

David drew back and clenched his fists.

Then the man added, "And Uriah the Hittite is among the deceased."

David slowly exhaled and his hands unfurled. "Tell Joab not to let this matter trouble him. War is deadly. The sword devours this one today and that one tomorrow. Just keep fighting."

When Bathsheba learned her husband was dead, she let forth a wail of lamentation. She wept and cried for seven days, the proper period of time for mourning.

When the week had passed, David sent for Bathsheba, and she became one of his wives.

Later that year, she bore a son.

• • •

The day after the boy was born, God sent a prophet named Nathan to speak with David. He was a bent and studious man. "There is an urgent matter for you to consider, O King," Nathan said. "There are two men in a certain town in your kingdom. One is rich, the other poor. The rich man owns a great many sheep and cattle. The poor man has nothing but one little lamb which he has raised along with his children. The little lamb ate from his own table, and he cuddled it in his arms like a baby daughter.

"Now a traveler arrived at the home of the rich man. But instead of killing and cooking an animal from his own flock, the rich man took the poor man's lamb and slaughtered it and served it to his guest."

When David heard this, he was outraged. "I swear the rich man should die! He must pay for the lamb four times over."

Nathan fixed his gaze on the king. "David, you are the rich man."

David's face froze.

Nathan spoke again. "God anointed you king of Israel. He has given you wealth, power, and wives. If that were not enough, he would've given you more. Why, then, have you despised God and done this horrendous deed? Why have you murdered Uriah with the sword of the Ammonites and then stolen his wife?

"Now, David, this is what God says: Because of what you've done, I will bring calamity upon you from within your own household. Your children will rebel against you. I will give your wives to another man before your very eyes, and he will bed them publicly. You did your deed in private, but I will make this happen in the sight of all Israel."

David went pale with grief. "I have sinned," he cried, thick with regret.

"Yes," Nathan concurred. "And one other thing: Bathsheba's son will die."

David looked up at the man of God, and then hunched over in sorrow.

At that instant, God struck the infant, and it became very ill.

For six days, David pleaded with God to save the boy. The haggard king ate nothing and lay on the ground in anguish day and night. No one could console him, and he could not even bare to be in the presence of his tiny, sickly son.

On the seventh day, the baby died. He had not been named or circumcised.

David's attendants were afraid to inform him the child had passed. "How can we tell him?" they said to one another. "He might do something crazy or harm himself."

David heard them whispering among themselves. "Is my son dead?" he asked.

"Yes," they answered shakily.

David got up from the ground, washed himself, put on lotions, and changed his clothes. He went to the Ark and worshiped God. After that, he returned to the palace and called for food and drink.

His advisers gaped at him. "We don't understand," they said. "While the child was still living, you wept and refused to eat. But now that he's dead, you have ceased your mourning and are eating again."

David replied, "I fasted and wept while my son was alive, for I thought perhaps God would be gracious to me and let him live. But that did not happen; he has passed. So why should I continue fasting? Nothing can bring him back to life. He is gone forever."

After he had refreshed himself with food, David made the long walk to Bathsheba's quarters. He had not seen her since the midwives hurried her off to the birthing room a week before.

This time, it was she who sat on a couch as he nervously entered the room. He nestled up to her and held her in his arms. Neither spoke. The king spent many days comforting Bathsheba.

In time, Bathsheba once again became pregnant and gave birth to a son, and they named him Solomon. And God loved the child.

● ● ●

David had many sons older than Solomon. Most of them were born years ago in Hebron and were now grown, strong men in their own right. Besides Abigail, who bore him one son, and Michal, who had none, David had a number of wives who were the mothers of his children.

Ahinoam was the mother of Amnon, the oldest son. He was an impulsive and passionate man.

Maacah was the mother of Absalom, the second living son. He was handsome, with long, thick hair, a keen mind, and a prolific personality.

Haggith was the mother of Adonijah, the third living son. He was a bit withdrawn, but also witty, cunning, and articulate.

David had daughters, too. One of them was a beautiful girl named Tamar. She was just entering womanhood, a virgin with bright eyes and a colorful disposition. Her mother was Maacah.

In the course of time, Amnon, the firstborn of David, fell in love with Tamar, his half-sister. Amnon became so obsessed with Tamar that he became ill, for he knew he could never have her.

Now Amnon had a very crafty friend named Jonadab. One day Jonadab said to Amnon, "What's the trouble? Why should the son of a king be so dejected day after day?"

Amnon told him about Tamar.

"Well," Jonadab said, "here is what you should do. Pretend you are sick—God knows you do look terrible. When your father comes to see you, ask him to let Tamar come and prepare some food for you. Tell him you'll feel better if she prepares it as you watch and if she feeds you from her own hands."

Amnon followed Jonadab's counsel.

When David came to see him, Amnon said to his father, "Please let my sister Tamar come and cook my favorite food in my presence. Then she herself can serve me."

David granted his request and sent Tamar to Amnon's house.

Once there, she took dough and kneaded it and made cakes in his sight. But when she set the tray before him, he refused to eat. Amnon turned to his personal aide and said, "Send all the attendants out of the house, and that includes you. Get out of here."

When they were alone, he said to Tamar, "Now come here and feed me."

Tamar obeyed. She took one of the little cakes and reached it carefully toward his mouth.

Suddenly he seized her by the wrist and said, "Come to bed with me, my sister!"

The girl recoiled. "No, my brother!" she cried. "No! No! . . ." But he would not let go of her. "Don't be so stupid," she pleaded. "Don't do this evil thing to me. Where could I go in my shame? And you . . . you would be called the greatest fool in Israel." He tightened his hold and jerked her toward him. "Please, please," she begged, "just speak to our father about it, and he will let you marry me."

"We both know that's a lie," Amnon growled. He tore open her robe and shoved her backward onto the floor. Then he raped her. As soon as he finished, he stood up and looked at her disgustedly. "Get out of here!" he snarled.

Tamar shook her head, her face blotched red. She drew up her knees, contracting herself into a tiny ball.

"Get out now," Amnon demanded.

"No," she whimpered. "I'm staying. For sending me away now is worse than what you've already done to me."

Amnon, seething with hatred, called in his assistant. "Take this woman out of here. And bolt the door behind her." So the servant gathered up Tamar and carried her from the room and locked the door.

In the courtyard, Tamar scooped some ashes and rubbed them in her hair. With her face in her hands, she went away crying to the house of her full-brother Absalom.

"What happened, Tamar?" Absalom asked, as she caved into his arms.

"Amnon, he . . . Amnon . . ." she whispered.

"Be still, my sister," Absalom said, rubbing her back. "Stay here with me and you will be safe."

So Tamar lived as a desolate woman in her brother Absalom's house.

Soon King David heard what had happened. He was very angry, but he did not punish Amnon. As for his part, Absalom never spoke to Amnon about the matter, but he hated him deeply because he had disgraced his sister.

● ● ●

Two whole years passed.

Then Absalom invited all his brothers, sons of the king, to join him for the annual spring feast in a little town just north of Jerusalem. It was a grand celebration. They ate the best food and enjoyed the finest fruits of the vine for a week.

In the evening of the final day, Absalom's servants entered the banquet hall, clutching daggers beneath their robes. Amnon, merry with wine, sat at the head of the table. At Absalom's signal, his servants surrounded Amnon, drew their weapons, and killed him.

At this, the rest of the king's sons arose and fled back toward Jerusalem so as not to be implicated in the murder. Before they arrived, a report reached David: "Absalom has killed all the king's sons. Not one of them remains!" The king tore his robe and threw himself on the ground in horror and sorrow.

But just then Jonadab came in and said, "You've been given bad information, O King. All your sons are not dead. Only Amnon. Absalom has been plotting his murder ever since Amnon raped his sister Tamar. Just Amnon is dead."

The watchman on the Jerusalem wall cried out, "A crowd of people is coming on the northern road."

"See," Jonadab said to the king, "there they are now—your sons, just as I said."

The men soon stumbled into the king's quarters. They told their father what occurred, and they all lifted their voices and wept bitterly.

Absalom, in the meantime, escaped in the opposite direction, to Geshur, a small city where his grandfather—his mother's father—ruled as king. When David learned of this, he issued a decree for Absalom to remain there as an exile, forbidden from returning home. That was his punishment.

41. FATHER AGAINST SON

In time, David's heart began to ache for Absalom. "Why should I lose two sons?" the king would say to himself as he wandered aimlessly through his rooftop gardens. "Amnon is gone forever, and now Absalom is as good as dead, banished."

Joab saw how the king pined for his son Absalom. He observed the toll it was taking on him. David's eyes no longer flashed; his gait slowed; he looked empty. The king had lost something, and the general worried that the success and security of the kingdom would be compromised. Thus, he took matters into his own hands.

He sent for a woman from Tekoa who had a reputation for great wisdom. He dressed her in the garments of one who is mourning and sent her to the king with a story. When the woman came to David, she bowed with her face to the ground and cried out, "O King, help me!"

"What's the trouble?" David asked.

"Alas, I am a widow," she replied. "All I have are two sons. But they got into an argument and one killed the other. Now the rest of the family is demanding I hand over the one living son so they can execute him. They say he doesn't deserve to live. But he is the only heir, so if he too dies, my husband's name and family will disappear from the face of the earth. Please don't let them extinguish the only coal I have left."

"I will not let them," David told her. "Go on home, and I'll see to it no one touches him."

"Do you swear in the name of God?" she asked.

"I swear it," the king assured her.

Immediately, the woman stood up, cleared her throat, and said, "Why don't you do the same thing for the people of God as you have promised to do for me? Don't you see you have convicted yourself in making this decision, because you've refused to allow your own expelled son to return home? Yes, the heir of your own kingdom is in exile." David stepped back, perplexed. "All of us must die," the wise woman went on. "Our lives are like water spilled out on the ground, which cannot be gathered up again—like Amnon who cannot be brought back. But God also does not sweep away life, and Absalom is alive, so he can be returned to you, to the kingdom of Israel—just as you decreed for my son."

David focused his eyes attentively on the woman. "I must know one thing," he said. "And tell me the truth. Is Joab behind this?"

She answered, "O King, you are as wise as an angel of God. Yes, Joab sent me and told me exactly what to say."

David stroked his chin. "Send for Joab."

When the general arrived, David said to him, "Fine. Go and bring back Absalom from Geshur." Joab cracked a smile. Then the king added, "But he may go only to his own house. He must never come into my presence."

"But, my lord the king," Joab challenged.

David interrupted with a wagging finger, and so Joab bowed humbly and departed. He went at once to Geshur and brought Absalom back to Jerusalem, but not to the palace.

• • •

Absalom lived in the capital for two years without seeing his father. Then the handsome, long-haired prince sent for Joab to ask him to intercede with David on his behalf. But Joab sent word back, saying, "I've washed my hands of this matter. It is now between you and your father. I'm only a military man, not an arbiter."

Absalom sent a second message to Joab, but again he refused.

So Absalom set fire to one of Joab's barley fields. Then he sent a third communication: "Go ask my father why he brought me back from Geshur if he had no plans to see me. I might as well have stayed there. I want to see my father. If he finds me guilty of anything, then let him kill me."

Reluctantly, Joab sought an audience with the king and conveyed Absalom's sentiments to him.

"Kill him?" David murmured. "Does he really think I would do that?"

"I am simply delivering the message," Joab replied.

At last, David summoned Absalom. When his son entered his chambers, David ran and embraced him and kissed him. "Absalom!" he cried. "My son, Absalom. Oh, how I've missed you!"

• • •

Now Absalom was praised as the best looking man in all Israel. He was tall, bronzed, and chiseled. His luxuriant hair was legendary and he was flawless from head to foot. He had three sons and one daughter whose name was Tamar, and she was very beautiful, like her aunt after whom she was named.

It was not long after his return that Absalom obtained for himself a chariot and horses, and he hired fifty bodyguards to go before him wherever he went. He would arise early every morning and go to the main gate of the city. There he met the people who came to Jerusalem seeking a decision from the king on some matter. The prince would ask which tribe they were from, what city they lived in, and what judgment they were seeking. After the person answered, Absalom would say, "Your claims are good and right—you have a strong case. It's too bad the king is busy and there is no one who can help you." Then he'd shake his head sympathetically. "If only I were the judge in the land, then everyone could bring their cases to me, and I would give them justice."

When people tried to bow before him, Absalom would gently raise them up, take them by the hand, and kiss them. His benevolent words and charming manner had great effect on those who came to the city of David. And in this way, he stole the hearts of all the people of Israel.

One day, Absalom requested a formal meeting with his father. "I ask your permission to go to Hebron to fulfill a vow I made to God," he said. "While I was in Geshur, I promised to worship God in Hebron if he would bring me back to Jerusalem."

David looked lovingly at his son. "I thought I might use this occasion to speak with you about a promise God made about my son building a temple here in Jerusalem, and about an everlasting dynasty through my offspring." He waited for Absalom to respond with curiosity, but he did not. So David acquiesced. "But I see you have your mind on honoring God in Hebron, the city from which I first ruled." He smiled reminiscently, as Absalom waited. "Sure," David said, "go fulfill your vow."

"I also request that two hundred men from Jerusalem go with me as invited guests for the sacrifices I intend to offer," Absalom said.

"Whatever you'd like," David consented.

So Absalom climbed into his chariot and went to Hebron with a retinue of unsuspecting men. As soon as he arrived, he conferred secretly with various leaders in Israel. He met his cousin Amasa, who was a captain in the army. He called for Ahithophel, an old man who had served as his father's chief advisor for many years before retiring back to his hometown. Absalom sent emissaries throughout the land to rally support for his cause. In each city and town and village, the messengers would say, "As soon as you hear the ram's horn, you will know Absalom has been crowned king in Hebron."

Now the citizens of Israel had grown to love the winsome and dashing Absalom, and they eagerly flocked to his side. In addition, the prince had many friends in Hebron, and the city still harbored resentment against David for abandoning them and setting up his capital in Jerusalem. Yes, Absalom was gathering an army and planning to overthrow his father. It was a full-fledged coup. And it gained momentum quickly.

Soon, rumors buzzed in the city of David:

"There's a rebellion in Hebron. All Israel has joined Absalom in a conspiracy."

"Amasa and Ahithophel are now with the prince. The elders of the twelve tribes have declared Absalom king."

"They plan to march on Jerusalem."

David's heart hurt. But he had little choice. He sent messengers to his officers and advisors. "We must flee at once, or it will be too late. If we can get out before Absalom arrives, both we and the city will be spared from disaster."

So the king and his household set out at once, with Joab and six hundred loyal soldiers leading the way. David left no one behind except ten concubines to look after the palace. The citizens of Jerusalem wept as David's entourage passed through the city gate where Absalom had so often stood. The last to come were Abiathar and the priests who carried the Ark of God.

"Go back," David said. "Take the Ark of God back into the city. If I find favor in God's eyes, he will bring me back home to see the Ark again. But if he is not pleased with me, then let him do to me whatever seems best." Abiathar looked at him sadly. "And send me a report," David added, "with any information you can gather about Absalom and his plans."

Abiathar and a select few other priests took the Ark back to Jerusalem and stayed there.

David turned and followed the procession up the road toward the Mount of Olives east of his capital, his mantel drawn over his head and his feet bare as a sign of mourning. The people with him also covered their faces and cried out as they climbed the hill.

When David reached the summit, one of his counselors, a man named Hushai, came up to him with dirt on his head and his robe torn in grief.

David embraced him and said, "Hushai, it would do more good for me if you returned to Jerusalem. When Absalom takes over the city, tell him you will be his advisor just as you were mine. That way perhaps you can counter the advice Ahithophel might give him, for, as you know, Ahithophel has joined the revolt. When you learn of my son's intentions, tell Abiathar who has also returned to the city. He will pass the word on to me."

So Hushai bowed and departed for Jerusalem. No sooner had he left than another man came to David. His name was Ziba, and he was the caretaker of Mephibosheth. Now Mephibosheth was the son of David's dearly departed friend Jonathan. He was just a boy of five when his father Jonathan and grandfather King Saul died in battle. When his nurse heard the news of their deaths, she picked up Mephibosheth and fled. But as she hurried away, she fell and dropped the boy, and he became crippled. Then, when David established himself in Jerusalem, he invited Mephibosheth—along with his attendant Ziba—to live with him in the royal headquarters. It was the least he could do for Jonathan.

Ziba, a wealthy man in his own right, stood before David with two donkeys loaded with two hundred loaves of bread, one hundred clusters of raisins, one hundred bunches of fruit, and a skin of wine.

"What are these for?" David asked.

"These are for you, my lord the king," Ziba replied fawningly.

David stared at the overloaded beasts. "Where is Mephibosheth?" David puzzled.

"He's a man now. He can make up his own mind and he wanted to stay in Jerusalem," Ziba replied. "I couldn't get him to come with us. He said he was joining Absalom's insurgency in honor of his grandfather Saul. He sees it as revenge for your taking Saul's kingdom."

David looked at him narrowly. "In that case," he said, "I hereby give you everything Mephibosheth owns."

"I humbly bow before you," Ziba replied, bending at the waist. "May I forever find favor in your eyes, my lord."

Then David and Ziba turned and together continued their flight eastward.

• • •

As they approached the small village of Bahurim, a man came out and began yelling curses at them. It was Shimei who was from the same clan as Saul's family. He hurled stones at David, his officers, and the mighty warriors surrounding the king. "Get out! Get out, you murderer, you scoundrel!" he shouted at David. "God is paying you back for all the blood you shed in Saul's household. You stole his throne, and now Absalom has stolen yours. Sweet, divine justice!"

David's men pressed in close, their shields deflecting the rocks.

"How can we let this dead dog curse the king like this?" Abishai said. "I'm going to cut off his head."

"No!" David said sharply. "Who asked your opinion, Abishai? If God has told him to curse me, who are you to stop him?"

Then David said loudly, but to no one in particular. "My own son—my own flesh and blood—is trying to take my kingdom and my life. Doesn't this relative of Saul have even more reason to do so? Leave him alone and let him curse me, for God has told him to. Perhaps God will see my persecution and will repay me with good because of the curses I am receiving today."

David and his men continued down the road, and Shimei kept pace with them on a nearby hillside, cursing as he went and throwing rocks down on them and tossing dirt into the air.

The king and his entourage eventually arrived, weary and worn out, at the Jordan River. There they stopped to refresh themselves.

42. O ABSALOM!

In the meantime, Absalom and his forces entered into Jerusalem and captured it easily, as it was mostly empty. The dashing prince donned royal robes and rode triumphantly to his father's palace. He ascended the throne, attended by a large and boisterous retinue, and proclaimed himself king of Israel.

At the conclusion of the coronation, Hushai approached Absalom, fell before him, and said with contrived enthusiasm, "Long live the king! Long live the king!"

Absalom recognized the man. "Is this the kind of loyalty you show to your friends, Hushai? Why didn't you go with David?"

Hushai exclaimed, "No, no! My loyalties are with the one whom God and the people of Israel have chosen. His I will be, and with him I will remain. Just as I served your father, so I will serve you."

"Good," Absalom answered. "Then you and Ahithophel will be my chief advisors."

The next morning, Absalom called the two men. "Tell me what I should do now that I've taken the capital. What would you recommend as my next move?"

Ahithophel spoke up confidently. "Go in to your father's ten concubines, the ones he left behind to look after the house. Then all Israel will know you've fully usurped the throne. They will see you have made yourself odious to your father, which will strengthen the hands of all who are with you."

"Excellent counsel!" Absalom beamed. "Whoever has the women has the throne—everyone knows that. No need to hear anything more."

So they set up a tent for Absalom among the gardens on the roof of the palace. The new king took the women, one by one, into the tent and lay with them in the sight of all Israel.

Then Absalom once more sent for his two counselors. "Now that my place of power is solidified, what should I do about my father?"

Again, Ahithophel answered quickly. "Choose twelve thousand men and pursue David immediately. You will catch him beat and discouraged and throw him into a panic. All those who are with him will flee. In your attack strike down only David, and then all his people will come back to you as a bride comes home to her husband."

Absalom mused over the advice. Ahithophel waited anxiously.

Then the king turned to Hushai. "Tell us what you think."

"This time the counsel Ahithophel has given is not good," Hushai replied, shaking his head. "You know your father and his men are mighty warriors. Now they are enraged, like a bear robbed of her cubs. So it would not be prudent to attack at this time. Besides, your father has gone into hiding—he is not with the rest of his men. It will be nearly impossible to kill him alone. Furthermore, if we attack, and a few of our men fall, the rumors will start, 'There's been a slaughter among Absalom's troops.' Then even our most valiant warrior will melt with fear.

"My counsel, therefore, O King, is to wait. First, gather all Israel to you, from north to south. Then, and only then, descend on David as the dew covers the ground, and he and those with him will perish. If he happens to escape into some city, all Israel will bring ropes to that city and drag it down the mountain until not even a piece of it can be found. Then, my lord, there will be no doubt who is king in the land."

Absalom stood up and declared, "Hushai's advice is better. We should attack, but I should first patiently gather the forces to launch that attack."

Hushai bowed and went out to tell the priest Abiathar what had happened. Abiathar, in turn, passed the news on to David.

Ahithophel also bowed and left the king's presence. He saddled his donkey and went back to his hometown, depressed that his advice had not been followed. Once there, he set his house in order and hanged himself.

David and his men had crossed the Jordan and were camping in the town of Mahanaim when the word from Abiathar arrived. David promptly called a meeting with his officials. "There's no telling what Absalom will do," he said gravely. "He might change his mind and do what Ahithophel said, or he might do something different altogether. We need to prepare immediately."

David divided his men into three large companies, one under Joab, one under Abishai, and one under a man named Ittai. It was not long before scouts reported that Absalom and his army led by Amasa had crossed the Jordan.

"My son is indeed unpredictable," David said to his generals. "Or else that was one quick gathering of troops. We must go forth to meet them—we cannot fight a defensive battle." He paused and looked at each man directly. "And I will march forth with you."

"No, you must not go," they urged in one voice, "especially if he's now following Ahithophel's advice and trying to kill only you."

David stood fast with a cold confidence.

"It makes no sense for you to go," Joab said. "Even if half of us die, they won't care; they will be looking only for you. You are worth ten thousand of us. You cannot go."

David did not bat an eye, but he relented. "I will do whatever seems best to you."

David positioned himself at the gate of the town. As each brigade marched forth, David called loudly for all to hear: "For my sake, deal gently with the young man Absalom."

And so the forces of David went out to battle the army of Absalom. The fighting took place on wooded mountainsides and in the valleys below; the terrain was a vast stretch of trees and brambles and thicket. Here Joab was at his best. He led David's army fearlessly as they beat back Amasa and his men. The battle raged through the endless forest. Thousands of Absalom's soldiers fell by the sword; others fled through the confusion of bark and vines, which seemed to devour more men than the sword. In this way, the army of Absalom was utterly defeated that day.

Absalom, too, fled for his life on the back of his mule. His long hair blew behind him as he searched desperately for a way out of the dark woods. In the bedlam, his frightened animal darted under a tree, and Absalom's hair caught fast in its low branches. The mule galloped on, leaving him hanging there, suspended between heaven and earth.

Absalom's face wrenched in pain. His scalp pulled from his skull. He tried frantically to free himself, but could not.

One of David's soldiers emerged from the bushes and stared aghast. Then he bolted for Joab. "Absalom—I saw him," he puffed when he came to the general. "He's hanging from a tree by his hair."

"What?" Joab exclaimed. "You saw him and didn't kill him? I would've rewarded you with ten shekels of silver."

"I wouldn't lay a hand on the king's son for even a thousand pieces of silver," the man replied. "For we all heard what David commanded regarding Absalom. And if I had killed him, you would've been the first one to point the finger of blame at me."

"I don't have time for your nonsense," Joab snorted. "Show me where he is."

When they returned to the tree, there was Absalom still writhing and tugging at the tangle above his head. Joab walked slowly toward him; then he took a dagger and plunged it into Absalom's stomach. The prince stopped kicking. Joab took two more daggers and thrust them deep into Absalom's chest.

"Finish him off," Joab rasped to his ten body guards. Then he sounded the trumpet, and the war was over.

● ● ●

As the blast of the horn faded with the setting sun, a young man named Ahimaaz stepped forward and said to Joab, "Let me run to King David and tell him the good news."

"No," Joab said. "It won't be good news to David that his son is dead. There will be no reward for you. In fact, David has a bad way with messengers. Remember when Saul died?"

Joab turned to a mercenary from Ethiopia and commanded him, "Go tell the king what has happened." The man bowed and ran off.

But Ahimaaz continued to plead with Joab, so he sent him too. Ahimaaz took a short cut and ran to Mahanaim ahead of the Ethiopian.

Now David was sitting at the gates of the town. A watchman on top of the wall looked out and observed a lone man running toward them. He shouted out the news.

"If he is alone, he must have word of the war," David said.

As the man came closer, the watchman saw another soldier running toward them at a terrifying pace. "Here comes a second one!"

"He also will have news."

"I think the first man in front is Ahimaaz—that's the way he runs," the watchman called.

"Ahimaaz is a good man; he will have good news," David said hopefully.

Ahimaaz cried out, "All is well! Victory is ours!"

David rose to meet him, and the messenger did obeisance.

"Praise be to God," Ahimaaz panted, "for he has defeated those who dared to stand against my lord the king."

"What about Absalom?" the king asked. "Is he safe?"

Ahimaaz's eyes dropped. "Um . . . I don't have news of that. When Joab sent me, there was a lot of commotion, but I'm not sure what it was."

"Hold on for a moment," the king told him. Ahimaaz stepped aside with a sinking heart.

Then the Ethiopian arrived and announced enthusiastically, "I bring good tidings to my lord the king! Today God has given you vengeance on those who rebelled against you."

"What about Absalom?" David asked. "Is he safe?"

The Ethiopian hesitated, weighing his words. "May all your enemies be as that young man is now."

David winced and hunched over. He stumbled up the stairs to the chamber above the gate, groaning as he went. "O my son Absalom! My son, my son Absalom! If only I had died in place of you! O Absalom, my son, my son!"

Ahimaaz and the Ethiopian watched until David was out of sight. Glancing at each other, they turned and broke into a sprint back toward Joab.

When word spread through David's troops that he was weeping and mourning for Absalom, the joy of victory turned into deep sorrow. The king's men crept back into Mahanaim that night as though they had lost the battle.

Still, David covered his face and kept on bawling, "O my son Absalom! O Absalom, my son, my son!"

By the next morning, Joab could take it no longer. He went to David and tore into him with a speech of elemental power: "My soldiers and I put our lives on the line for you and your kingship. We saved your life and the lives of your sons, your daughters, and your wives—Michal, Abigail, Bathsheba, and the others. Have you forgotten that?" Joab was shouting. "Some of our men did not come back. What will you tell their wives and their sons and daughters who no longer have a husband and a father? Did you ever think about that? Those were flesh and blood men who died fighting for you, for your family, for your kingdom. We have put you back on the throne.

"Yet you act like this? You can do nothing but weep for Absalom? You love those who hate you and hate those who love you. You've made it clear today that we mean nothing to you. You'd be happier if Absalom had lived and all of us died.

"Now get up! Go speak to your troops. Thank them for what they did for you. For I swear to God if you don't address them right now, not a single one of them will be here by sundown. Then what will you do?"

So David composed himself, washed, and went out to speak with the troops, just as Joab demanded.

• • •

The king gave orders and they started the march back to Jerusalem to reclaim the seat of power. On the way, David sent word to Amasa, Absalom's general who had survived the civil war. The message read: "You deserve to die for treason, Amasa. But when I return home, I will appoint you the commander of my army in place of Joab. For I need to secure the support of those who followed you and Absalom. And besides, Joab killed my son."

When David and his men came to the Jordan River, a large group of people, many from the tribe of Judah, greeted them and escorted them across the waters. Among them was Shimei who fell prone before David.

The king did not know who he was until he spoke.

"My lord, please forgive me," Shimei beseeched. "Forgive me for cursing you and throwing stones as you fled Jerusalem. It was a terrible and sinful thing I did. I am here to beg your mercy and to welcome you back as king of the land."

Abishai interjected, "You should die, Shimei, for you cursed God's anointed one."

"No, no," David said, looking down at Shimei. "This is not a day for execution, but for celebration. For today I am once again the king of Israel. I swear to you, Shimei, your life is secure."

No sooner had David finished pardoning Shimei than another man approached. He was hobbling, helped along by two others. David knew him immediately. It was Mephibosheth. He had not trimmed his beard or washed his clothes since the king had left Jerusalem.

David folded his arms across his chest and waited. Mephibosheth could barely walk.

"Why didn't you come with me, Mephibosheth?" David asked.

"O King," Mephibosheth cried, "it was my servant Ziba. He betrayed me. I told him to saddle my donkey so that I, a lame man, could go with you. But he didn't, and now he has slandered me by saying I refused to go. But that is not true. Listen, my lord. I know that since I am a descendant of Saul, you should've killed me long ago. But instead you honored me by allowing me to live in the palace. So how could I possibly ask for any more kindness?"

David stared into Mephibosheth's heart.

"I already decreed that Ziba is entitled to all you own," David replied measuredly. "But now I will modify that decree such that you and Ziba will divide your possessions equally between you."

"Give him all of it," Mephibosheth said. "I'm happy just to have you safely back as king."

David nodded and then continued his journey home to Jerusalem. He was once again the king of Israel.

people of Israel for their support of the revolts of Absalom and Sheba—revolts against his anointed king, revolts against the man through whom he promised to build his everlasting kingdom.

The anger of God burned against Israel and he incited David against them, saying, "Go and take a census of all the people."

David sent men throughout the land to count the citizens and the warriors. When they returned and gave him the numbers, David suddenly felt pangs of guilt. His conscience was stricken and he said to God, "I have sinned greatly by what I've done. Please, I beg, forgive me for my foolish actions."

God replied, "I will give you three options. Choose one of them for me to carry out against you. Do you want three years of famine in the land, three months of running from your enemies, or three days of plague in Israel?"

"They're all terrible," David groaned. "But I choose the third. For it is better to fall into the hands of God, whose mercy is great, than into human hands."

Accordingly, God sent an angel into the kingdom, killing by a pestilence. After seventy thousand were dead, the angel turned and advanced menacingly toward Jerusalem. Just as death was about to descend on the city, God grieved because of the great calamity and said to the angel, "Enough! Withdraw your hand!"

David looked and saw the angel on a hill outside the gates, hovering above the threshing floor of a man named Araunah. "O God," David cried out, "I'm the one who has sinned and done wrong. But the people of the land are innocent as sheep—what have they done? Let your anger fall only on me and my family."

God said, "Build an altar on the threshing floor of Araunah."

So David went to Araunah. "I have come to buy your threshing floor so I can build an altar to God there."

"You may have it, my lord, for whatever purpose you wish," Araunah answered. "You may take my oxen for the burnt offering, and you may use the threshing boards for wood to build a fire. It's all yours."

"No, I will buy it from you at a price, for I will not present offerings to God that have cost me nothing." David insisted. Then he paid him fifty pieces of silver for the threshing floor and the animals. He laid stones for the altar and made offerings on it. Thus the anger of God was quenched.

• • •

David was becoming an old man and his days drawing to a close. His eyes drooped, his skin sagged, and he had terrible circulation. He was always cold. His attendants searched for a beautiful young virgin to look after the king and to keep him warm. They found no one more perfect than Abishag. She dutifully served the king and put her warm flesh next to his. David was never intimate with her, for he was no longer able.

The aging king spent much of his time now reflecting quietly on his rooftop. Despite some revolts and other setbacks, he had successfully united all Israel under his rule. He had built a legacy. He thought often of his wives and his many children, both living and deceased. Yes, God's punishment for his sin against Bathsheba and Uriah had come to pass: Trouble had surely arisen from within his own household.

But God had been with him through it all. His only lingering regret was that he had not been permitted to build a temple for God. He cherished the thought that his successor would one day carry out that task. And he rested in God's promise to build a dynasty through his offspring.

With the deaths of Amnon and Absalom, it was the third son, Adonijah, who was next in line to inherit the kingdom. As David's faculties declined, Adonijah prepared to take the throne. He gathered fifty powerful bodyguards and procured for himself the king's best chariots and charioteers. He met with Joab and Abiathar the priest, and they gave him their support. He then proclaimed himself king and held a grandiose coronation ceremony. There he sacrificed sheep, cattle, and fattened calves. All his brothers—the other sons of King David—and all his father's royal officials were with him. Except three whom Adonijah did not invite: his brother Solomon, the son of Bathsheba; Nathan, the prophet; and a military captain named Benaiah.

Nathan met secretly with Bathsheba. "Your life and the life of your son Solomon are in serious danger," he said to the graying queen. "For Haggith's son, Adonijah, is proclaiming himself king this very moment. David doesn't even know what is happening. Here is what we must do. You go to David and say to him, 'My lord the king, didn't you make a vow to me that my son Solomon would succeed you and sit on your throne? Why then has

Adonijah become king?' Then, in the middle of your meeting with him, I will arrive and confirm everything you've said." Nathan looked at her mischievously—and desperately.

That afternoon, Bathsheba called upon the king. He was resting in his bedroom when she entered. Abishag sat attentively next to him; she slipped her hands beneath the old man and helped him sit up.

"What can I do for you?" he said, managing a toothless smile.

She replied, "My lord, you made a vow to God that your son Solomon would be the next king. But instead, Adonijah is exalting himself, and you're doing nothing about it. Now, O King, all Israel is waiting to hear the announcement of who will rule after you. If you do not keep your word, my son Solomon and I will be in mortal danger—we will be treated as criminals when my lord the king is laid to rest."

At that moment, Nathan appeared in the doorway. He entered and did obeisance. "My lord, have you declared Adonijah king?" He is holding a coronation feast at this very hour. Joab and Abiathar are celebrating and crying out, 'Long live King Adonijah!' Everyone was invited—everyone but Benaiah, your son Solomon, and me."

David turned and looked at Bathsheba. Mustering all his strength, he said to her, "I swear in the name of God that your son Solomon will be the next king and will sit on my throne."

Bathsheba sank to her knees. "May my lord the king live forever."

David shifted his attention back to Nathan, his energy gaining momentum. "You and Benaiah are to lead Solomon and my loyal officials down to Gihon Spring. Solomon is to ride on my own mule. When you get there, call an assembly and anoint Solomon. Blow the ram's horn and shout, 'Long live King Solomon!' Then the whole city will know whom I have announced as king."

"May God be with Solomon as he's been with you, my lord," Nathan said. "And may he make Solomon's reign even greater than yours."

Nathan did as David commanded. When all the people heard the ram's horn, they raised their voices with shouts of joy. The dancing and singing was so noisy that the earth shook with the sound. When David heard the uproar, he bowed his head and prayed, "Praise the God of Israel who today has allowed my eyes to see a successor on my throne."

Adonijah and his contingent also heard the hoopla and cheering. "I wonder what that's all about?" Joab questioned. Just then a messenger burst in. "David has declared Solomon king! Jerusalem is rejoicing. Solomon is now sitting on the royal throne."

At that, all Adonijah's guests arose in panic and scattered. Adonijah rushed into Jerusalem, to the sacred tent that housed the Ark of God, and grabbed on to the altar in front of it. For it was a place of asylum—anyone holding on to the altar could not be executed.

When word reached Solomon of Adonijah's whereabouts, he immediately dispatched men to the tent.

"Let King Solomon swear that he will not kill me," Adonijah pleaded as the guards shackled him and led him to the palace.

Adonijah bowed before Solomon, who watched him quizzically and declared, "If you prove yourself to be loyal, not a hair on your head will be touched. But if you act treacherously, you will surely die." Adonijah raised his head and the two brothers locked eyes for a long moment. Then Solomon dismissed him, and Adonijah returned home.

● ● ●

It was barely a week later that David summoned Solomon to him. The stalwart man knelt before his father. David placed his worn hands on his son's shoulders and said, "My days are short. I am about to return to the earth as every man does. You must be strong. Show yourself to be a man. Keep the commandments of God and follow all his decrees. Obey him and you will prosper in all that you do and wherever you go. If you do this, then God will keep the promise he made to me—the promise that if my descendants live as they should and follow God faithfully with all their heart and soul, then one of them will sit on the throne of Israel always and forever."

David paused pensively. Then he bent forward and said, "And there are a few other things, my son. You know that Joab murdered both Abner and Amasa in peacetime. He has stained his belt and sandals with innocent blood. Do with Joab what you think best, but don't let his gray head go down to the grave in peace."

Solomon pressed his lips into a firm line and nodded once slowly. David went on in low tones. "And remember Shimei who cursed me and hurled stones at me as I fled from Jerusalem? When he later met me on my return home, I swore in God's name I wouldn't kill him. But that doesn't make him innocent, nor does my oath bind you. See to it that his bald head also goes down to the grave in blood."

Then David spoke no more. Solomon arose, embraced his father, and went out.

Three days later, David died. He had reigned over Israel for forty years, and there was great mourning and lamentation in Jerusalem.

Solomon sat upon the throne of his father David, and his kingdom was firmly established.

44. KING SOLOMON

Not long after David's funeral Adonijah went to see Bathsheba, Solomon's mother. It was an unusual meeting—the king's half-brother speaking with the queen mother. Bathsheba granted the audience, but she was apprehensive.

"Have you come with peaceful intentions?" she asked Adonijah.

"Yes," he answered, "I come in peace. I'm here to ask a favor of you."

"What is it?" Bathsheba frowned.

Adonijah replied, "As you know, the kingdom was rightfully mine. All Israel was expecting me to be the next ruler. But then things changed, and the kingdom went to my brother Solomon instead—maybe that's the way God wanted it. Now here is my request: Speak to King Solomon on my behalf, for I know he will do anything you request, and ask him to let me marry Abishag."

Bathsheba straightened up, a curious expression spread across her face. She had nearly forgotten about Abishag—the beautiful virgin who attended her elderly husband prior to his death. "Okay, I will speak to the king for you."

When Bathsheba met with her son the next morning, the new ruler rose from his throne and bowed down before her.

"I have one small request to make of you," she said.

"What is it, Mother? You know I won't refuse you."

She cleared her throat and said, "Let your brother Adonijah marry Abishag."

Solomon jerked to attention. He had not forgotten Abishag. She was now among the palace harem, though he had not yet slept with her. His mind raced. This was treachery of the highest order. How could his mother not see the treason in her request—was she growing too old to discern Adonijah's intentions?

"How can you possibly ask me to give Abishag to Adonijah?" King Solomon demanded. "You might as well ask me to give him the kingdom! You know he's my older brother, and Abiathar and Joab supported his campaign to become king."

He looked at her, exasperated and confused. "No, Mother, he cannot have Abishag. In fact, I swear to God Adonijah has sealed his fate with this request. God put me on the throne of my father David, and thus all contenders to the throne must be subdued. Adonijah, Abiathar, and Joab will meet their fate this very day."

So King Solomon called Benaiah, his freshly appointed general, and said, "Go to Adonijah's house and kill him."

Immediately Benaiah turned and went and struck down Adonijah.

While he was doing that, Solomon summoned Abiathar. The old priest trudged in falteringly. "You deserve to die," Solomon declared to him. "But I will not kill you now because you carried the Ark of God for David my father and you shared all his hardships."

"Thank you," Abiathar shuddered.

"But you can no longer reside here in Jerusalem," Solomon announced. "You must return home; for I am deposing you as a priest of God."

● ● ●

Meanwhile, news of Adonijah's death reverberated through the capital. When Joab learned of it, he ran to the sacred tent of God and clung to the altar. When this was reported to Solomon, he sent Benaiah to execute him too.

"The king orders you to come out of the tent!" Benaiah shouted to Joab.

"No, I will die here!" Joab yelled back.

Benaiah, honoring the rule of asylum, returned to Solomon and told him what Joab said.

"Do just as he asked," the king snarled. "Kill him there. This will remove the guilt of Joab's senseless crimes from me and my father's family. God is about to repay him for the murders of Abner and Amasa, two men more righteous and better than he. May their blood be on Joab and his descendants forever."

So Benaiah returned to the sacred tent and ran his sword through Joab.

Solomon now continued down the list of his father's dying commands. He sent for Shimei and said to him, "Move into Jerusalem and live here. You are never again to set one foot outside this city. On the day that you so much as take a step beyond the gates, you will surely die; and your blood will be on your own head."

Shimei bowed low. Then he moved his entire household into Jerusalem and remained there. But three years later two of his slaves ran away to another town, and Shimei saddled his donkey and went to search for them. When he found them, he brought them back home. Solomon heard what Shimei had done, so he summoned him and said, "Didn't I command you never to set foot outside this city? And didn't I explain clearly that if you did, you would die?"

Shimei crumpled to the floor. "But . . . but . . ."

Solomon continued, "You certainly remember the evil curses you called down on my father David. May God now bring that evil on your own head." Then Solomon beckoned Benaiah who was standing in the shadows. The general emerged, his sword drawn. He grabbed Shimei by the collar and dragged him outside and slew him.

And so the kingdom was firmly in Solomon's grip.

One night God appeared to Solomon in a dream and said, "What do you want? Ask for anything, and I will give it to you."

Solomon replied, "You showed great kindness to my father David because he was faithful to you and righteous and upright. And you have continued your kindness to him by giving him a son to sit on his throne. Yes, O God, you've made me king. But I am like a little child who doesn't know what to do. Here I am in the midst of your chosen people, a nation so great and numerous they cannot be counted. Give me, I ask, a discerning and wise heart so I can govern your people well and distinguish between right and wrong. For it is a mighty task to lead your people."

God was exceedingly pleased with Solomon's request. "Because you asked for wisdom and knowledge to rule my people with justice, and did not request a long life or wealth or the death of your enemies, therefore I will grant what you asked. I will indeed give you a wise and understanding heart such as no one else has had or ever will have. Moreover, I will also bestow upon you what you did not ask for—riches and honor and fame, so that in your lifetime you will have no equal among the kings of the earth."

Then Solomon awoke and realized it had been a dream. In the morning, he arose and went and stood before the Ark of God, where he sacrificed burnt offerings and peace offerings.

As promised, God conferred upon Solomon very great wisdom and a breadth of understanding as vast as the sands of the seashore. His wisdom exceeded that of all the sages of the East and the sages of Egypt, and his fame spread throughout the nations round about.

It seemed that there was nothing Solomon did not know. He composed three thousand proverbs and wrote one thousand songs. He spoke learnedly about all kinds of trees and plants, from the great cedar of Lebanon to the tiny hyssop that grows from cracks in a wall. He taught about beasts and birds, reptiles and fish. Some said he could even speak the languages of the animals and talk to them in their own tongues. So great was Solomon's knowledge that dignitaries from many nations came to listen to him.

When the queen of Sheba—a neighboring land—heard of Solomon's great mind, she came to test him with hard questions. She arrived in Jerusalem with a large group of attendants and a great caravan of camels loaded with spices, gold, and precious jewels. Solomon welcomed her as he did all his guests. The two talked at length in a private room in the palace. They talked about whatever the queen wanted, and Solomon had answers for all her questions. Nothing was too difficult for the king to explain to her.

"Everything I heard about your wisdom is true," she marveled. "I didn't believe it until I heard it with my own ears. In fact, I had not heard the half of it! Your wisdom is far beyond what I was told. How happy your people must be. How wonderful for your officials to stand in your presence day after day. Praise be to your God who delights in you and placed you on the throne of Israel. He made you king so you can rule with justice and righteousness."

Then she presented him with gifts; no one had ever brought to Israel as many spices as those the queen of Sheba gave to Solomon.

● ● ●

It was not only royalty who came to see Solomon, but ordinary folks as well. They would bring their disputes before the king, and he would render justice. One day two prostitutes came to have an argument settled.

"My lord," one of them began, "this woman and I share the same house. We both gave birth in the same week to baby boys. But then this woman's baby died during the night when she rolled over on it. So she got up and took my son from beside me while I was asleep and laid her dead child in my arms. When I awoke in the morning to nurse my son, he was dead! But then I looked more closely and saw it wasn't my baby at all. It was hers."

The other woman cried, "No! The living child is mine. The dead one is yours."

The first woman shot back, "No, the dead one is yours!"

And so they argued back and forth before the king.

Then Solomon declared, "Bring me a sword."

So a sword was brought. "Cut the living child in two," Solomon decreed. "Give half to one woman and half to the other."

Instantly the first woman screamed, "No, don't kill the baby! Give him to her!"

But the other woman said, "Neither one of us will get the baby. Cut him in two."

Solomon said, "Give the child to the first woman, and do not kill it. For she is his mother."

When all Israel heard the verdict, they held Solomon in awe. And his fame spread throughout the land and beyond.

● ● ●

It spread as far north as the city of Tyre where Hiram ruled as king. One day Hiram sent good will ambassadors to Solomon, for Hiram had been on friendly terms with David. Solomon graciously received the emissaries and sent them back with this message to Hiram: "You know my father David could not build a temple to honor the name of our God, for he had too many wars to fight. But now our God has given me peace on every side; I have no enemies, and all is well in my kingdom. Thus I'm planning to build a temple, which will fulfill the promise God made to my father.

"Therefore, I request cedars from Lebanon be cut for me. Let my men work alongside yours, and I will pay your men whatever wages you set. As you know, there is no one among us who can cut timber like your people."

Hiram received Solomon's message with delight. "God has given David a wise son to be king of the great nation of Israel." Then he sent word back to Solomon: "I will supply all the timber you need. My servants will haul the logs from the Lebanon mountains down to the Mediterranean Sea and make them into rafts and float them along the coast to whatever place you specify. Then we will break apart the rafts so you can carry the logs away. You can pay by supplying food for my household."

In this way Hiram furnished as much wood as Solomon desired. In return, Solomon sent him countless bushels of wheat and gallon upon gallon of pure olive oil.

And so it was that Solomon built the house of God in Jerusalem. It was a grand edifice, with three major areas. Its beams were made of cedar and the interior walls were paneled with cedar boards which featured the most exquisitely shaped carvings—cherubim, palm trees, and flowers. The inner most and holiest room was overlaid with gold from floor to ceiling. In it were a golden lampstand, a dazzling incense altar, and an expertly crafted table.

Solomon spent seven years building the house of God, and when it was done there was nothing as magnificent in all the earth. Then the king called together the elders of Israel and the heads of the tribes in order to bring the Ark of God into the temple. In a solemn procession, the priests transported the Ark from the sacred tent where David had set it up to its new resting place. As always, it contained the two tablets of stone inscribed by the finger of God.

On this sacred occasion, a thick cloud filled the temple, for it was the presence of God.

That day Solomon and the people sacrificed so many sheep and cattle that they could not be recorded or counted. When they finished, Solomon stood before the Ark and addressed the whole assembly of Israel. "Blessed be the God of Israel who has today fulfilled what he promised with his own mouth to my father David. I have built for you, O God, a house in which to live, and I have provided a place where the Ark may rest eternally."

The people applauded reverently. Solomon then knelt down, stretched forth his hands toward the heavens, and prayed aloud, "O God, there is no God like you in the heavens above or on earth below. The heavens—even the highest heaven—cannot contain you. How much less this temple I have built. Nonetheless, hear my prayer, O God. May you hear the humble and earnest requests from me and your people Israel when we pray toward this place.

"When your people Israel are defeated by their enemies because they have sinned against you, then hear from heaven and forgive the sin of your people. When the skies are shut up and there is no rain because your people have sinned against you, then hear from heaven and forgive their sin. When there is a famine in the land, or a plague, or crop disease, or an attack of locusts—whatever disaster or pestilence there is—then hear from heaven and forgive. May you always listen to your people when they cry out to you. For you have singled them out from all the nations of the world to be your own possession and you have fulfilled your covenant with our ancestors Abraham, Isaac, Jacob, and Moses, and my father David."

When he finished praying, Solomon arose and blessed the congregation. The king and the people celebrated at the temple for fourteen days. Then they went to their homes, joyful and glad in heart for all the good things God had done.

After completing the house of God, King Solomon devoted himself to strengthening his kingdom. He built a palace for himself. It was a stunning structure of cedar and stones, with a throne of ivory overlaid with gold. Six high and wide steps led to the throne. Twelve lions stood on the six steps, one on each side. There was nothing like it in all the kingdoms of the world.

Solomon had a fleet of trading ships that sailed to far off places and brought back gold and silver, apes and baboons. He fortified the great wall around Jerusalem. He built towns throughout the land. Treasures of all kinds flowed into Israel from distant places—whether by forced tribute or free trade. Vessels of silver and gold, fine linens, exotic spices, horses and mules, harnesses and armor, cedar and pine, and all manner of riches accrued to the kingdom of Solomon. He made silver as common as stones in Jerusalem. He accumulated fourteen hundred chariots and twelve thousand horsemen. Indeed, Solomon was wiser and wealthier than all the kings of the earth.

● ● ●

When Solomon had accomplished all he set out to do, God once again appeared to him in a vision of the night. This time, however, he did not ask the king what his heart desired; he offered a sobering word instead: "If you will follow me with integrity and uprightness, as David your father did, and if you obey my commands and adhere to my decrees and laws, then I will establish your royal throne over Israel forever.

"But if you or your descendants turn away from me and disobey my statutes, and if you serve and worship other gods, then I will remove Israel from this land I have given them. I will reject this temple that honors my name. I will make Israel an object of mockery and ridicule among the nations. And though this temple is impressive now, all who pass by will be appalled and will scoff and say, 'Why did God do such terrible things to this land and this temple?'

"And the answer will be, 'Because his people forsook God who brought their ancestors out of Egypt, and they worshiped other gods and bowed down to them. That is why God has brought these disasters.'"

45. TORN ASUNDER

Now King Solomon loved many foreign women. When he made political alliances, he married the daughters of the kings of surrounding lands. He wed the daughter of Pharaoh the king of Egypt, as well as many women from the countries of Moab, Ammon, and Edom. In all, Solomon had seven hundred wives and three hundred concubines.

These women led Solomon astray; for when they came to live in Israel, they longed to continue the religious traditions of their homeland. Solomon tried to please them by allowing them to worship their native gods. With the passing of time, however, they turned his heart away from the God of Israel. Solomon built altars for Ashteroth, Chemosh, Molech, and all the detestable gods of his many wives. Though he continued to make sacrificial offerings to the God of Israel, he also bowed down and worshipped many strange deities.

So God became very angry with Solomon. He spoke to the king in a third vision and said: "Since you have violated my covenant and disobeyed my decrees, I will most certainly tear the kingdom away from you and give it to one of your servants. Nevertheless, in honor of your father David, I will not do this during your lifetime. Instead, I will take the kingdom away from your son. Even then, I will not take away the whole kingdom from him. I will allow him to rule one tribe, for the sake of my servant David and for the sake of my chosen city Jerusalem."

Although the nation of Israel prospered mightily under Solomon's rule, it came at a price. It required much manpower to construct the temple and the palace and the king's massive building projects. And it required much money: taxes were extremely high. "David never burdened us this way," people began to grumble.

"Saul managed to rule from a rough fortress barely bigger than an average house," others said.

"The palace is twice as nice as the temple and took almost twice as long to build," still others observed. And so seeds of discontent took hold.

From this restlessness, God raised up a rebel to oppose Solomon and to carry out his word. Jeroboam, one of the king's high ranking officials, was an industrious and well-respected man. He heard the complaints of the Israelites and saw their faces shiny with the king's sweat. He knew the royal greed and felt the creeping oppression. One day, as he went about his daily work in Jerusalem, a prophet named Ahijah approached him and led him out into the open country.

Ahijah was wearing a new cloak. When they reached a solitary place, he took hold of the garment and tore it violently into twelve separate pieces. "Take ten pieces," he said to Jeroboam, holding forth the shredded cloth. "For thus says the God of Israel: Because Solomon and his throne have forsaken me, I am about to tear the kingdom from his hand and give ten tribes to you. Yet, for the sake of my servant David and the city of Jerusalem, I will leave one tribe for him and his offspring."

Jeroboam fixed his eyes firmly on the prophet and slowly reached out his hands. Ahijah pressed ten fragments onto his palms.

Ahijah continued, "As for you, Jeroboam, you will reign over the ten northern tribes of Israel. If you follow God's commands and do what is right in his eyes, then God will be with you and will build for you a dynasty as enduring as the one he promised David."

Jeroboam went on his way, pondering the prophet's words. When Solomon learned of the prophecy, he tried to kill the future rebel. But Jeroboam fled to Egypt to await the king's death.

Not long thereafter, Solomon passed way. He had reigned over Israel forty years. He was buried in Jerusalem next to his father David. And his son Rehoboam succeeded him as king.

● ● ●

By this time, the people of Israel, particularly those in the northern part of the land, were wholly dissatisfied with their lot under Solomon, and they hoped for more benevolent treatment from Rehoboam. Upon hearing of Solomon's death, Jeroboam returned from Egypt and led the congregation of Israel in a formal petition to the new king.

The hearing took place on a cloudy, foreboding day in the city of Shechem. Jeroboam raised his voice and declared, "We the people of Israel say to you Rehoboam: Your father Solomon was a hard master. Our work was burdensome and our taxes extreme. The kingdom was rich, but we were not. Please, we ask, lighten the heavy load your father imposed on us, and we will be your loyal subjects."

Rehoboam sized up Jeroboam. "Give me three days to think this over," the king declared. "Then I will give you my answer." So the people went away.

King Rehoboam met with the advisors who had counseled his father. The older men among them urged him to listen to the people. "Be good to them, and they will be good to you."

But the young cabinet members, the ones whom Rehoboam had grown up with, were of a different opinion. "Answer these people like a real king. Tell them your little finger is thicker than your father's loins. You must answer them harshly, for only the strong are respected."

Three days later Jeroboam and all the people gathered to hear Rehoboam's decision. The king ascended the platform and spoke. "If my father laid heavy burdens on you, I will make them even heavier. My father beat you with whips, but I will beat you with scorpions."

There was silence for a moment, then a rising murmur of outrage. Jeroboam stood and lifted his voice to the multitude, "Go home, Israel! Go home! For we have no share in the house of Israel and of David. This man will never be our king."

Then he pointed at Rehoboam and said, "You, O great one, had better look out for your own house!"

As the din of rebellion rose, Adoniram, one of Rehoboam's body guards, tried desperately to restore order, but the people of Israel stoned him to death. At this, Rehoboam jumped into his chariot and fled to Jerusalem.

And so it came to pass the ten northern tribes of Israel turned their backs on Rehoboam and crowned Jeroboam as their king. Only the tribe of Judah in the south remained loyal to the kingdom of David. Thus, the land of Israel was torn apart, just like the prophet's cloak.

There had been civil war in the past, but this time it was different. It was permanent. Though they had the same history and the same blood, they were now two separate kingdoms: Judah in the south, and Israel in the north. And those two kingdoms were at war.

Jeroboam, king of the newly formed Israel, established his capital at Shechem, the seat of the schism. But he feared his people would continue to go to the temple in the sacred city of Jerusalem in order to offer their sacrifices to God, and in this way they might be persuaded to rejoin Rehoboam and the house of Judah.

For that reason, he quickly established two places of worship within his territory, one in the city of Bethel to the south, the other in Dan to the north. Priests were installed in both locations and festivals held at the same time as those in Jerusalem. Both sacred places also featured a golden calf. "These are the gods who brought you out of the land of Egypt," Jeroboam proclaimed. "Worship them here in our land."

The people did.

One day, a man sent by God from the kingdom of Judah came to Bethel during one of Jeroboam's sacrificial feasts. He arrived just as Jeroboam was ascending the steps of the altar, a bowl of incense poised above his head about to be poured on the burning coals.

"O altar, altar!" the man from Judah cried out. "This is what God says: A child named Josiah will be born into the dynasty of David. On you he will sacrifice the priests who offer incense on you." Jeroboam peered down at him in amazement. "And human bones will be burned on you!" the man shouted. "And this altar will be torn down and its ashes poured out."

"Seize him!" commanded Jeroboam. He aimed a finger at the man and repeated, "Someone seize him!"

But in that instant the king's outstretched hand withered. It shrank, the skin cracked, and he could not pull it back to his body.

"Man of God," the king cried, "restore my hand."

Without blinking, the man said, "Please, O God, restore his hand."

Immediately the blood flowed back into Jeroboam's hand and the flesh fattened around the bones. The king looked in disbelief at his hand, then at the lone man below him. After a moment, he composed himself and said, "Come to the palace with me and have something to eat, and I will give you a gift."

The young man shook his head. "No. Even if you gave me half your kingdom, I would not go with you, for God forbid me to eat or drink anything in this land."

Then he turned and departed through the crowd in great haste.

● ● ●

As it happened, there was an old prophet in Bethel whose sons were at the feast that day. They hurried home and told their father about the incident.

"Quick, saddle my donkey," the old man said. "I must meet this man of God from Judah."

They saddled the animal, and he rode off into the blazing afternoon. Two miles down the road toward Judah, he came upon the man resting beneath a huge oak tree.

"Are you the man of God who came from Judah?" the old prophet called out.

"Yes, I am."

"I thought so. Come home with me and eat some food."

"No, I cannot," he replied. "God instructed me not to eat or drink anything until I return home."

"Yes, I heard about that command," the gray-haired man said. "But, you see, I am a prophet just as you are. And an angel of God bid me to bring you home and to nourish you with bread and water."

Still the young man shook his head.

But the old man urged him. "You are fatigued and it is a long way to Judah. Please make the short trek back to my house with me." He walked over and gently tugged on his arm.

So the man from Judah arose and together they went back to the prophet's house in Bethel. They ate and they drank and they talked.

While they were sitting at the table, a command from God came to the old prophet. He stood and cried out to his guest, "You have defied the word of God! You came back to this place and ate and drank. Because of this, you will not be buried in the tomb of your ancestors."

The young man keeled over, but made not a sound. The old prophet went out, saddled his own donkey, and told the man from Judah to ride it back home.

On the way, the man from Judah stopped to rest under the same oak tree. As he dozed in the shade, a lion leapt from the thicket and mauled him to death. The beast, as it were, neither ate the man nor attacked the donkey. The shredded corpse lay there beside the road—the donkey and lion stationed on either side of it.

Some passersby recognized the donkey and they sent word to the old prophet: "Your donkey is under the huge oak on the road to Judah. A lion is next to it, and there is a dead man."

When the prophet heard the report, he went and found the morbid scene just as he had been told. "God has fulfilled his word," he said aloud, "for he disobeyed God's command."

Then the prophet walked gingerly past the jaws of the lion and gathered up the young man's body. He laid it on the back of the donkey that stood waiting, as if for this very task, and led the animal back to his house in Bethel, mourning as he went: "Oh, my brother! My brother!"

The next day he buried the man from Judah in his own tomb, and he said to his sons, "When I die, lay my bones beside the bones of this prophet. For the message he proclaimed against the altar in Bethel will certainly come to pass."

● ● ●

After the festival in Bethel, King Jeroboam of Israel returned to his capital city, Shechem. He soon forgot the bizarre encounter with the man of God from Judah and continued about the business of ruling his new kingdom.

One day his son Abijah became very sick, and the king was troubled. He said to his wife, "Disguise yourself so no one will recognize you and go to the prophet Ahijah in Shiloh—the man who tore his robe and told me I would become king."

The small woman listened, cradling her boy. "Take him a gift," her husband continued. "Say, ten loaves of bread, some cakes, and a jar of honey. Tell him you have a son who is ill, and ask him what will happen to the boy."

Jeroboam's wife put on the clothes of a peasant, pulled a shawl tightly around her face, and headed for Shiloh bearing the gifts.

Now Ahijah was an old man and could no longer see. But God was with him. When he heard footsteps at the door, he called out, "Come in, wife of Jeroboam. Why the disguise?"

"How did you . . . Well, I . . . I . . ." she stuttered.

"I have bad news for you," Ahijah announced. "Tell your husband this is what God says: I made you ruler over my people Israel. I ripped the kingdom away from the line of David and gave it to you. But you've not been like David, who obeyed my commands and followed me with all his heart. Instead, you have done great evil by setting up golden calves.

"Since you have turned your back on me, I will bring disaster on your house and I will destroy all your male descendants—every last one of them. I will burn your royal dynasty as one burns up a trash heap. Those who die in the city will be eaten by dogs, and those who perish in the field will be devoured by vultures. I, God, have spoken."

Jeroboam's wife doubled over and began to sob. "But I only wanted to know about—"

"Go back home," Ahijah said with a raised palm. "As soon as you enter your city, your child will die. He is the only one in Jeroboam's house who will have a proper burial, for this boy is the only good thing God has found in it."

The woman's sobs grew into wailing. Ahijah waited a minute and then pressed on: "Furthermore, God will raise up a king over Israel who will destroy the family of Jeroboam. God will shake Israel like a reed whipped about in a stream. He will uproot the people of Israel from this good land and will scatter them abroad; for they have angered God. Yes, he will abandon Israel because your husband, King Jeroboam, abandoned God with his idols of worship."

The king's wife could take no more. She got up and ran from the house, arms flailing. The moment she stumbled across the threshold of her home, the child breathed its last.

All Israel mourned, and they buried him with a prince's funeral.

Shortly thereafter, Jeroboam also died. He was memorialized and eulogized and interred next to his son. He had been a central figure in the story of Abraham's descendants, for he established the nation of Israel, breaking free from the oppressive rule of Solomon's son Rehoboam. But he also led the people astray by setting up bogus idols and not remaining true to the covenant of his ancestors.

After Jeroboam died, his son Nadab became king of the nation of Israel.

46. ELIJAH AND AHAB

King Rehoboam of Judah had seen his kingdom reduced to a small plot of the once great Promised Land. He could not, and did not, rule with the iron fist he had threatened. He maintained, nonetheless, his grand capital in Jerusalem, the city of David, and he enjoyed control over Solomon's magnificent temple of God. Even so, Rehoboam, like Jeroboam in the north, did not worship God alone. He set up sanctuaries to foreign gods in various places throughout Judah. He raised a sacred pole to Asherah and endorsed worship of the fertility gods of Canaan.

God was displeased with Rehoboam, but for the sake of David he raised up a son, Abijah, to succeed him as king. Abijah committed all the sins of his father, and then he died, and his son Asa ruled Judah. Asa was a good king whose heart was fully devoted to God. He cleaned up much of the idol worship, and even deposed his grandmother because she encouraged repulsive practices in the land. Then he passed away and his son Jehoshaphat became king.

● ● ●

In the northern kingdom of Israel, Nadab succeeded his father Jeroboam as king. He did evil in the eyes of God as well. Soon a certain man named Baasha plotted against Nadab and killed him. Baasha then took the throne and mercilessly slaughtered every one of Jeroboam's descendants, just as Ahijah foretold. But Baasha himself was no better for it: He too worshipped many graven images.

So God sent a message to Baasha: "I am about to destroy you and your household as I destroyed Jeroboam and his family. You were the instrument of my wrath against him; now you will be the object of my vengeance. Those in your house who die in the city will be eaten by dogs, and those who perish in the field devoured by vultures."

When Baasha died, his son Elah ruled after him. It was not long before Zimri, a high ranking court official, conspired against him. One day when Elah was drunk at a feast, Zimri entered and assassinated him. Then he declared himself king and destroyed every male relative of Baasha's, as God predicted. Zimri's rule, too, was short lived, for when the army of Israel learned what had happened, they proclaimed Omri, their commander, king. When Zimri saw he did not have the support of the military, he barricaded himself in the palace and set it on fire. Thus he died. He had been king for seven days.

Then Omri ruled over Israel. He moved the capital of the kingdom to Samaria and there he did more evil in the eyes of God than all the kings who had come before him. He provoked the anger of the Almighty with his worthless idols and sinful ways. Then he died and his son Ahab took the throne.

● ● ●

Ahab was worse yet. He married Jezebel, the daughter of a nearby king. She was a devotee of the Canaanite god Baal and his consort Asherah.

Wishing to appease her, Ahab ordered a temple built in Samaria for the deities of his new wife. On a high place within the city walls, the land was dug, pillars were raised, and a lovely house was hewn of stone and cypress and cedar. In it were an ornate and magisterial altar to Baal and a sacred pole to Asherah. Now all Israel could worship these foreign gods who, it was believed, controlled the rains which made the earth fertile. Baal, the god who rode on the clouds, was now the god of Ahab; and Asherah, the great goddess, the lord of Israel.

Baal and Asherah, of course, required priests who needed a place to live. So Ahab commanded that houses be built for four hundred fifty priests of Baal and four hundred priests of Asherah.

Jezebel was delighted with the luxurious temple in honor of her native gods and with the warm welcome extended to the priests, but she intended to do more than keep the traditions of her homeland. She wanted to wipe out worship of the God of Israel. To that end, she began to persecute the prophets and priests of God, who were forced into hiding in caves and in the wilderness. And so it was that the name of God was rarely heard in Ahab's court.

Then one day a strange figure with a ragged robe, full head of bushy brown hair, and tangled beard appeared before King Ahab just as he was about to enter the temple of Baal. The man's eyes burned with a fierce intensity and he spoke with terrifying eloquence. His name was Elijah, and he was a prophet of God sent to deliver a short and dire message to the king: "As surely as the God of Israel lives, the God whom I serve, there will be neither dew nor rain in the next few years—except by my word."

Then he was gone.

When Jezebel heard of it, she was incensed. "Except by *his* word?" she scoffed. "Baal is the god of the rains. I will not tolerate such blasphemy."

God said to Elijah, "Get away from this place. Turn eastward and hide by the brook Cherith. You can drink from the waters while they still flow, and I have commanded ravens to feed you."

Elijah did as God said. The ravens brought him bread and meat each morning and evening, and he drank from the brook. But after a while, the brook failed because there was no rain anywhere in the land, as Elijah said.

Drought and famine fell together on Israel like a dreadful plague. Jezebel twitched with fury, but she could not find the prophet of God.

Then God ordered Elijah, "Go to the town of Zarephath and stay there. I have instructed a widow in that place to take care of you."

Elijah left the dried-up brook and travelled though the arid countryside to Zarephath. When he arrived at the gates of the village, he saw a widow gathering sticks for a fire. She looked tired.

He called out to her. "Would you please bring me a little water in a cup, so that I may drink?" She turned and looked at the strange man speaking to her. Then she went to get the water. "And bring me, please, a piece of bread to eat as well."

She spun around. "I cannot," she said sorrowfully. "I swear I don't have a single piece of bread in the house. I have only a handful of flour left in the jar and a little cooking oil in the bottom of the jug. I was just gathering a few sticks to make one last meal for myself and my son. We will eat; then die."

"Don't be afraid," Elijah said. "Continue with your plan, but first make a little bread for me. Then use what's left to prepare a meal for yourself and your son. For God has said your jar of flour will not be empty and your jug of oil will not run dry until the day God sends rain upon the earth."

The widow went to her house and did as Elijah told her. When she had baked a small cake for the prophet, she found enough flour and oil to feed herself and her son. And it was the same every day thereafter, for many weeks—there was a sufficient amount to feed three people.

● ● ●

As time passed, it happened that the woman's son became sick. His condition grew worse and worse, and finally he died. The woman's heart was broken, and in her sadness she turned upon Elijah. "O man of God, what have you done to me?" she cried. "Have you come here to remind me of my sins and punish me by killing my son?"

"Give me the boy," Elijah replied gently. He took the child's lifeless body from her arms, carried him up the stairs to the loft, and laid him on the bed. Then he cried out to God, "Why have you brought tragedy to this widow who is taking care of me? Why have you caused her son to die?"

Elijah stretched himself over the boy three times and each time he prayed, "O God, please let this child's life return to him." The heat from Elijah's body warmed the body of the child, and the breath from his mouth entered the mouth of the child. God heard Elijah's prayer, and the boy's breathing became deep and regular, and he revived. Then the prophet carried the child down to his mother. "Look," he said. "Your son is alive."

The woman clung to her boy with tearful joy and amazement. "Now I know you are a man of God," she said. "And God truly speaks through you."

● ● ●

For nearly three years there was flour in the jar and oil in the jug and drought throughout the land. King Ahab was hard pressed to feed his household, and his fleet of horses barely hung on. He searched desperately for Elijah, but each time his messengers returned without any news of the prophet. As for Jezebel, she continued her relentless persecution of the prophets and priests of God.

As the hunger crisis deepened, Ahab called his chief household servant, Obadiah, and said to him, "Go to every spring and valley in the land to see if we can find enough grass to save at least some of my horses and mules." Obadiah obeyed.

Late in the afternoon on the following day, Obadiah looked up and saw Elijah coming toward him. He hurried forward and bowed low. "Is it really you, my lord Elijah?"

"It is," Elijah replied. "Now go tell your master I need to meet with him. For God has ordered me to announce that the rains will soon return."

Obadiah began to shake. "Oh, no, I cannot do that. Why would you send me to my death at the hands of Ahab? For I swear the king has searched the earth from one end to the other looking for you. He's made each city and town and outpost take an oath that they've not seen you. And now if I go back and tell Ahab I know where you are, he will assume I've been aiding you this whole time. And he will kill me. No, I cannot risk being identified with you."

He looked pleadingly at the stout man of God. But he received only a narrow stare in return. So Obadiah continued, "I've been a true servant of God all my life. Has no one told you about the time I hid one hundred prophets of God in two caves and supplied them with food and water in order to save them from Jezebel's reign of terror? I've risked my life once before in the name of our God. But that was secretly; this time it would be out in the open."

Still there was only a penetrating gaze from Elijah.

"Besides, as soon as I leave you," Obadiah resumed, "the spirit of God will carry you away to who knows where. Then when you don't show up to meet Ahab, he will kill me for deceiving him."

Finally Elijah spoke. "I swear in the name of God, in whose presence I stand, that I will present myself to Ahab."

It was then Elijah's turn to receive a hard stare, before Obadiah wheeled and ran to tell Ahab.

The next day, before the sun had risen above the horizon, Elijah looked up and saw Ahab coming across the parched earth. Neither man bowed. "So, is it really you, you troublemaker of Israel?" Ahab said.

"I've made no trouble for Israel," replied Elijah. "You and your household are the troublemakers, for you've refused to obey the commands of God and have worshiped Baal instead."

Ahab started to protest, but he knew Elijah spoke the truth three years earlier and he knew the land was in dire need of rain, so he held his tongue.

Elijah went on. "Summon all Israel to join me at Mount Carmel, along with the four hundred fifty priests of Baal and the four hundred priests of Asherah. There we will have a contest to see who is mightier: God or Baal."

So Ahab sent messengers throughout the land of Israel, and great crowds soon climbed Mount Carmel, covering it with a curious and hungry congregation. The priests of Baal and Asherah were also there, but Jezebel was not. She would not leave her palace at the behest of a lone prophet of God.

On the mountainside were scattered the old stones of an altar to God torn down by Jezebel. Two bulls were tethered nearby. Amidst the stones stood Elijah, wrapped in his cloak of camel's hair. Then he raised his voice and said, "How much longer, O Israel, will you waver between two opinions? If the God of Israel is the Truth, then follow him. But if Baal is the Truth, then follow him."

The people answered not a word. Only the sound of the mountain winds filled the air.

"Here are two bulls," Elijah called to the priests of Baal. "Choose whichever one you wish and cut it into pieces and lay it on the wood of your altar. But put no fire to it. Then call on the name of your god. I will do the same with the other animal on my altar and call on the name of my God. The deity who answers by setting fire to the wood is the true God."

Excitement rolled through the great assembly.

"You go first," Elijah said to the Baal worshippers.

Forthwith, they slaughtered one of the bulls and butchered it. They placed the bloody meat on the dry wood and began to pray. "O Baal, answer us. Lord of the clouds, hear our cries."

All morning long they shouted their request to Baal, while Elijah carefully placed the stones of God's altar back into place. The foreign priests danced wildly around their altar, begging their deity to show himself.

But nothing happened to the pieces of flesh.

About noontime Elijah began mocking them. "You'll have to shout louder. Perhaps he's taking a nap. Maybe he is relieving himself. Or maybe he's away on vacation."

The priests drew their swords and cut themselves until blood streamed down their arms and legs. They raved and shrieked all afternoon. But still there was no sound. No one answered.

Suddenly Elijah called to the people of Israel, "Come near to me!" They drew near and saw the repaired altar of God, with twelve large stones. They saw he had piled wood on the altar, cut the bull in to pieces, and laid the pieces on the wood. They also saw a deep and large trench around the altar.

Elijah said, "Fill four barrels with water and pour it over the offering and the wood."

They did.

"Do it again," he ordered, and they did.

"Now do it a third time." So they did as he said, and the water soaked the altar and filled the trench around it.

Then Elijah lifted his hands and prayed, "O God of Abraham, Isaac, and Jacob, prove today that you are God in Israel and that I am your servant. O God, answer me. Answer me so these people will know you are God."

Immediately fire forked down from heaven. It burned up the bull, the wood, the stones, and the dust. It even consumed the water in the trench.

The people of Israel fell flat on the ground, screaming, "The God of Israel is God! The God of Israel is the only God!"

Elijah, full of holy zeal, called out, "Seize the prophets of Baal! Don't let a single one escape." Instantly the multitude of people descended on the priests and bound them. Then Elijah and the Israelites dragged them down the mountain into the Kishon valley below. "Kill them," the prophet ordered, and Israel slaughtered the priests of Baal and Asherah. Not one of them survived.

● ● ●

Ahab watched all the day's happenings from a distance. As the people trickled away to their homes, Elijah turned to him and said, "I hear a mighty rainstorm coming." Ahab stared at the carnage on the ground and at the cloudless sky and he shrugged. Then he walked slowly, as if in a daze, to his chariot.

There was no one else around, except a lingering young man. Elijah called to him. "Come with me, boy," and the two of them climbed the mountain again. When they came to the spot of the great sacrifice, Elijah sat down, pulled his legs up, and put his face between his knees.

Then he said to the youth, "Go and look out toward the sea and tell me what you find."

The boy went and looked, then returned to Elijah and said, "I didn't see anything."

"Go again."

The boy went and came back. "I don't see anything."

Six times the lad went to the top of the mountain and peered westward. Finally, the seventh time, he said to Elijah, "I see a little cloud about the size of a man's hand rising from the sea."

"Run back down to King Ahab," Elijah replied, "and tell him to hurry home, for a mighty rain is on the horizon. Hurry! For God has spoken."

In a short while the sky was black. A heavy wind rose and huge drops of water began to fall. Then the power and strength of God came upon Elijah. He tucked his cloak into his belt and bounded down the mountain. As sheets of rain swept over the thirsty land, he sped past the king in his chariot and sprinted ahead of him all the way to the gates of the palace.

● ● ●

Jezebel was not in the least bit happy about the torrential rains. When Ahab told her what occurred on Carmel, and that Elijah killed all the priests of Baal and Asherah, she flew into a violent rage. "Tell Elijah I have a message for him: May the gods deal with me, as severe as it may be, if by this time tomorrow I do not make your life like the lives of my priests."

When Elijah received the word, he was afraid. He headed south as fast as he could go, through the kingdom of Judah all the way to the desert region. At dusk, he collapsed under a broom tree. "I've had enough, God," he despaired. "Take my life; for I am no better than my ancestors."

Night descended and the air grew cold. Elijah pulled his cloak tightly around him and drifted off to sleep under the tree.

All at once an angel touched him and said, "Arise and eat." He looked around, and there by his head was some bread baked over hot coals and a jar of water. He ate and drank and then lay down again.

The angel came a second time and touched him and said, "Get up and eat, or else the journey will be too much for you." So he got up and ate and drank. Strengthened by that food, he traveled forty days and forty nights until he reached Sinai, the mountain of God and of Moses, deep in the wilderness.

He entered a cave at the foot of the mountain. Darkness covered the place. Then the word of God came to him: "What are you doing here, Elijah?"

"I have been very zealous for God Almighty," he answered. "The Israelites have forsaken your covenant, the covenant you established here on this mountain. They have torn down your altars and killed your prophets. I am the only one left—I alone—and now they are seeking my life too. So I am here to save myself."

God said, "Go out and stand on the mountain, for I am about to pass by."

Before Elijah could move, a great and powerful wind ripped down the mountainside, shattering the rocks. But God was not in the wind.

After the wind died, the entire mountain began to tremble. Boulders split and huge stones tumbled down. But God was not in the earthquake.

After the earthquake, fire shot up from the clefts in the rock. Crackling flames and billowing smoke ascended into the sky. But God was not in the fire.

After the fire, came the sound of silence, a mysterious and holy calm. When Elijah heard it, he pulled his mantle over his face and went out and stood at the opening of the cave. A voice said to him, "Elijah, what are you doing here?"

Elijah whispered, "I have been very zealous for God Almighty. The Israelites have forsaken your covenant—"

"You are not alone," the voice of God interrupted. "There are seven thousand people in Israel whose knees have not bowed to Baal and whose mouths have not kissed him."

Elijah knelt to the ground and began to whimper.

God continued, "Now go and find Elisha and anoint him as prophet in your place when you are gone. He will be your successor. Take heart."

So the next morning Elijah made the trek back through the wilderness and the land of Judah to the kingdom of Israel. He found Elisha, a bald and lanky man with an aquiline nose, supervising twelve yoke of oxen plowing his father's fields. He himself was driving the twelfth pair. Elijah took off his mantle, shook it open, and laid it around Elisha's shoulders. Both men knew what this meant: The younger man was to continue the older man's work when the time was right. Elisha also knew he must follow the senior prophet that very day.

"Let me kiss my father and mother goodbye," Elisha said to Elijah, "and then I will come with you."

"You may go," Elijah replied.

So Elisha rushed back to his team of oxen. He led them home, slaughtered them, and used the wood from the yokes to cook the meat. He then served the beef to his parents and his whole household.

When they completed the farewell meal, Elisha set out to follow Elijah and to become his apprentice.

47. PROPHETS AND VINEYARDS

While Elijah was meeting God at Mount Sinai, King Ahab and Samaria came under attack. King Ben-hadad of Aram mobilized his army, supported by the chariots and horses of thirty-two allied kings, and besieged Samaria. When he had cut off all the supply lines to the city, Ben-hadad sent a message to Ahab: "Give to me all your silver and gold and your wives, and we will withdraw."

Ahab, as it were, had acquired significant power and wealth and, like all kings, he enjoyed a large harem. But he had little choice. He had to capitulate. So he loaded carts with silver coins and gold bullion and sent them ahead of his entourage of wives to the enemy outside his gates.

But the Aramean king did not retreat. Instead, he sent a second message: "I've taken your money and your women, but I'm coming for more. My officials will search your palace and the homes of your people. They will take away anything and everything their eyes desire."

Ahab replied, "I've given you enough already, and you still did not withdraw. Your officials will not enter this city."

Ben-hadad sent word back: "May the gods strike me if there remains enough dust from Samaria to give each of my men a handful."

Ahab responded, "A warrior putting on his sword for battle should not boast like a warrior who has already won."

That night a certain prophet of God—one whom Obadiah had saved from Jezebel's wrath—came to see Ahab of Israel and told him, "This is what God says: Do you see all these enemy forces? Today I will hand them over to you. Then you will know I am God."

Emboldened by this surprisingly sanguine word, Ahab mustered his troops. About noontime, as Ben-hadad and his generals were in their tents drinking themselves into a stupor, the first of Ahab's soldiers marched forth from Samaria.

Ben-hadad's scouts reported to him, "Men are advancing from the city."

"If they've come out for peace, take them alive," Ben-hadad shouted, with a raised jug of wine. "And if . . . and if they've come out for war, take them alive," he slurred, laughing.

Suddenly a vast horde of soldiers emerged from the Israelite capital and fell upon the Arameans. Ben-hadad's army panicked and fled. The Israelites chased them down the hill, slaughtering them along the way, man and horse alike.

God had indeed kept his word.

But Ben-hadad and many of his generals managed to escape. As they regrouped, Ben-hadad's officers said to him, "The Israelite gods are gods of the hills; that's why they won. If we fight them on the plains, we will win. We must only rebuild our forces."

Ben-hadad did as they suggested.

The following spring, he marched out against Israel, this time in the lowlands near Aphek. Ahab in turn summoned his forces, which looked like two little flocks of goats next to the massive Aramean army blanketing the countryside.

Then the same prophet of God appeared again to Ahab and said, "This is what God says: The Arameans think my power is limited to the hills. So I will defeat them for you on the plains. Then you and they will know I am God of the hills and the valleys."

The two armies camped opposite each other for a week before both forces attacked simultaneously. Once more, the Israelites routed their enemies. Countless Arameans fell on the plain. The rest absconded into the town of Aphek, but the wall fell on them and killed many more, though Ben-hadad was not among them.

As he hid in the defenseless Aphek, Ben-hadad's officers said to him, "We've heard the kings of Israel are merciful. Let's humble ourselves and surrender. Perhaps Ahab will let us live. You stay here, and we'll go out and give ourselves up."

The Aramean king looked at them skeptically. "Your last advice—something about being only a god of the hills—hasn't worked out so well. Nonetheless, do as you say."

So the king's men came out with sackcloth around their waists and ropes tied around their necks. "Your servant Ben-hadad begs for his life and ours," they cried out to the Israelite warriors who quickly sent for King Ahab.

"Is Ben-hadad still alive? He is my brother," Ahab said to the now shackled prisoners.

The Aramean men took quickly picked up on his words. "Yes," they said, "your brother Ben-hadad. He's alive and hiding in Aphek."

"Go get him," Ahab ordered.

When Ben-hadad arrived, Ahab invited him up into his chariot. There the two talked for quite some time. Finally, a new treaty was agreed upon, and Ben-hadad was set free.

• • •

Meanwhile, God again called upon the company of his prophets who had survived Jezebel's purge. He instructed one of them, "Go find one of your comrades and tell him to punch you in the face. Then I will instruct you what to do after that."

Perplexed and not a little hesitant, the man went and found another prophet of God and said, "Hit me in the face as hard as you can."

"What? No. What are you talking about?" the man answered

"Do it. Now."

But the second prophet just stared at him. So the first one said, "Because you've not obeyed the voice of God, a lion will kill you as soon as you walk away from here." The man shook his head disbelievingly and departed. He had not gotten very far when a lion jumped from behind a pile of rocks. The beast sank his teeth into the man's soft flesh and shredded him to pieces.

Then the prophet found another man and said, "Hit me." Immediately the prophet clenched his fist, drew back, and struck him in the left eye.

The man wrapped a bandage around his head and over his wound; then he waited beside the road for Ahab to pass by on his way back to the palace. "O King," he said, "I was in the thick of battle today, and suddenly a man brought me a prisoner and said, 'Guard this man. If for any reason he gets away, you will surely die.' But we were in the middle of fierce fighting, and the prisoner disappeared."

"That is your sentence," the king replied. "You have spoken it yourself."

The man of God pulled the bandage from his eyes, and Ahab instantly recognized him as one of the prophets. The king's chin dropped.

"This is what God declares," the prophet said. "You have spared a man—Ben-hadad—I determined should die. Thus, it is your life for his life, and your people for his people."

So Ahab went home to Samaria angry and sullen.

● ● ●

Ahab remained in a foul state for some time. God's prophets and their messages—whether Elijah's famines or a deceptive disguise—were a perpetual thorn in the king's side. Yes, they had foretold the victory over his foes to the north, which happily restored peace and security to his nation. But the joy of that success was immediately overshadowed by the proclamation of his death. This made the king terribly unsettled. He needed to get out of Samaria. So he and Jezebel moved to a second, less extravagant palace in the city of Jezreel a bit to the north.

It happened that there was a man named Naboth who owned a vineyard in Jezreel. One day Ahab said to him, "Since your lovely property is adjacent to my house, I would like to buy it from you at a very good price to use as an herb garden. Or if you prefer, I will give you a better vineyard in exchange."

The elderly Naboth replied, "God forbid I should give you the inheritance passed down to me by my ancestors."

Ahab tried mightily to convince him to sell, but Naboth would not be moved. So the king stomped back home in a huff. He crawled into his bed, faced the wall, and refused to eat.

"What's the matter?" Jezebel asked him. "What's made you so upset that you're not eating?"

"I asked Naboth to sell me his vineyard or trade it, but he won't. Says it's been in the family a long time."

Jezebel's brow furrowed. "Are you not the king? Get up and eat something. Stop being so glum. I'll get Naboth's vineyard for you."

The queen wrote a letter in Ahab's name, sealed it with his seal, and sent it to the councilmen and other leaders of Jezreel.

In her letter she ordered: "Call the citizens together next week for a day of fasting and give Naboth a place of honor. Seat two scoundrels across from him and have them accuse him of cursing both God and king. Then take him out and stone him to death."

The town leaders followed the instructions exactly. Then they sent word to her: "The old man Naboth is dead."

When Jezebel received the message, she said to her husband, "The vineyard Naboth wouldn't sell you—you can have it now. He's passed away."

Ahab looked at her inquiringly. Then he hurried out to claim the vineyard, happily envisioning his new garden.

• • •

At that moment, God spoke to Elijah. "Go and see King Ahab. He's in Jezreel. Tell him this is what God says: You have murdered a man and seized his property. Because you've done this, dogs will lick up your blood in the very same place where they licked up the blood of Naboth."

So Elijah went.

Ahab was resting unawares in the courtyard of his palace when he looked up and saw the prophet at the gates. His demeanor changed in a flash. "So, my enemy, you've found me," Ahab exclaimed.

"Yes," Elijah answered, "I have come because you've done evil in the sight of God." Ahab raised his palms innocently. "So here is what God says," Elijah declared. "I will bring disaster on you. I will consume every one of your male descendants. I am going to destroy your family as I destroyed the family of Jeroboam and the family of Baasha. Those in your house who die in the city will be eaten by dogs, and those who perish in the field will be devoured by vultures. For you have provoked my wrath and have caused Israel to sin."

Ahab dropped his arms; his face blanched.

Then the fiery-eyed prophet added: "And regarding Jezebel, God says that dogs will devour her by the wall of Jezreel."

Ahab tore his clothes and scooped dust on his head. For the next three days he fasted and went about in deep mourning.

God saw this and gave another word to Elijah. "Ahab has humbled himself before me. Because of this, I will not bring disaster during his lifetime. I will bring it on his house in the days of his son."

● ● ●

In time, Ahab's spirits rose and his kingdom enjoyed a period of peace and prosperity. The treaty with Ben-hadad and Aram made for good relations with the nation to the north. Ahab also signed a truce with King Jehoshaphat of Judah to the south. To ratify the agreement, Ahab and Jezebel gave their daughter, Athaliah, to Jehoshaphat's son Jehoram. The two sister kingdoms—Israel and Judah—were finally no longer at war. And now they were bound not only by a common history, but also by marriage.

Then Ahab grew restless. The city of Ramoth-gilead was supposed to have been given to Israel as part of the agreement with Ben-hadad. The transaction, however, never occurred and the important town remained under Aramean authority. Consequently, Ahab asked Jehoshaphat to join him in a campaign to take Ramoth-gilead. The king of Judah agreed. "You and I are as one. My troops are your troops, and my horses are your horses. But let us first seek the counsel of God."

Ahab summoned the prophets. Nearly four hundred of them assembled before the two kings who had donned their royal robes and seated themselves on two thrones. "Should I go to war against Ramoth-gilead, or should I refrain?" Ahab called out to them.

They answered loudly and in unison, "Go to war. For the God of Israel will give you victory."

Jehoshaphat looked at Ahab doubtfully. Then he leaned over and said, "Is there not also a prophet of God whom we can ask?"

Ahab bit his lower lip. There was Elijah, of course, though his whereabouts were always unknown. One other name came to mind. "There is one more man who could consult God for us," Ahab said. "But I hate him because he never prophesies anything good about me. His name is Micaiah."

"You should not say that," Jehoshaphat replied. "Summon him and let's hear what he has to say."

So Ahab ordered one of his officials to fetch Micaiah. As they waited for him to return, a prophet from among the crowd, Zedekiah by name, stepped forward. He held iron horns above his head with both hands. "This is what God says," he shouted. "With these horns you will gore the Arameans to death!"

A cheer rose from the multitude of prophets and they began to chant, "Go up to Ramoth-gilead and attack, for God will give you victory!"

In the meantime, the messenger who went to get Micaiah said to him, "Look, all the prophets are promising success in battle. Let your word agree with theirs."

Micaiah replied, "I say only what God tells me to say."

The official ushered Micaiah before the king, and silence fell.

"Micaiah," Ahab said confidently, "should we go to war against Ramoth-gilead, or refrain?"

"Attack and be victorious," Micaiah answered with a grin. "For God will grant you success." He held his smile for several seconds.

Ahab replied sharply, "How many times must I make you swear to tell me nothing but the truth when you speak in the name of God?"

Micaiah's visage changed. "In a vision I saw all Israel scattered on the mountains, like sheep without a shepherd. And God said, 'These have no master.'"

Ahab's face hardened. "Didn't I tell you?" he said to Jehoshaphat. "He never prophesies anything favorable for me, only bad."

Then Micaiah continued, "I saw God sitting on his throne with all the hosts of heaven around him, on his right and on his left. And God said, 'Who will entice Ahab to go into battle against Ramoth-gilead so he can be killed?'

"One suggested this and another that. Finally, a spirit stepped forward and said, 'I will entice him.' God asked, 'How will you do this?' The spirit replied, 'I will go out and become a lying spirit in the mouths of all his prophets.' God answered, 'Go ahead and do it.' So you see, God has done this, for he has pronounced your doom."

Zedekiah threw down his iron horns, walked up to Micaiah, and slapped him across the face. "Since when did the spirit of God leave me to speak to you?"

Micaiah replied, "You will find out on the day when you go to hide in a secret room."

"What?" Zedekiah ridiculed. "What does that mean?"

Before Micaiah could explain, Ahab pointed at Micaiah and roared, "Seize him! Put this man in prison, and feed him nothing but bread and water until I return safely from battle." The guards moved quickly to bind Micaiah.

"If you come back, then God has not spoken through me," Micaiah said, surrendering his hands and feet. Then he turned to the pack of prophets. "Mark my words, all you people."

● ● ●

King Ahab of Israel and King Jehoshaphat of Judah prepared for battle. Ahab said to his counterpart, "When we march out, I will disguise myself by wearing plain armor so no one will recognize me, but you wear your royal robes as you normally would."

The next morning, then, it was Jehoshaphat who commanded the troops to charge, while Ahab blended in with the common soldiers.

As it turned out, the king of Aram had issued these orders to his captains: "Attack only the king of Israel. Don't worry about anyone else."

When the Aramean captains saw Jehoshaphat in his royal attire, they pursued him. As they drew closer, they realized he was not Ahab and stopped giving chase.

An Aramean soldier, in the course of battle, drew his bow and shot blindly into the melee and happened to hit Ahab. The arrow lodged between the joints of the king's armor.

"Turn around and get me out of here," Ahab groaned to his chariot driver. "I've been hit."

The fighting waged into the afternoon, with Ahab looking on from a nearby hill, propped up in his chariot.

As the shadows lengthened, a messenger approached and found the king dead. The blood from his wound covered the floor of the chariot. Then a cry rang through the troops: "Retreat! The king has been killed!"

The Israelites, indeed, were like sheep without a shepherd.

King Ahab's body was taken back to Samaria, where he was buried. They washed his chariot by the pool of Samaria, and dogs came and licked up his blood.

48. CHARIOT OF FIRE

After Ahab died, his son Ahaziah reigned over Israel. Like his father, he stirred up the anger of God by worshipping Baal when the dry ground needed nourishment. Baal, however, was not the one to consult for advice about going to war, or for an oracle of personal well-being. There were other gods for that.

So when Ahaziah fell through the latticework of an upper room in his palace, he sent messengers to the priests of Zebub, the god of Ekron, to ask whether he would recover from his injury.

Once again God called on Elijah. "Go and confront the messengers of Ahaziah—they are on the road to Ekron—and say to them, 'Is there no God in Israel that you consult Zebub? Now here the word of God: You, Ahaziah, will never again arise from your bed. You will surely die.'"

Elijah went and delivered the message. When the king's envoy heard it, they reversed course and went back to Samaria. "Why have you returned so soon?" Ahaziah asked them.

"A man stopped us on the road and told us to go back and give you a message," they replied. Then they told him, word for word, what Elijah said.

"Who was this man?" the king demanded. "What did he look like?"

"He was a hairy man, and he wore a leather belt around his waist."

"Elijah!" the king exclaimed. "He was my father's nemesis and now he's become mine."

Ahaziah immediately dispatched a battalion of fifty soldiers to arrest the prophet. They hurried out, swords in hand, and found him resting on top of a hill under a terebinth tree. The captain of the troops approached and said, "Man of God, the king orders you to come down."

Elijah chomped some grain between his teeth and spit the husk to the side. "If I am a man of God," he said with raised eyebrows, "let fire come down from heaven and destroy you and your men."

Instantly, red and yellow flames fell from the clear skies. The green hillside went up in vapors of black, and the king's men were incinerated.

Ahaziah beat his fists against the cushions of his bed when he heard. Then he barked out orders for another battalion of fifty to apprehend the hairy man.

They went and found Elijah on the same hill under the same tree. And the same thing happened: A firestorm burnt them all to death.

Rage consumed Ahaziah, and he sent a third company to seize Elijah. But this time the captain ascended the ash-covered hill and fell to his knees. "O man of God, I beg you to spare my life and the lives of my men. Please don't call down flames from heaven on us. Please."

Then God said to Elijah, "Go down with him, and don't be afraid."

So Elijah arose, looked down at the prostrate captain, and said, "Take me back to Samaria."

With gratitude, they led him to the capital, unshackled, and escorted him to the king's cool chambers. Before Ahaziah could say a word, the prophet started in: "This is what God says: Why did you send messengers to Zebub to ask whether you would recover? Is there no God in Israel for you to consult? The answer to your questions is: No, you will never recover. You will never leave the bed you are lying on, and there you will surely die."

"You . . . You . . ." Ahaziah pouted.

Then the prophet was gone.

Soon thereafter Ahaziah closed his eyes for the final time, in his bed. Since he did not have a son to succeed him, his younger brother Joram took the throne of Israel.

● ● ●

After delivering his word to the king, Elijah returned to Gilgal, a small town where he and Elisha shared a humble abode. Elisha had been learning diligently from his master, and now the time had come for the younger to succeed the older.

It was a misty morning when Elijah said to Elisha, "God has sent me to Bethel today; you stay here."

"I remain behind too often," Elisha protested. "I swear this time I will not let you go by yourself."

Elijah slung his mantle over his shoulder and set out. Elisha followed wordlessly all the way.

When they entered Bethel, a company of prophets took Elisha aside and said, "Do you know God will take your master from you today?"

"Yes, I know," Elisha answered. "Say no more." Then he hurried to catch Elijah who was toiling along the path.

Elijah stopped and said to him, "Stay here, Elisha. God has sent me to Jericho."

"No," the younger man said. So Elijah turned and headed down to Jericho, and Elisha followed.

Again a band of prophets in Jericho went up to Elisha and asked him, "Do you know God will take your master from you today?"

For a second time he answered, "Yes, I know. Please say no more."

Yet again the master said to his understudy, "Stay here. God has sent me to the Jordan."

This time Elisha only stared at him. So the two of them walked on. A chilly evening wind was blowing when they reached the banks of the Jordan. The waters churned before them; it was an impossible crossing. Fifty men from the company of prophets in Jericho stood at a distance watching.

Elijah rolled up his mantle and struck the water with it. The Jordan parted to the right and to the left, and the two men crossed over on dry ground. Then the river rushed back into its place behind them.

As they came up out of the river basin, Elijah said, "What can I do for you before I am taken from you?"

"Let me inherit a double portion of your spirit," Elisha answered solemnly.

The old prophet put a hand on his companion's shoulder. "You've asked a difficult thing. If you see me when I am taken from you, it will be yours; otherwise, it will not."

They walked on slowly together, talking. Darkness had nearly overtaken the day. Suddenly a blazing mass descended from the sky. Elisha looked and saw a chariot of fire and horses of fire. They rushed downward and then between the two men of God. A great whirlwind gathered up Elijah and carried him up toward the heavens.

"My father! My father!" Elisha cried out. "The chariots and horsemen of Israel!" Then it all vanished. And the air was still again. Elisha tore his garment in two. He fell to his knees and gazed into the sky, where he saw the mantle of his master floating gently to the earth.

Elisha picked up the cloak of camel hair and went back and stood on the bank of the Jordan. He rolled the mantle and struck the waters and cried out, "Where now is the God of Elijah?" As before, the Jordan split and Elisha walked across the stony riverbed.

The company of prophets from Jericho observed from the other side. They said to one another, "The spirit of Elijah is resting on Elisha." And they went to meet him and bowed before him. Then they returned to Jericho.

● ● ●

Presently, the people of Jericho learned what had occurred at the Jordan. They approached Elisha and said, "We see the power of the Almighty is on you, and you have authority over the waters of the land. As you know, we have a fine city, but the water here is bad which is a burden on us. Can you purify our spring?"

"Bring me a new bowl full of salt," Elisha said. So they brought one to him.

He led them out to the spring, reached into the clay container, and began tossing handfuls of salt into the water, saying, "This is what God declares: I have healed this water. Never again will it be bitter." The water was instantly cleansed, and the people of Jericho were amazed.

● ● ●

The next morning, while it was still dark, Elisha arose, took a jar of fresh water, and set out for Bethel. The sun ascended and a hot breeze blew; sweat glistened on Elisha's scalp. As he neared the town, some boys came out toward him shouting, "Get out of here, baldy! Get out of here, baldy!"

Elisha stopped, raised his hands above his head, and declared, "In the name of the God of Israel, I call down a great curse on you." Then he lowered his arms and quietly resumed his walk. In that instant, two black she-bears emerged from the shadowy woods. They charged toward the children and mauled them, their teeth tearing easily through skin and bone. Hideous screams split the muggy air. When it was over, forty-two youths lay strewn about the field.

Now Joram, son of Ahab, had assumed the throne of Israel after the death of his brother Ahaziah. Joram followed in the ways of his father by doing evil in the eyes of God. But, also like his father, he maintained peaceful and healthy relations with King Jehoshaphat of Judah.

When King Mesha of Moab made war on Israel, Joram sent emissaries to Jehoshaphat asking for aid. "You helped my father in his war against Ramoth-gilead. Now please join me in the fight against Moab."

The king of Judah agreed, and so the two armies assembled and began a ten day march through the wilderness of Edom. But on the seventh day, every water jug was empty. There was not even a sip for the soldiers or the animals.

"What should we do?" Joram cried out. "God has brought us here to defeat us."

"Is there no prophet of God whom we can consult?" Jehoshaphat asked.

One of Joram's officers spoke up. "There's Elisha. He's back in Samaria. He used to be Elijah's student."

Jehoshaphat said, "Yes, he speaks the word of God. Let's summon him."

Joram was reluctant. He knew what happened the last time Jehoshaphat insisted on a prophet of God: Micaiah delivered a deathly message to his father. But he had little choice, so they sent for Elisha.

"Why are you calling on *me*?" Elisha asked Joram. "Why don't you find the prophets of your father Ahab and mother Jezebel? Surely they will tell you what you want to hear."

"No!" Joram retorted. "For it was God who—"

"As surely as the Almighty lives, whom I serve, I wouldn't even be here were it not for my respect for King Jehoshaphat. Now bring me someone who can play the harp." Immediately they obtained a musician from among the troops.

While the melody played, the power of God came upon Elisha, and he prophesied. "This is what God says: This dry land will be filled with pools of water. You will see neither wind nor rain, but this place will be drenched. Furthermore, God will make you victorious over the army of Moab. You will cut down their good trees, stop up their springs, and ruin their good land with stones."

The next day water suddenly appeared. It rippled like a gentle wave through the desert, filling every creek bed, trench, and gulley. Man and beast gulped greedily.

When the armies of Moab looked out and saw the sun shining across the water, it appeared red to them. "It's blood!" they cheered. "The armies of Israel and Judah have turned on each other like squabbling sisters. Let's go collect the plunder."

But when the Moabites drew near, the soldiers of Joram and Jehoshaphat rushed out and attacked them and drove them back. They destroyed Moabite towns, threw stones on their fertile fields, stopped up the springs, and chopped down the trees.

When the king of Moab saw the battle had gone against him, he took his firstborn son and climbed the wall of his palace. There he sacrificed the crown prince as a burnt offering to his god Molech. The smell of charred flesh wafted upward, and the fury against Israel was great, and the soldiers of Joram and Jehoshaphat withdrew.

49. MIRACLES

Elisha walked alone through the soggy desert back to Israel, a solitary man of God under an endless sky. A shawl covered his hairless head from the bright sun. He went to Gilgal, to the house he had shared with his departed master. There he lived, ministering among the company of prophets.

One day, a widow of one of the prophets came to Elisha and said, "As you know, my husband feared God and served you. But now he's dead, and we are in debt and cannot repay it. One of his creditors is threatening to take my two sons as slaves."

"What can I do to help you?" the prophet asked. "Tell me. What do you have in the house?"

"Nothing whatsoever of any value, except maybe a flask of olive oil," she replied.

"Go to your friends and neighbors and borrow as many empty jars as you can," Elisha told her. "Then go into your house with your sons and shut the door. Pour olive oil from your flask into the jars, setting each one aside when it is filled."

She did as Elisha said. She took the first empty container and poured oil from her flask until it was full. Then she did the same with a second and a third. Her sons kept bringing jars to her, and she filled one after another. Soon every container in the house brimmed with olive oil.

"Bring me another jug," she said to her sons.

"There aren't any more."

She looked around the room, dumbstruck. Then she ran to the man of God and fell at his feet in tears.

"Now you can sell the olive oil and pay your debts," he smiled at her. "And there will be plenty left over for you and your sons to live on."

Shortly thereafter, Elisha called his personal servant, a man named Gehazi. "Order the men to gather wood for a large fire. Get the biggest kettle you can find and let's make some bread and stew for everyone in town."

Gehazi, a hefty man with a soft voice, told some of the prophets to fetch logs for a fire and others to collect herbs and vegetables. As one of them was splitting wood, his ax head flew off and landed in a nearby pool of deep water. "Oh, no, I've lost my only blade," he said. "And it was borrowed."

He turned around to go home, and there was Elisha. "Where did it fall?" the senior prophet asked. The man pointed to the place. Elisha took a stick and tossed it into the water at that spot. In a few moments, the ax head surfaced.

"You made it float!" the man exclaimed.

"Now you can finish your work," Elisha said. The man did, and soon a fire was crackling.

Meanwhile, one of the other young men went into the field and filled his cloak with wild gourds for the stew. He diced them and put them in the pot. No one knew what they were, but Gehazi cooked them anyway.

"Taste this," Gehazi said to one of his companions, handing him a spoonful of steaming broth.

The man put it in his mouth and then spewed it forth. "It's poison! Don't eat it."

Elisha came over and said, "Bring me some flour, Gehazi." Gehazi obeyed, and Elisha poured it into the caldron and said, "Now it's fine; go ahead and eat." The man took another bite, and the poison had gone out of the pot.

"But now there's hardly any flour, and we only have twenty loaves of bread," Gehazi observed. "It will be impossible to feed everyone with so little."

"Get the loaves and serve them with the stew," Elisha said.

"But it won't be nearly enough," Gehazi persisted.

"Just do it," Elisha commanded. "For this is what God says: Everyone will eat, and there will even be some left over."

So they called the townspeople and served the food. There was plenty for all and much more besides.

● ● ●

Sometimes God would send Elisha to the king with a message. Other times he sent him to various cities and towns throughout the land. Gehazi usually went with him. When Elisha traveled, he commonly stopped in the village of Shunem and stayed with a wealthy woman who lived there with her husband. She always prepared a delightful meal for the prophet and his servant, and they would enjoy a pleasant evening together.

One day the woman said to her husband, "Elisha is a holy man of God. Let's build a small room upstairs for him, with a bed, table, chair, and lamp. Then he will have a place to stay whenever he comes by." And so they did.

"We appreciate the generosity you've shown to us," Elisha said to the woman on his next visit. "What can we do for you in return? Can we put in a good word to the king on your behalf?"

"No, thank you," she replied. "I have all I need."

That night Elisha asked Gehazi, "What can we do for her?"

Gehazi replied, "Well, as you know, she doesn't have a son, and her husband is an old man."

As they readied to leave the next morning, Elisha said to his host, "Next year at this time you will hold a son in your arms."

"No, my lord!" she cried falling to her knees. "O man of God, don't trick me and get my hopes up like that."

Elisha and Gehazi only waved goodbye.

Sure enough, the woman soon became pregnant and gave birth to a son. The child grew strong, and the woman loved him.

One morning the boy went out to help his father harvest the crops. Suddenly he collapsed clutching his skull. "My head! My head!" he cried out.

"Quick, carry him home to his mother," the father said to a servant.

The servant lugged him back to the house, and the woman wrapped her son's forehead in a cool cloth and gave him water to drink. Then she cradled him in her lap, and the boy went to sleep.

But he never woke up.

Her eyes glazed with tears, the woman carried the child upstairs and laid him on the bed of the man of God. She closed the door gently behind her and sent a message to her husband: "I'm going to Carmel to see Elisha." She saddled a donkey and rode off to the northwest.

The prophet was high on the mountain, not far from the spot where Elijah defeated Jezebel's prophets of Baal. The man of God might have expected to see the queen approaching, for she still had it out for men of God. But as Elisha scanned the countryside, he saw the woman of Shunem bouncing along on her beast of burden.

"Gehazi," he said, "look who's coming." The servant peered down the hillside. "Run to meet her and ask if everything is alright with her and her husband and son."

Gehazi went and called out the greeting.

"Yes," the woman said to him, without slowing down, "everything is fine." She rode directly by him. Gehazi shrugged and turned to follow her up the mountain.

The woman fell to the ground before Elisha and caught hold of his feet. Gehazi reached down and pulled at her shoulder. "Come now," he urged.

But Elisha scolded him. "Leave her alone. She is deeply troubled. But God has hidden the reason from me."

"Did I ask you for a son, my lord?" the Shunammite said to the prophet. "And didn't I tell you not to get my hopes up?"

Elisha's face flickered perceptively. He turned to Gehazi and ordered, "Take my staff and go quickly. Don't talk to anyone along the way. Hurry straight to the boy—he's in the loft in her house—and lay the staff on the child's face."

"In the name of God," the woman swore, "I won't go home unless you go with me."

Elisha motioned Gehazi to go on ahead. Then the prophet went to saddle his mule.

Gehazi ran all the way to Shunem and laid Elisha's staff on the child's face. But nothing happened. There was no sign or sound of life. So he headed back up toward Carmel. About half way, he met Elisha and the woman coming toward him. "The child is still dead," he said.

The two nodded and continued their journey.

When they reached the house, Elisha went upstairs alone and shut the door. He bowed, prayed to God, and stretched himself out upon the child's body, mouth to mouth, eyes to eyes, hands to hands. As he lay there, the boy's body began to grow warm. But he did not stir. Elisha got up, walked back and forth across the room once, and then stretched himself out on the child again. This time the boy sneezed seven times and opened his eyes.

The prophet went to the door and called the woman.

"Here's your son," he said as she entered. She took one look at her boy sitting up on the bed and she bowed to the ground before Elisha. Then she took her son in her arms and carried him downstairs.

50. ELISHA AND THE ENEMY

King Ben-hadad and the nation of Aram to the north of Israel represented a perpetual threat to King Joram and the Israelites. An enduring tension marked the relationship between the two, and bands of raiders were frequently sent out by both rulers—though full-fledged war had been avoided since the reign of Ahab.

At this time, a certain man named Naaman was the commander of Ben-hadad's army. Ben-hadad had great admiration for Naaman, for he was a mighty warrior who won many victories. But the great general suffered from terminal leprosy.

Now it came about that Aramean raiders captured a young Israelite girl and gave her to Naaman's wife as a maid. One day, when Naaman was particularly ill and bedridden, the girl said to her mistress, "I wish my master would go to see the prophet Elisha in my homeland. He would heal him of his leprosy."

The woman told her husband, who in turn told Ben-hadad what the girl said. "May I go to Israel in search of this man," Naaman asked the king.

"Yes, you may," the king replied. "I will send a letter of introduction for you to take to King Joram of Israel."

So Naaman set off carrying gifts of silver and gold and clothing. The note in his hand read: "With this letter I present to you my honored and esteemed servant Naaman. He has come to your land to be cured of his leprosy."

When Joram read the letter, he tore his clothes in dismay. "What does this mean? Am I God? Can I give life and take it away? Ben-hadad is trying to pick a quarrel with me."

"No, my lord," Naaman said meekly. "Elisha. I am here to see Elisha."

"Oh," Joram sobered. "Well, send for Elisha then."

When Elisha received the message, he sent back, "I am here in Samaria. Send Naaman to me, and he will see there is a true prophet in Israel."

So the Aramean commander, with his horses and chariots and sacks of coins and garments, made the short trip to the other side of the capital. He waited at the door of Elisha's house. But the prophet did not come out. Instead, he sent a messenger with this word: "Go and wash yourself seven times in the Jordan River, and your flesh will be healed, and you will be cured of your leprosy."

Naaman threw his hands in the air. "I thought he would surely come out to see me. I expected him to wave his hand over the leprosy and call on the name of his God and heal me. But no, he can't even come out of his house! Aren't the rivers of Aram better than any of the waters in Israel? I could've just gone and washed in one of them."

His servants tried to reason with him. "Sir, if the prophet told you to do some great and difficult thing, wouldn't you have done it?" Naaman was silent. "So why not do this simple thing?" they admonished. "What do you have to lose?"

Naaman went down to the Jordan River, took off his gear, and waded into the muddy water. He slowly bent his knees until his head was covered; then he stood up and looked at his flaky and shriveled arms. He dipped himself again and again. When he emerged from the water the seventh time, his skin was as healthy as that of a young child. He was healed. The leprosy was gone.

Naaman sloshed excitedly to the riverbank and led his entire party back to Elisha's house. "Now I know there is no God in all the world except in Israel," Naaman declared. "Please, O man of God, accept a gift from me, your servant."

Elisha refused. "As surely as God lives, I will take nothing."

"I beg you. Take the goods. I brought them for you."

Elisha shook his head. Naaman pressured him further, but still the prophet would not relent.

"Well," Naaman said finally, "then allow me to take something. May I load two of my mules with earth from this place to take back home. There

I will build an altar to the God of Israel. From now on I will never again make burnt offerings or sacrifices to any other."

"Do as you wish," Elisha replied.

Naaman genuflected gratefully, before adding, "May God mercifully pardon me in this one thing: When my master, King Ben-hadad, goes into the temple of his god to worship, he expects me to join him. Please forgive me when I bow down too."

"Go in peace," said Elisha.

So Naaman headed for home, but not before he gathered two large piles of dirt.

● ● ●

After Naaman and his entourage had traveled some distance, Gehazi, the servant of Elisha, said to himself, My master should not have let this Aramean leave without accepting any of his gifts. I will chase after him and get something from him.

So Gehazi started off after Naaman.

When Naaman saw him coming, he climbed down from his chariot and went to meet him. "Is everything alright?" Naaman asked.

"Yes," Gehazi said, "but my master has sent me to tell you that two visitors have just arrived, and he would like two silver coins and two sets of clothes to give them."

"By all means," Naaman answered cheerfully. He put the money and clothes in two bags and gave them to Gehazi.

Gehazi took the gifts and hid them in his room.

At dinner that evening, Elisha asked his servant, "Where did you go today, Gehazi?"

"I haven't been anywhere."

Elisha eyed him closely. "This is no time to receive money and clothing, olive groves and vineyards, sheep and cattle, and male and female servants."

"I only—"

"Because you have done this, Naaman's leprosy will cling to you and your descendants forever."

When Gehazi finished eating and arose from the table, he was covered with leprosy. His skin was white as snow.

• • •

Shortly after Naaman returned home, King Ben-hadad of Aram grew restless. He was not naturally a man of peace, and, on second thought, he did not particularly care to have his top military man journeying to Israel to be healed—though he was happy for Naaman's sake.

Ben-hadad determined to mobilize his troops for a strike against Israel who was thriving under King Joram and now posed a serious danger to Aram. "I'll attack them," Ben-hadad said, "before they attack me."

But the Israelites were seemingly always one step ahead of Ben-hadad. He would plan to draw up his troops in one place for a surprise raid only to discover Israel had fortified its border at just that spot. Or he would put soldiers in a location where they could ambush unsuspecting Israelites only to learn that, suddenly, no more Israelites passed that way.

Eventually, Ben-hadad became very upset and suspicious. He called his officers together and demanded, "Which of you is the traitor? Who has been informing King Joram of our plans?"

No one answered; a few looked in Naaman's direction.

Then one of them spoke up. "It's Elisha, the prophet in Israel, the one who healed Naaman. It's Elisha who tells the king of Israel every word you speak, even what you say in the privacy of your own room."

"Elisha," the king said pensively. "Then let's find out where he is, so we can send troops to seize him."

They sent spies who soon returned with news: "Elisha is in Dothan."

The next night the king of Aram sent a large contingent of soldiers with many chariots and horses to surround the city of Dothan.

Gehazi was the first to arise the following morning. He dragged his pale flesh to the window and peered out. "Oh, no!" he shrieked. "The city is surrounded. There are soldiers everywhere."

Elisha sat up in bed. "Don't be afraid," he said easily. "For there are more on our side than on theirs."

"What?" Gehazi frowned. "Come look at this."

Elisha bowed his head and prayed, "O God, open his eyes and let him see."

God opened Gehazi's eyes, and he saw the city filled with horses and chariots of fire around Elisha.

Elisha prayed once more. "God, please make these Aramean soldiers blind." So God struck them with blindness.

At once the prophet dressed, took Gehazi by the arm, and went out to the city gate. "You have come to the wrong place," he shouted to the Aramean army. "This isn't the right city. Follow me, and I will take you to the man you're looking for."

Elisha told the blind men to join hands, and he led them south to the city of Samaria. When they entered the capital, the prophet cried loudly, "O God, now open their eyes and let them see." God did as Elisha asked.

The Arameans looked up, and there before them was the king of Israel.

"Should I kill them? Should I kill them?" King Joram blurted eagerly to Elisha.

"No," answered Elisha. "Even if you'd captured them with your own sword and spear, would you've slaughtered them? How much less men who have been led sightless into your own city. Instead, give them food and drink and send them home to Ben-hadad."

Joram obediently made a great feast, and they ate and drank, and then went back to Aram.

● ● ●

Ben-hadad simmered with rage. Elisha had humiliated his men. He could not bear the thought of being outwitted, outdone, by one measly prophet.

To satisfy his anger, Ben-hadad mustered his troops and besieged Samaria. The army surrounded the city and cut off every supply of food and every channel of water. "Now let's see how much feasting there will be in Samaria," Ben-hadad laughed.

There was no feasting, only famine—severe famine as the siege wore on. Food became so sparse that a donkey's head sold for eighty pieces of silver, and a cup of dove's dung for five pieces.

King Joram's spirit dwindled. As he meandered through the city one day, a woman called out to him, "Please help me, my lord the king."

"If God doesn't help you, what can I do?" Joram replied. "I have no food or water to give you." He looked pitifully at the bony woman and then added, "What's the matter?"

She answered, "This woman said to me, 'Let's kill and eat your son today, then we'll eat my son tomorrow so we won't die of starvation.' So we cooked my son and ate him. Then the next day I said to her, 'Kill your son so we can eat him,' but now she's hidden her boy, and I am faint with hunger."

When the king heard this, he tore his clothes in despair. And his despair needed a scapegoat. "May God kill me if Elisha's head remains on his shoulders by sundown! For this is all his fault."

Elisha sat in his house with some companions and he said to them, "A murderer is coming to cut off my head." Soon, Joram and his men knocked on the door. Elisha arose and opened it. Standing on the threshold, the prophet declared, "This is what God says: By this time tomorrow, five quarts of premium flour will sell for only one piece of silver, and ten quarts of barley grain for the same price."

The king's chief attendant chuckled. "That couldn't happen even if God opened the windows of heaven."

"You will see it with your own eyes," Elisha replied. "But you won't eat of it."

● ● ●

Now there were four men with leprosy who would sit outside the city gates of Samaria and beg for food. "Why should we stay here and perish?" they asked each other. "We might as well surrender to the Arameans. Maybe they will give us something to eat and we will live. If they kill us, we've lost nothing."

At twilight they set out for the enemy camp. As they drew near, they could see no movement. They could hear no noise. "Very strange," they whispered to one another. They kept moving cautiously forward, step by step, their hands raised in surrender. Finally, they came to the edge of the camp. No one was there! The place was deserted. For God had caused Ben-hadad's army to hear the clatter of a thousand chariots and the galloping of ten thousand horses and the sounds of a mighty army approaching. They had panicked and fled into the night, abandoning their tents, horses, donkeys, and everything else.

The four Israelite lepers stared in stunned silence. They crept into one tent after another, devouring food still on plates and drinking wine from half empty jugs. They exchanged their rags for beautiful garments; they stuffed their pockets with gold and silver; they laughed and danced in the moonlight. Eventually, they said to each other, "This is not right. This is a day of victory and celebration for all. If we wait until morning, some calamity will certainly fall upon us. Come on, we must return to Samaria and tell everyone."

They ran jubilantly back to the city and informed a night watchman. The guard immediately went to the palace with the information.

King Joram awakened his counselors and conferred with them. "I will tell you what has happened," he said. "The Arameans know we are starving, so they've abandoned their camp and hidden in the fields. They're trying to lure us from the city. When we come out, they will ambush us and burn our citadel."

One of the advisors replied, "Yes, we need to send out scouts first. We cannot trust the word of four beggars. We have five healthy horses left. Send them out with two chariots. If they don't come back, it won't be any worse than if they'd stayed here."

So King Joram ordered a reconnaissance mission. It slipped out of the sleeping capital and went toward the enemy base. They found it just as had been reported: vacant. The scouts went all the way to the Jordan River, following a trail of strewn clothing and equipment the Arameans had jettisoned in their confused escape.

Just before sunrise, the news was shouted throughout the city of Samaria. The people awoke, rushed out, and plundered the Aramean camp. So it came to pass that five quarts of premium flour sold that day for only one piece of silver, and ten quarts of barley grain for the same price.

King Joram's chief attendant was stationed at the gate of Samaria. As the starving Israelites stampeded forth, he was knocked down and trampled to death. He had witnessed Samaria's salvation, but he did not taste of it.

• • •

When Ben-hadad saw his army hurtling toward Damascus, his capital city, he was distraught. "The Israelites must have hired the Egyptians to attack us," his generals told him. "We heard the sounds of a massive army coming and we fled in fear." At this, Ben-hadad fell into a deep depression, which soon wracked his entire body with disease.

When the pain became unbearable, the king said to his personal servant, Hazael, "Take a large gift and go find Elisha, the prophet from Israel whom I despise, but must respect. Ask him to consult God to see if I will recover from this illness."

Hazael went, taking with him forty camel-loads of the finest wares of Damascus. He did not have to go far, for Elisha, as it were, was on the way to Aram. Hazael bowed before him and said, "Your servant Ben-hadad sent me to ask you if he will recover from his sickness."

Elisha dabbed at the sweat on his neck and looked Hazael up and down. Then he answered, "Go and say to him, 'You will certainly recover.' However, God has revealed to me that he will in fact die." Hazael pulled back, perplexed. The prophet continued to stare at him until Hazael was embarrassed. Then the man of God began to weep.

"Why are you crying?" asked Hazael.

"Because I know the harm you will do to the Israelites," Elisha managed to say. "You will set fire to their fortified places, kill their young men with the sword, dash their little children to the ground, and rip open their pregnant women."

Hazael recoiled. "How could I, a mere dog, accomplish such a thing?"

"God has shown me that you will become king of Aram," answered Elisha.

Hazael trembled at this word. Then, in a daze, he went back to Damascus. Elisha looked through blurry eyes at the forty camels still standing beside the road.

"What did Elisha say to you?" Ben-hadad asked when Hazael came in.

"He assured me that you would get well," Hazael replied. The king heaved a sigh of relief.

The next day, as Ben-hadad napped in his private chambers, Hazael took a thick cloth, soaked it in water, and spread it over the king's face, suffocating him to death.

Then Hazael summoned the military officers and proclaimed himself king.

51. TREASON

While all this had been taking place in the kingdoms of Israel and Aram, life in the southern kingdom of Judah plodded along. Judah was not only a smaller nation, but it was also protected by Israel to the north, the Sinai desert to the south, and the great Mediterranean Sea to the west. As a result, it was not the target of attacks from surrounding nations like its sister kingdom. Although not as rich or prosperous, Judah was blessed to have the sons of David sitting on the throne in Jerusalem, even if they did not always please God.

At this time, Ahaziah was the king of Judah. He and King Joram of Israel were on good terms, so when Ahaziah learned Joram had been wounded in battle, he journeyed north to see his friend.

Now Elisha was meeting with the company of prophets of God and he said to one of the young men, "Tuck your cloak into your belt and get ready to run. Take this flask of olive oil with you and go to Ramoth-gilead. There the army of Joram is locked in battle against King Hazael of Aram. Joram himself has been injured, and they've transported him back to his palace in Jezreel to rest. It is indeed the beginning of the end for Joram.

"Your task is to find the Israelite military commander name Jehu. Call him to a private place and pour the oil over his head and say: 'God has anointed you the king over Israel.' Then run for your life."

The young man took the flask and hurried out. When he arrived in Ramoth-gilead, he went to the generals' quarters. "I have a message for you, commander," he said, looking at no one in particular.

"For who?" one of them asked.

"For Jehu," the prophet replied.

Jehu looked around at the others, then slowly arose and went with the prophet into another shelter. The young man of God put his hand on Jehu's shoulder, pushed him down to one knee, and declared. "This is what the God of Israel says: I anoint you king over my people Israel." Then he emptied the oil on his hair.

Jehu shut his eyes and wiped his face as the prophet continued speaking: "You are to destroy the family of Ahab, beginning with his son, King Joram. By this means, I, the God of Israel, will avenge the blood of my prophets and the blood of my servants shed by Jezebel. The whole family of Ahab must be purged from the earth. I will cut off every one of his male descendants—slave or free. I will eliminate the family of Ahab like the families of Jeroboam and Baasha. As for Queen Jezebel, dogs will devour her in Jezreel, and no one will bury her."

Then the young prophet opened the door and fled.

Jehu went back to his fellow officers who asked him, "What did that madman want? Is everything alright?"

"Yeah, it was nothing," Jehu brushed them off.

"You're hiding something," they said, watching him closely. "Tell us what he said."

Jehu looked at each man in turn. "He anointed me king over Israel," he said resolutely. The other commanders quickly spread out their cloaks on the bare steps. They blew the trumpet and shouted, "Jehu is king!"

● ● ●

So it was that Jehu led a conspiracy against King Joram. The upstart mounted his chariot and rode to Jezreel to find the king.

The watchman on the tower of the palace saw the cloud of dust. He shouted to the king, "I see a band of troops coming!"

Joram was in a corner room talking with his mother Jezebel and his visiting friend and ally King Ahaziah of Judah. When they heard the watchman, the pulse of the two kings quickened. "Send out a horseman to ask if they are coming in peace," Joram ordered.

A horseman rode forth and said, "The king wants to know if you are coming in peace."

"What do you know about peace?" Jehu replied. "Fall in behind me."

The watchman called out to the king, "The messenger went out and spoke with them. But now he's joined them. He's riding with them!"

"Send a second horseman," Jezebel commanded brusquely. So another one was dispatched.

"The king wants to know if you come in peace," the rider said to Jehu.

Again Jehu answered, "What do you know about peace? Fall in behind me."

The watchman exclaimed, "The second messenger has met them, and now he too has fallen in behind them! It looks like it's Jehu, for he's driving like a madman."

The queen snapped upright. "Jehu? Our own forces?"

"Yes, Israelites," confirmed the lookout.

"I will handle this," Joram said. "Hitch up my chariot and Ahaziah's chariot."

Straightway, the king of Israel and the king of Judah rode out to meet Jehu, while Jezebel went to an upper room in the palace to observe. The two rulers came to Jehu at the plot of land that had belonged to Naboth. King Joram demanded, "Do you come in peace, Jehu?"

The grim commander replied, "How can there be peace when the land is filled with the idolatry and witchcraft of your mother Jezebel? She has turned this nation into a whore who worships any god that passes by."

Suddenly Jehu and his men raised their swords in unison.

Joram wheeled his chariot around and fled, shouting to King Ahaziah, "Treason, Ahaziah! Treason! Run for your life!"

Jehu drew an arrow from his quiver and pulled it taut in his bow. It sailed through the air in a spectacular arc and sank into Joram's back between the shoulder blades. He sank down dead in his chariot, and as the horses raced along his body bounced to the ground.

Jehu turned to the warrior next to him and said, "Go pick him up and throw him into the vineyard over there. For God has finally avenged the blood of Naboth spilled by his father Ahab and his mother Jezebel."

King Ahaziah, too, whipped his chariot around and fled.

"Shoot him," Jehu ordered.

His men looked at him in surprise. "That's the king of Judah," one of them said. "What does he have to do with anything? Why kill him?"

"Shoot him," Jehu repeated. So they pursued and pierced him with arrows until he was dead.

Jezebel watched the unfolding coup from an upper window in the palace. When she saw Jehu turn his chariot toward her, she retreated to an adjacent room where she sat down at a table with ointments and powders. She dabbed makeup on her face and drew lines on her eyelids. She coiled her long hair onto her head and splashed on perfumes. Then she returned to the window, threw open the lattice, and stood there.

As Jehu entered the gate of the palace, she called down to him in a thick voice, "Do you come in peace, you murderer?"

Jehu looked up and saw her. He gazed for a moment and then cried out, "Who is on my side? Who?"

Instantly, three eunuchs stood at the window next to Jezebel. "Throw her down!" Jehu yelled. The eunuchs grabbed the queen mother, one on either side and one behind her. Together they lifted and set her on the edge, then pushed her out. She dropped without a sound, turning once in the air and smashing her head on the pavement. Blood spattered on the wall. Jehu tugged on his horse's reigns, and the animal trotted over and trampled Jezebel's body until its legs were drenched in red.

Then Jehu and his men went into the palace and they ate and drank. On their way out, Jehu said, "Someone bury that cursed woman, for she is royalty after all." But when they went to the place where she had fallen, they found only her skull, her feet, and her hands.

"Dogs must've eaten her," Jehu said, "just as Elijah, the prophet of God, foretold long ago. She's been scattered like dung on the ground."

● ● ●

Jehu was now the king—at least in Jezreel. In order to consolidate his coup and establish control of the kingdom of Israel he would need to take Samaria, the powerful and original capital of Israel where Ahab's descendants held sway.

Now Jehu was not royalty; he was not nobility. He was a brutal boor, a man of the sword only. Fittingly, then, he sent a message to the elders and officials of Samaria. "Crown one of Joram's sons as king," he said. "You have a fortified city, as well as chariots, horses, and weapons. Arm yourselves and prepare to defend Joram's honor and the dynasty of his father Ahab."

The leaders of Samaria sent word back. "We know you've killed two kings. We are powerless before you and the military. We will not put one of Joram's sons on the throne. We are your servants and will do anything you tell us."

Jehu responded: "If you support me as the new king and intend to obey me, then do this: Bring the heads of the seventy sons and grandsons of Joram to me at Jezreel by this time tomorrow."

So the people of Samaria rounded up Joram's offspring, from toddlers to grown men. They bound their hands behind their backs and sliced off their heads one by one. They placed the bloody heads in baskets and sent them to Jezreel.

"Dump them out and pile them in two heaps on either side of the city gate," Jehu ordered. "And leave them there until tomorrow morning."

They did, and flies swarmed on the rotting and foul flesh.

The next day, Jehu went out and spoke to the crowd gathered around the ghastly sight. "I am the one who conspired against Joram and assassinated him," he declared. "But who decapitated all these people? Not me, but rather the citizens of Samaria, for they now recognize my kingship. You can rest assured the word of God spoken through Elijah concerning the descendants of Ahab will not fail."

"Long live King Jehu!" the people shouted.

That very night, Jehu's army slaughtered all Ahab's relatives who were living in Jezreel, as well as his officials, his friends, and his priests. So Ahab was left without a single survivor.

As Jehu set out to take control of Samaria, he met a group he did not recognize. "Who are you?" he asked them.

"We are relatives of King Ahaziah of Judah, God rest his soul," they replied. "We are going to visit the sons of King Ahab and Queen Jezebel. And who are you?"

"Take them alive," Jehu commanded. So his armed soldiers seized all forty-two of them and hacked them to pieces there on the roadside.

With the throne securely in his hands, Jehu called together the people of Samaria and said to them, "Ahab and Jezebel worshiped Baal a little; I will worship him much. Now summon the prophets and priests of Baal. See to it that every one of them comes—whoever does not will be put to death—for I am going to offer a magnificent sacrifice to the great storm god."

Accordingly, messengers were sent to the clergy of Baal throughout the land. The priests journeyed to the capital and crowded into the temple of Baal until it was full from one end to the other. Not one of them was missing. Each was adorned in their sacred vestments.

"Go through the hall and make sure no one who worships God is here," Jehu instructed his officers. "Then station yourselves outside the building and wait for my command."

When they had done so, Jehu approached the altar and sacrificed a burnt offering to Baal. As the smoke ascended and the men chanted and danced, Jehu stepped outside. "Go in and slay all of them," he said to his guards. "If anyone escapes, you will pay with your own life."

The guards drew their swords, stormed the temple, and slashed and gored to death everyone inside. Shrieks and screams mixed with pools of blood in mad chaos. When it was over, every prophet and priest of Baal lay dead. Jehu's soldiers dragged the corpses outside and then entered the inner shrine of the temple and smashed it to pieces. They hauled out the sacred stone of Baal and urinated on it.

And so Jehu destroyed every trace of Baal worship from Israel. Queen Jezebel was dead and so was her foreign god.

52. ISRAEL DESTROYED

Down in the nation of Judah, the queen was not dead. In fact, she was on the throne. When King Ahaziah was killed by Jehu, Ahaziah's mother, Athaliah, took control of the Davidic kingdom. She won the support of the military and then ruthlessly and systematically eliminated the entire royal family—except for one: Joash, a newborn baby who a priest of God by the name of Jehoida managed to steal away and keep hidden in Solomon's temple for six years while Athaliah ruled the land.

In the seventh year of her reign, Jehoida summoned five of the top army men to the temple in Jerusalem and showed them the boy Joash. They were astounded, and then persuaded by Jehoida to support Joash as king.

On the next Sabbath day, Jehoida led Joash to the altar in the temple. The throng of people in the courtyard looked on curiously as the five generals stationed themselves around the youth with their swords drawn. Jehoida raised his priestly flask and poured oil on the boy. He then placed a crown on his head and shouted, "Long live King Joash!" The crowd echoed the refrain, rejoicing and singing and blowing trumpets.

When Queen Athaliah heard the commotion, she rushed to the temple. There was the boy king. She tore her robes and cried out, "Treason! Treason!"

Jehoida gave a signal, and the troops charged at the queen. She turned and fled in her royal chariot back toward the palace. But they caught her, pulled her down, and executed her on the spot.

Jehoida, in turn, led a grand procession of prophets, priests, and warriors to the palace. There they placed Joash on the throne, and Judah had a new ruler. He was eight years old.

Joash grew into a good and righteous king who devoted countless resources to renovating the temple of God. But in time, he too was assassinated, and his son Amaziah was crowned king.

● ● ●

After King Jehu of Israel died, his son Jehoahaz succeeded him as king, followed by his son, Jehoash. These peaceful transitions of power created stability and security in the northern kingdom. But problems remained. Although Baal worship had been expunged, the people of Israel continued to bow down to the golden calves set up by Jeroboam years before. This angered God greatly, and so he punished them by the oppressive hand of the Arameans who reduced Israel's military strength, without taking over altogether.

God continued to speak to the king and people through his prophets, but with little success. Elisha had led these prophets for years, but now he was old and tired and dying. King Jehoash went to visit him in his house, for the prophet could no longer travel.

The withered man of God and the young ruler talked for a long while. "The Arameans have been a thorn in Israel's side because of her sin," Elisha said. "But God has been gracious and compassionate toward his people because of his covenant with Abraham, Isaac, and Jacob. That covenant is what has sustained this kingdom; it is the reason God has not destroyed Israel or banished them from his presence."

Jehoash listened.

"Open this window to the east," Elisha barked abruptly, gesturing to his left.

The king stood at attention and quickly obeyed.

"Get a bow and some arrows," Elisha called. So the king went outside to his chariot and retrieved the weapons. "Take the bow in your hand," Elisha instructed. The king drew his bow, faced the open window, and waited. Elisha pulled himself to his feet and placed his own hands on the king's hands. "Shoot," Elisha commanded.

Jehoash released, and the arrow whizzed out of the house into the open sky.

"God's arrow of victory!" Elisha proclaimed. "The arrow of victory over Aram, for you will completely destroy the Arameans."

Then the man of God said, "Pick up the other arrows and strike them against the ground." So the king clenched a handful of arrows and banged them on the floor three times.

Instantly, Elisha's countenance dimmed. "You should've struck the ground five or six times. Then you would've beaten Aram until it was entirely shattered. Now you will only be partially victorious."

Jehoash's shoulders slumped as the prophet shooed him out.

Two days later, Elisha died and was buried in a nondescript tomb in the cleft of a rock. Months later, some Israelites unwittingly threw a corpse into the same tomb. When the body rolled over Elisha's bones, the dead man revived and jumped to his feet. The prophet had passed, but his power had not.

● ● ●

Jehoash successfully defeated the armies of Aram—in exactly three battles—and thus regained control of several important cities. Jehoash also entered into war with King Amaziah of Judah, who, after certain military successes of his own, sent a message to Jehoash. "Come and meet me face to face in battle."

Jehoash replied to him with a parable: "In the mountains of Lebanon, a tiny thistle sent a message to a mighty cedar tree: 'Give your daughter in marriage to my son.' But just then a wild beast came along and stepped on the thistle, crushing it.

"You, King Amaziah, have indeed overpowered Edom, and now you are arrogant. Be happy with your victory and do not pick fights with kings you cannot defeat. Why ask for trouble that will only cause your downfall and the destruction of the people of Judah?"

But Amaziah did not withdraw his taunts, so Jehoash mobilized his army and easily routed the forces of Judah. Then he marched to Jerusalem and demolished six hundred feet of the wall around the capital city. Jehoash also ransacked the palace and the temple of God, carrying off gold and silver, and he took hostage Judean dignitaries and officials.

And so the years of peace between the two kingdoms of Abraham came to an end.

● ● ●

After Jehoash's death, his son Jeroboam reigned as king over Israel. Jeroboam followed the ways of the first king of Israel—with whom he shared a name—by promoting the worship of false gods and graven images. Every Israelite king thereafter would do the same, though not every one of them died in peace as Jeroboam did.

Jeroboam's son Zechariah ruled after him until he was assassinated by a man named Shallum, who reigned one month before he himself was murdered by a certain Menahem.

During Menahem's rule, the mighty nation of Assyria invaded Israel. Menahem, fearing for the safety of his relatively tiny kingdom, paid a large tribute to the Assyrian ruler in order to keep the peace. This required a heavy tax on the people of Israel. When Menahem died, his son Pekahiah became king; but he was soon killed by one of his chief officers, Pekah.

Pekah joined the king of Aram in a revolt against the Assyrian empire, which provoked the huge northern power to conquer a large portion of Israel's territory and deport many of its people. A growing faction in Israel favored a policy of cooperation or submission to the Assyrians, as Menahem had done. Thus it was not long before internal squabbling erupted in Samaria, and Pekah was killed. Hoshea then became king.

Hoshea surrendered to the Assyrians and again bought peace with a sizable tribute. But when the king of Assyria died, Hoshea thought he might, with the help of armies from Egypt, break free from the oppressive yolk of foreign occupation. So he stopped sending payments to Assyria.

The new ruler of Assyria, Shalmaneser, wasted little time in responding to the rebellion. He marched west and attacked Israel who received no aid from the Egyptians. Shalmaneser rolled easily through the land, until only Samaria remained. He laid siege to the well-fortified capital. For three years Hoshea held out. But then on a hot summer day, the Assyrians stormed in and took the city. They arrested Hoshea, the elders, officials, and nobles, and carried them away to Assyria.

The nation of Israel was no more.

God's patience finally ran out. The people of Israel had worshipped other gods for too long. They sinned against their God who brought them out of bondage in Egypt and delivered them into a land of milk and honey. They polluted that good land with their idolatry, and they failed to heed God's repeated warnings sent through the mouths of prophets. They were stubborn; they would not listen.

They rejected God's first two commandments: You shall have no other gods besides me. You shall not make for yourself an idol of any kind or an image of anything in the heavens or on the earth or in the seas. Instead, Israel fashioned two calves made from metal and bowed down to them. They served Baal and Asherah. They even sacrificed their own sons and daughters in the fire. They broke their covenant with God. Therefore God was angry and broke his covenant with them and wiped them from the face of the earth with the hand of Assyria.

53. TWO GOOD KINGS AND ONE VERY BAD

Only the kingdom of Judah remained now, and even Judah did not keep the commandments of God. After King Amaziah died, his son Azariah ruled. God afflicted him with leprosy until the day of his death, whereupon his son Jotham succeeded him. Then came Ahaz who walked in the ways of the kings of Israel, which included offering his own children as burnt offerings, like the detestable practices of the surrounding peoples.

Next, Hezekiah became king, and he did what was pleasing in God's sight. He destroyed the shrines to foreign gods, cut down the Asherah poles, and committed his people to serve God alone. There had never before been a king like him. He remained faithful to God in everything, and he carefully obeyed all the words God gave to Moses. So God was with him, and Hezekiah was successful in all that he did.

But his life was not without its trials. The Assyrian army launched a sustained and prolonged attack on the land of Judah. To make matters worse, Hezekiah became deathly ill during the ordeal.

God sent a prophet named Isaiah to visit him. Isaiah entered the king's room and stared at the thin, sallow man lying in the bed, boils festering on his limbs and face. Then, like Elijah and Elisha prior to him, the man of God delivered the word of God to the king. "This is what God says," Isaiah declared. "Set the affairs of your house in order, for you are about to die. You will not recover from this sickness."

Hezekiah clenched himself into a ball and rolled to the side, facing the opposite wall. "Remember, O God," he cried out, "how I've always been faithful to you and served you wholeheartedly and tried to do what is right in your eyes. Please . . ." his voice trailed off and he wept bitterly.

Isaiah looked on in icy silence and then walked out. But before he left the palace courtyard, a word from God came to him. "Go back to Hezekiah and say to him: The God of your ancestor David has heard your prayer and seen your tears. He will heal you. Three days from now you will arise and be restored. Moreover, God declares that he will rescue you and Jerusalem from the king of Assyria. He will defend this place for his own honor and for the sake of David."

Isaiah whirled around and returned to Hezekiah with the message. When the king heard it, his hands and lips began to tremble. Then the prophet spoke again. "Make an ointment from figs."

Hezekiah's servants obeyed and they spread the balm on the king's skin. Hezekiah looked up at the prophet and asked, "What sign will God give to prove he will heal me and defend our capital?"

Isaiah replied without hesitation. "Would you like the shadow on the sundial to go forward ten steps or backward ten steps?"

"The shadow always moves forward. So, of course, make it go back ten steps instead."

Isaiah called upon God, and God caused the shadow to retreat ten steps. Hezekiah was dumbfounded; he fell to his knees in gratitude and belief.

On the morning of the third day, the boils vanished.

● ● ●

Now it happened earlier in Hezekiah's reign that he offered a large tribute to the Assyrians to keep them from overrunning his country, like they had done to the nation of Israel. But now, after hearing Isaiah's promise of divine protection for Jerusalem, Hezekiah was no longer willing to accept his vassalage. So he revolted.

King Sennacherib, the new ruler of Assyria, immediately dispatched his chief officer, supreme commander, field general, and a huge army to Jerusalem. The Assyrians took up a position just outside the Judean capital.

Hezekiah sent three palace officials to negotiate with them: Eliakim, Shebna, and Joah. They stationed themselves at the entrance to the city gate. A large crowd gathered on the wall above.

The Assyrian field general stepped forward and said in a loud voice, "This is what the great king of Assyria says to King Hezekiah of Judah: What are you trusting in that makes you so confident? You claim to have great military strength, but we both know those are merely empty words. Surely your rebellion is based on the hope of receiving aid from another king. But who are you counting on? Egypt? If you lean on Pharaoh, he will be like a reed that snaps in two and pierces your hand. Look, if you need some help, I myself can give you two thousand horses—if you have enough riders for them." He chuckled, looking around at his comrades.

"Come now, Hezekiah, and be reasonable," he continued soberly. "Make a deal with us. You have no other choice. Your whole army couldn't even defeat our weakest contingent. And besides, do you think we've come to your land without instructions from your God? God himself told us to attack this city and destroy it."

Eliakim called out, "Please negotiate properly by speaking to us in Aramaic. Don't speak in Hebrew which our people here can understand."

Sennacherib's general answered, still in Hebrew, "Do you think this message is only for you and your king? No. It's for all your people, for when we lay siege to this city, they too will be so hungry and thirsty that they will eat their own dung and drink their own urine."

Then he looked up at the people on the wall and shouted, "This is what the great king of Assyria says to you: Don't let Hezekiah deceive you. He cannot rescue you from my power. Don't let him dupe you in to trusting your God. Have the gods of any other nations saved them from the king of Assyria? What happened to the gods of Hamath and Arpad, Hena and Ivvah? And what happened to your God when we destroyed Samaria and the kingdom of Israel? He didn't save his people then, did he? So why do you think he will save Jerusalem now?

"Here is what you must do: Surrender peacefully to us, and then each of you can continue eating from your own grapevine and fig tree and drinking from your own well. Some of you we might take to another land—but it will be a land of grain and new wine, bread and vineyards, olive trees and honey. Choose life, not death."

Not one person on the wall spoke; no one moved. There wasn't a sound.

Eliakim, Shebna, and Joah turned quietly and went to the palace.

When King Hezekiah heard their report, he rent his clothes. "Go find Isaiah," he said to them, "and tell him that today is a day of trouble, insults, and disgrace. It is like when a baby is ready to be born, but the mother has no strength to deliver it. Perhaps God heard the words of this Assyrian, and will deal with them accordingly."

So the officials delivered the king's message to Isaiah. The prophet disappeared into an inner room of his house and then returned a while later. "This is what God says to Hezekiah: Do not be afraid of this blasphemous speech against me. I will defend Jerusalem and protect it—for my own honor and for the sake of my servant David. Listen, I myself will move against the king of Assyria, and I will see to it he returns to his own country, and there I will have him cut down with the sword."

Hezekiah's men knelt to the ground.

Isaiah continued, "Here is God's message to Sennacherib: Who is it you have defied and ridiculed? Against whom did you raise your voice? Who did you look at with such haughty eyes? It was I, the Holy One of Israel! And now, because of your arrogant spirit and your raging against me, I will put my hook in your nose and my bit in your mouth, and I will make you return home by the same road on which you came."

Hezekiah, meanwhile, went to the temple and prayed, "O God, you alone are God of all the kingdoms of the earth. You alone created the heavens and the earth. Hear, O God, and listen to Sennacherib's words of defiance against you.

"It is true, O God, the kings of Assyria have laid waste countless nations and thrown their gods into the fire and burned them. But they were not gods at all—only idols of wood and stone fashioned by human hands. Now rescue us from the hand of Assyria, so all the kingdoms of the earth will know you alone are the true God."

Then Hezekiah arose and returned to the palace where Eliakim, Shebna, and Joah told him what Isaiah said. The four men embraced one another before retiring to their quarters, for it was late in the day.

That night the angel of God went forth and killed one hundred eighty-five thousand Assyrian soldiers. The next morning, the Assyrian officers awoke to find corpses everywhere. They went through their camp, poking one body after another for any sign of breath. There was none. They had all perished silently in their sleep.

So King Sennacherib withdrew to his own land. Not long thereafter, as he worshipped in the temple of his god, one of his men drove a dagger through his back. Thus Sennacherib died, cut down by the sword.

● ● ●

When King Hezekiah's life came to an end, his son Manasseh took the throne. He enjoyed a long, peaceful reign, even though he did evil in God's sight by following the abominable practices of the surrounding nations. Manasseh repudiated the reforms of his father. He rebuilt the shrines to foreign gods, reconstructed altars to Baal, and re-erected Asherah poles. He even placed some of these pagan altars in the temple of God. He added to the numbers of strange gods in Jerusalem by paying homage to the astral deities of the Assyrians. He sacrificed his own son in the fire and murdered many people until the capital was filled from wall to wall with innocent blood.

So God sent this message through the prophets: "I will bring such disaster on Jerusalem and Judah that the ears of those who hear it will tingle with horror. I will judge this nation and city in the same way I judged Israel and Samaria. I will wipe away the people of Jerusalem as one wipes a dish and turns it upside down. I will reject my own people and I will hand them over as plunder to their enemies. For they have done great evil in my sight and have angered me ever since their ancestors came out of Egypt."

But God did not carry out his word in Manasseh's day, and so the king died old and full of years, and his son Amon succeeded him. Amon continued the wicked ways of his father, welcoming and worshipping the gods of Canaan, until his officials conspired against him and assassinated him and put his young son Josiah on the throne.

● ● ●

Like his great grandfather Hezekiah, King Josiah did what was right in the eyes of God. He cleansed the temple of the pagan altars and oversaw major improvements to God's dwelling place. He took the articles used to worship Baal, Asherah, and the foreign gods and burnt them outside Jerusalem. He ground the ashes to dust and threw the dust over the graves of common folks.

Then Josiah went throughout the land destroying every altar to a pagan deity. He smashed them to pieces and desecrated the places where they had stood by scattering human bones over them. He even went into the territories of the former northern kingdom Israel and demolished the adulterous shrines still in use there. He executed the priests of these shrines on their own altars.

When he came to the city of Bethel and saw the golden calf Jeroboam had fashioned years earlier, he fumed with ire. "Dig up those graves!" he bellowed, pointing to the tombs on a nearby hillside. Soon he held a bag of skulls and long white bones and hip sockets. He ascended the altar near the graven calf and emptied the bag on it. Then he set it on fire. Thus Josiah defiled the altar in Bethel, just as the man of God from Judah had predicted centuries ago.

• • •

While the high priest Hilkiah was repairing and purging the temple of God in Jerusalem under Josiah's direction, he found the Book of the Law written on a long scroll, wedged between two stones in a dusty corner. He stood there holding the parchment in his hand, rigid with astonishment. He called Shaphan, the king's secretary, who began to read it silently. Then Shaphan spun and hurried to the king.

"Look at this," he said, holding up the scroll. "Hilkiah just uncovered it."

"What is it? And what does it say?" Josiah asked.

Shaphan began to read aloud the ancient statutes of the covenant of God, the holy code given to Moses on Mount Sinai generations ago. The old words echoed through the chambers. When Josiah heard them, he tore his clothes and wept. "Great is the wrath of God! For our fathers have not obeyed the words of this book. And we are not living in accordance with what was written by the finger of God."

The scroll quivered in Shaphan's hands.

"Go to the prophets and ask them what God would have us do," the king said to his secretary. So Shaphan gathered Hilkiah and other officials and they went to the prophetess Huldah. They found her sitting in a dimly lit corner of her house.

"This is what God says," she pronounced to the group of somber men huddled before her. "I am going to bring disaster on this city and its people. I will banish Judah from my presence just as I banished Israel. And I will reject my chosen city Jerusalem and the temple where my name was to be honored. For my people have abandoned me and offered sacrifices to strange gods. My anger burns against this place for all the wicked things Manasseh and others have done, and it will not be quenched."

Huldah took a breath. "But go back to Josiah," she continued slowly, "and tell him that because he has humbled himself and been a good and righteous king, God will not unleash the disaster until after he's dead and buried in peace. No, Josiah won't see the destruction that God will wreak on this nation."

The men turned and walked with heavy steps back to the palace and delivered the message. Josiah received it stoically. Then he summoned to the temple courtyard all the elders, priests, prophets, and people of Judah, from the least to the greatest. There he took a stand by the pillars and read to them the entire Book of the Law of Moses. When he finished, he pledged to keep every one of its commands, laws, and decrees. He then bade the whole assembly to renew and reaffirm the covenant with him. This they did in verbal unison. And so the nation of Judah bound themselves once again to the covenant of God.

54. FINAL DEFEAT

It happened during Josiah's reign that the Assyrian empire began to crumble as a new empire rose to power: Babylon. The Assyrians retreated and regrouped for one last stand against the Babylonians. They sent word to Pharaoh Neco of Egypt asking for help, and he complied. Neco mustered an enormous army and marched northeast out of Egypt to form a coalition with the Assyrians. He would have to pass through Josiah's kingdom in order to reach them.

When Josiah received news of the massive forces approaching from the south, he rushed his armies out to Megiddo to block Neco's passage.

Neco sent a message to Josiah, saying, "I am not here to fight against you. I am on my way to battle the Babylonians. Please let me pass through."

But Josiah did not withdraw. Instead, he led his soldiers into war against the Egyptians. During the battle, a marksman drew his bow and shot Josiah in the back, and the king fell dead in his chariot. The army of Judah fled to Jerusalem where they buried King Josiah. He was thirty-nine years old.

Josiah's son Jehoiakim was crowned king of Judah, but not by the people of Judah. He was placed on the throne by Pharaoh Neco; for the kingdom of David was now a vassal of Egypt and forced to render a very high tribute. Jehoiakim paid the Egyptian ruler the required silver and gold by levying a heavy tax on the people. No one was exempt, and the nation suffered. But the Davidic plate had not yet been wiped clean with God's anger and turned upside down with his wrath. And for that they were thankful.

• • •

King Nebuchadnezzar of Babylon soon defeated the Egyptians, and Judah had a new master. Jehoiakim now sent his tribute to Babylon to keep the peace. But after three years, and prompted by apparent weakening of Babylonian forces, Jehoiakim withheld his payment. In response, God sent Nebuchadnezzar to carry out the divine punishment on his people. But before the Babylonian ruler arrived, Jehoiakim died and his son Jehoiachin became king.

Within a few weeks of Jehoiachin's coronation, Nebuchadnezzar laid siege to Jerusalem. Jehoiachin had little recourse. He surrendered to the Babylonian army.

Jehoiachin, his mother, his wives, and all the nobles, officials, and elders were shackled and led out through the city gate. The Babylonians rounded up the artisans, craftsmen, soldiers, and priests—ten thousand in all. Only the poor people who worked the land were left. They stood and watched the procession of prisoners being exiled to Babylon. Then Nebuchadnezzar's troops took all the treasures from the temple and the palace and they loaded them on carts which followed the trail of captives.

The city of David was nearly empty now. But its walls were still standing, the temple remained, and a descendant of David was on the throne. For Nebuchadnezzar appointed Zedekiah, the last son of good King Josiah, to rule over Judah.

For nearly a decade, Zedekiah rendered tribute to Babylon. But then a new Pharaoh came to power in Egypt, and Zedekiah saw in him a much stronger ally. So he revolted against the king of Babylon.

Nebuchadnezzar answered by marching his army to Judah. They occupied its cities and towns until they came to Jerusalem. There they encamped and built siege works all around it. The famine in the city soon became severe.

Then late on the ninth day of the fourth month of the siege, the Babylonian soldiers broke through the wall and entered the city. Zedekiah escaped in the darkness with a small band of soldiers. They fled at breakneck speed. Nebuchadnezzar sent his swiftest chariots in pursuit. When Zedekiah's men turned and saw the enemy, they deserted him and scattered. The king was captured, bound in bronze chains, and brought back to Jerusalem.

The next day he was taken to Babylonian headquarters in the city of Riblah, along with the whole royal family, the descendants of David. There Nebuchadnezzar pronounced judgment on Zedekiah.

His hands were tied behind his back and he was escorted, head bowed, to a podium in the center of camp. Soldiers led his oldest son, also bound at the wrists, into the courtyard and ordered him to kneel. They forced Zedekiah to raise his eyes, and then with one tremendous blow, they cut off the boy's head.

Zedekiah cowered. But the guards did not allow him to turn away. They brought his second child and beheaded him. Then the third. When all Zedekiah's sons had been decapitated and bodiless heads littered the yard, the soldiers seized Zedekiah by the hair, yanked back his head, and plunged butcher knives into his eyes. Blood flowed from the sockets and fell to the earth. The death of his children would be the last sight Zedekiah ever saw. He was then taken to Babylon where he disappeared forever.

Back in Jerusalem, Nebuchadnezzar's army looted the temple and the royal palace. They loaded the silver and gold accoutrements on carts, the six magnificently carved lions that lined the steps of the throne were stacked on one of them. When they had ransacked the rest of city, they lit torches and went through the streets lighting houses and buildings on fire. Soon Jerusalem was ablaze. It burned with a holy fury. The Babylonians then tore down what remained of the exterior wall. Judah's capital now lay naked, a defenseless heap of charred ruins.

The important priests, dignitaries, and officials were arrested and executed. The remaining people in the city were detained and deported to Riblah and then finally exiled to Babylon.

Jerusalem was wiped out, the kingdom of David gone, and the nation of Judah ceased to exist.

● ● ●

King Nebuchadnezzar appointed Gedaliah as governor over Judah, the new province in his empire. Gedaliah, himself a Judean, established his headquarters in the city of Mizpah. There he called the people of the land who were left and vowed to them that he and the Babylonians meant them no harm. "Don't be afraid," he said reassuringly. "Live here and serve the king of Babylon, and all will go well for you."

But a few months later, a certain man named Ishmael gathered ten comrades and stormed the compound in Mizpah. They killed Gedaliah and the Babylonian officials who were with him. At this, all the people of Judah fled to Egypt for fear of reprisals from Babylon.

Egypt.

Israel had returned to the place of slavery. The children of Abraham no longer lived in the Promised Land.

• • •

About twenty years later, a new ruler ascended the Babylonian throne. He released King Jehoiachin of Judah from his chains. He spoke kindly to him and gave him a seat of honor higher than all the other exiled kings. Jehoiachin put aside his prison clothes and took his meals at the royal table in the palace of Babylon for the remainder of his days.

DISCUSSION QUESTIONS

Chapter 1: The Covenant of God

(Genesis 12-15, 17)

1. What challenges did Abram face by leaving his homeland? What if he decided not to go? How would you have responded to God's command?
2. Was Abram wrong to lie about Sarai? Was God's treatment of Pharaoh fair? Are there times when lying might be acceptable?
3. What caused the problems between Abram and Lot? Was their solution a good one? How else might they have addressed the issue?
4. The concept of "covenant" is central to the story. How are covenants (contracts, agreements, pacts) important in your life and the world around you today?
5. How do you imagine that Sarai is feeling at this point in the story? What would she say to God and Abram about what has happened thus far?

Chapter 2: A Son, a Promise, a Firestorm

(Genesis 16, 18-19)

1. Was it a mistake for Abraham and Sarai to have children through Hagar? How does God treat Hagar and Ishmael?
2. How do Abraham and Sarai respond to the promise of a son for Sarai? Does it show a lack of faith? Does God seem upset by their response?

3. Why does Abraham object to God's plan concerning Sodom? Do you agree with Abraham's reasons? Are you surprised by God's response to Abraham's challenges? Should we challenge God?
4. Does Lot act righteously when the men of Sodom surround his house? How do you think his daughters felt about what he did?
5. Is the punishment for Lot's wife too harsh? Who else is affected by it?

Chapter 3: Parents and Children in Crisis
(Genesis 19, 21-22)

1. The story does not indict Lot's daughters for their actions. Why? What might be the message here?
2. What would you say to Sarah, Abraham, and God about the way they handle Hagar?
3. Abraham does not question God about the command to sacrifice his son. Is this surprising? Does this suggest that we are to have an unquestioning faith? What would Sarah have said?
4. What might we learn from Abraham's willingness to sacrifice his son? Would you have followed God's command? How do you think Isaac felt on the way down the mountain?
5. For which character do you have the most sympathy: Lot's daughters, Ishmael, or Isaac?

Chapter 4: Isaac and Rebekah
(Genesis 23-26)

1. How do marriage practices in the biblical text compare to those in your culture? What are the advantages and disadvantages of arranged marriages?
2. How is Rebekah's leaving her family both like and unlike Abraham's leaving his homeland? If you were Rebekah, would you have gone with Abraham's servant?
3. What is Abraham's legacy? What would be a good epitaph or eulogy for him?

4. What might have been the conversation between Isaac and Rebekah after Abimelech left? The conversation between Abimelech and his men?
5. What are the different obstacles that characters in the story must overcome? And how do they overcome them? What can we draw from their experiences?

Chapter 5: Twin Boys
(Genesis 25, 27)

1. How does God's word to Rebekah during her pregnancy influence your interpretation of the story? Is Rebekah and Jacob's deception part of God's plan?
2. How does parental favoritism impact Jacob and Esau? Is it ever good to show more love and attention to one child over another?
3. Does Jacob "steal" Esau's birthright? Is Jacob to blame for tricking his father—or is it all Rebekah's doing? What words would you use to describe Jacob's actions and character?
4. Are Esau's murderous thoughts justified? Can you identify with Esau in any way?
5. Should Jacob have left the country as his mother directed? What else could he have done? What would you have done? When is it good to run away from a bad situation?

Chapter 6: Jacob in the House of Laban
(Genesis 28-30)

1. Does God still speak through dreams today, as he did to Jacob? If not, why not? And if so, how would one know which dreams represented the voice of God?
2. How does Jacob's encounter with Rachel at the well compare to Eliezer's meeting Rebekah at a well (chapter 4)?
3. What is somewhat comical or ironic about Leah being given to Jacob? How do you think Leah felt about it?

4. What is God's primary role in this chapter—that is, what does God do? Where else in this chapter might you have expected God to intervene that he does not?
5. How does the Leah-Rachel relationship compare to the Jacob-Esau relationship? For whom do you have more sympathy, Leah or Rachel?

Chapter 7: Homeward Bound
(Genesis 30-31)

1. Jacob has stayed with Laban for a long time. If he could do it over, what might Jacob do differently in his twenty years with Laban?
2. Is Jacob performing some sort of magic with the mating of the animals? Does God bless his actions?
3. Did Jacob leave in an appropriate manner? Was Laban right to be upset? Do Jacob's actions have anything to commend to us about how to get out of a difficult situation?
4. Why does Rachel take her father's talismans (or "household gods"—it is difficult to know what these are)? Is she too a "trickster" like her husband and father?
5. What is the nature of the relationship between Jacob and Laban? Is either man trustworthy? How does their relationship compare to your experience of in-law relationships?

Chapter 8: Brothers Reunited, a Daughter Defiled
(Genesis 32-35)

1. What kind of relationship does Jacob have with God in this chapter? What is the significance of the meaning of the name Israel (one who strives with God)?
2. Is Jacob making a genuine attempt to reconcile with Esau? Or is he trying to bribe him and buy forgiveness? How do our actions sometimes have complex motivations?
3. Why does Esau initially not accept the gifts from Jacob? Why does Jacob insist? How would you have received Jacob if you were Esau?

4. Why does Jacob not follow through on his word and live in Edom with Esau? What does this say about Jacob?
5. It is not clear if Dinah is raped or if it were "forbidden love" because Shechem was not an Israelite. What do you imagine is the case? Do the brothers go overboard in their response?

Chapter 9: Joseph

(Genesis 37, 39-40)

1. How does Joseph annoy his siblings? Could he have done anything differently to develop a better relationship with them?
2. Why do you think Potiphar's wife was interested in Joseph? Should Joseph have handled the situation differently after his first encounter with her? Is he partly to blame? Or is that blaming the victim?
3. How are the themes of "deception/betrayal" and "favoritism" manifest in the story? What "themes" animate the story of your life?
4. How do "dreams" and "clothes" play an important role in Joseph's life?
5. What obstacles does Joseph overcome? What is the key to his success? What can we learn from the way he handles adversity?

Chapter 10: Dreams and Deceptions

(Genesis 38, 41-43)

1. Pharaoh recognizes the "spirit of God" is with Joseph and promotes him. Does this make Pharaoh a believer in Joseph's God? What distinguishes "believers" from "non-believers"?
2. Joseph has an Egyptian wife, Egyptian children, an Egyptian name, and is second in command in the Egyptian government. Is he now essentially an Egyptian? Are there times when it is appropriate—even good and right—to assimilate into a different culture?
3. Judah says that Tamar is more righteous than he. Do you agree? How is Tamar alike and unlike Potiphar's wife (chapter 9)?

4. Why do you think Joseph initially accuses his brothers of being spies? How would you have reacted to seeing your siblings for the first time in years?
5. Has Jacob not "learned his lesson" since he continues to favor one son (Benjamin)? Does the brothers' concern for Simeon and treatment of Benjamin show how they have matured?

Chapter 11: Together Again

(Genesis 43-50)

1. Why does Joseph continue to test his brothers, as opposed to revealing himself immediately? Are there times when it is good to hide the truth?
2. What do you think of Joseph giving the best land (Goshen) to his family? How might the average Egyptian have felt about it?
3. As soon as their father died, Joseph's brothers feared he would exact revenge on them. What does this suggest about their relationship during all those years in Egypt?
4. Bestowing final blessings and being buried in the proper land are important ideas at the end of the Joseph story. In your estimation, are such practices important for having a "good death"?
5. Joseph understands his life in terms of the providence of God ("but God intended it all for good"). Do you resonate with such thinking? What about people's lives that don't end as happily as Joseph's?

Chapter 12: Moses

(Exodus 1-2)

1. What do you imagine other Israelite mothers did to try to hide their baby boys? Why doesn't the story focus on them?
2. How are women important in the early life of Moses? Which of them is the bravest—including Pharaoh's daughter who defied her father's orders to kill Israelites?

3. If you were Jochebed, would you have returned your son Moses to Pharaoh's daughter after he was weaned? Would it have been better for Moses to be raised by his enslaved mother, or as Egyptian royalty?
4. Was Moses wrong to kill the Egyptian slave master? Does this put a "blemish" on his record? What kind of record should we expect of our leaders?
5. How is Moses' escape similar to and different from that of Jacob's flight from his home (chapters 5-6)?

Chapter 13: A Burning Bush
(Exodus 2-7)

1. How does God's appearance in the burning bush compare to his previous appearances to Abraham, Jacob, and Joseph? How does God appear today?
2. Why does God decide beforehand to harden Pharaoh's heart? What might Moses have suggested as an alternative (like Abraham proposed that God reconsider his plan to destroy Sodom)?
3. What objections does Moses raise for not wanting to do what God has asked? Does this show a lack of faith? How does God respond to Moses' reluctance?
4. Why does God try to kill Moses? What does this suggest about God? Is Zipporah the un-sung hero of the story? Do you perceive God acting in unexpected ways today?
5. What is Pharaoh's initial response to Moses and Aaron? What might we take away from this concerning the challenges we confront in our own lives?

Chapter 14: Plagues and Pestilence
(Exodus 7-10)

1. Is it surprising that Pharaoh's magicians can duplicate the first couple of plagues? How does this heighten the drama of the story?

2. In your judgment, which of the first nine plagues would be the worst to live through? Do you feel badly for the Egyptians?
3. Why does Moses repeatedly ask Pharaoh for a three-day journey when that is not his intention? Should he have been fully upfront about his plan?
4. Why doesn't Pharaoh let the Israelites go? Is Pharaoh, too, a man of faith, remaining loyal to his gods in hopes that they will help him?
5. What is God's stated purpose for the plagues? What do you think of that purpose?

Chapter 15: The Angel of Death
(Exodus 11-15)

1. Why do you think God required the Israelites to put blood on their door posts, as opposed to the other plagues where Israel did not need to distinguish themselves from the Egyptians?
2. How has the relationship between God and Moses changed since the burning bush? How, if at all, has your relationship with God changed over time?
3. Miriam appears again in the story after a long absence. What do you think she has been doing this whole time?
4. What is your view of the enslaved Israelites celebrating the violent death of their Egyptian enemies?
5. How would you sum up the story of the Exodus? What are its main themes and how might we connect them to our contemporary lives?

Chapter 16: Through the Wilderness and to the Mountain
(Exodus 15-31)

1. What accounts for the people's desire to return to Egypt? How could they lose faith so quickly after witnessing God's power over Pharaoh? Do people today sometimes wish to return to their symbolic Egypt?
2. God clearly marks off the mountain as a sacred place. Do we have sacred places in our tradition, and how do we mark them off?

3. How is God's covenant with the people of Israel different from his covenant with Abraham in terms of what is required?
4. Do people follow the Ten Commandments today? Do they even try to follow them? Should religious laws be state laws?
5. In this chapter, God appears at once very powerful and even frightening, but also very human—talking with people face to face and writing with his own finger. What does this suggest about God?

Chapter 17: Broken Tablets and a Golden Calf

(Exodus 32-40)

1. Is Aaron breaking the first command not to worship other gods or the second command not to make an idol? If the latter, is that a lesser offense?
2. The people worship a god made of gold. What do people worship today that compromises their commitment to God?
3. Moses threatens to back out on God, just as God threatens to back out of his covenant with Israel. What does this reveal about each of them?
4. Moses sees God face to face. How do people see God today?
5. There is an emphasis on the written covenant as opposed to the spoken word. How do we think about written versus oral agreements in our contemporary context? In what context is one more valued than the other?

Chapter 18: The Promised Land

(Numbers 9-14)

1. Being a leader is difficult, and Moses is ready to quit. When is it good to delegate responsibility and when is it good to do things yourself?
2. Aaron and Miriam question whether God speaks only through Moses. How do we determine through whom God is speaking? Why did God punish only Miriam?
3. What does God mean when he says that he speaks to Moses clearly and not in riddles?

4. How do you think you would have responded when you heard the spies report? What causes failures of faith in our lives?
5. Why does God not give the people a second chance after they realize their mistake? Do they deserve a second chance?

Chapter 19: Forty Years of Wandering
(Numbers 16, 20-25, 31)

1. In ancient Israel the individual person was not valued above the group—there was not a concept of individual rights. How is that seen in this chapter?
2. Is God's punishment of Moses fair? How do you imagine Moses feels?
3. God punishes the people, yet he declares them blessed and will not allow Balaam to curse them. What does this suggest about God's relationship with the Israelites?
4. In what ways is the Balaam story comical? In what ways is it confusing?
5. Foreign women are a big problem for the Israelites. Who is held more responsible for the trouble—the Israelites or the Moabite women? How does this compare to holding women responsible for men's mistakes today?

Chapter 20: A Final Farewell
(Deuteronomy 28-34)

1. Moses commissions Joshua to lead the people into the Promised Land. How do transitions of power take place today?
2. What words would you use to describe the life of Moses? What would you say if asked to speak at his funeral?
3. Who are the Moses-figures in our day and time?
4. What is the significance of the statement that no one knows where Moses is buried? How has burial location been important in the story thus far?
5. What do you think happens next in the story?

Chapter 21: Taking the Land
(Joshua 1-4, 6)

1. How does the crossing of the Jordan River compare to the crossing of the Red Sea earlier? How are "boundary crossings" (literal or metaphoric) significant in our lives?
2. How do the actions of these spies compare with the earlier scouting of the land?
3. How would you describe Rahab? What alternative actions could she have taken? What do you think the other citizens in Jericho would have said if they knew what she did?
4. God's command to kill everyone in Jericho is a difficult issue. What are your thoughts on how to deal with this?
5. What kind of faith is required to walk around Jericho seven times? Did God have a purpose for this plan?

Chapter 22: Trials and Tricks
(Joshua 7-9)

1. Does Joshua's prayer to God after the initial defeat at Ai reveal a lack of faith? Should he have assumed, based on previous experiences in the wilderness, that a hidden sin was the cause?
2. Compare and contrast Rahab and Achan. Do their fates suggest that faithfulness to the covenant is more important than ethnic identity (whether or not you are an Israelite)?
3. Why do the Israelites not send the same small army to attack Ai the second time? Does sending everyone undermine God's point that the original defeat was due to Achan's sin?
4. What does the story of the Gibeonites imply about the power of oaths? What do you think of Joshua's negotiation with the people of Gibeon?
5. The story of treaty-making presents an alternative to the mass destruction done elsewhere in the Promised Land. Is there a time for one and a time for the other?

Chapter 23: Promise Fulfilled, Covenant Renewed

(Joshua 10-11, 23-24)

1. It is interesting that we are told the perspective of the people in the land (they hear of the Israelites and are afraid). What might we draw from this aspect of the story?
2. What do you think of the sun standing still? Should we read this literally? How is this different from God's other miraculous acts?
3. God intentionally hardened the hearts of the people in the land so that they would be exterminated. What is your reaction to God doing this?
4. What do you think Abraham would have said if he were at Joshua's meeting at Shechem?
5. Given their past actions, do you think the people will be faithful to their word and keep the covenant?

Chapter 24: A Fat King and Two Women

(Judges 2-4)

1. Why would the people worship Baal? Why do we do things that we know we should not do? What gods in our own time and place lure us away from God?
2. How is God's action in this chapter similar to his handling of the Israelites in earlier stories?
3. What humor do you find in the story of Ehud? What is the appropriate role of humor in our spiritual lives?
4. How is Deborah like the male leaders we have encountered so far? How is she different? Is Barak smart for insisting that she go to battle? Or is it a reflection of cowardice?
5. How does Jael compare to other women in the story thus far? Does the story of Deborah and Jael speak to the role of women in leadership positions today?

Chapter 25: Gideon

(Judges 6-8)

1. Gideon, like Moses and others, is reluctant to do God's bidding. Do you find this surprising? Why does God not pick braver, more confident people?
2. Is it appropriate for Gideon to test God, asking for signs? What do you make of the fact that God obliges Gideon's requests? Should we ask for God to show himself in our lives?
3. God wants Gideon and the people to know that credit for the victory goes to God. Are there times when we do not give God due credit? Are there times when we can and should take credit for our successes?
4. How has Gideon changed from the beginning of the story to the end?
5. Is Gideon humbly rejecting the offer to be king? Or is he running away from an opportunity, or even responsibility, to lead the people in a faithful relationship with God on a more permanent basis?

Chapter 26: Bastard Sons

(Judges 9-12)

1. How is Abimelech's story different from Jephthah's and the other leaders before (Ehud, Deborah, and Gideon)?
2. Abimelech instigates a civil war in Israel. What are the different factors that lead to the strife? How do they compare to the causes of conflicts today?
3. What is your view on the feelings and emotion that God expresses at the people's continual disobedience? Do you imagine God having the same sort of conflicted emotions about his relationship with people today?

4. What was Jephthah thinking when he made the vow? Why did God allow him to go through with it? Are there times to break our oaths?
5. If you were Jephthah's daughter, would you have willing submitted to the sacrifice?

Chapter 27: Samson

(Judges 13-16)

1. Do Manoah and his wife have different levels of faith or just different kinds of faith?
2. What are the roles and portraits of women in this chapter? Imagining you were Delilah, what would you have done when your Philistine leaders approached you?
3. Does Samson die a good death? Is his story one of tragedy or triumph?
4. What does this chapter teach about the nature of violence? What is your assessment of Samson's statement, "I have simply done to them what they did to me"?
5. Overall, how would you characterize Samson? What are his good and bad qualities? What do you make of the fact that the spirit of God is upon such an ambiguous person?

Chapter 28: Rape and Civil War

(Judges 19-21)

1. How does the rape and dismemberment of the concubine reflect the sad stories of women throughout history and around the globe today?
2. How does the Levite dodge his role and responsibility for his concubine's rape and death? How do we "pass the buck" in our lives?
3. Why does the Israelite coalition initially lose to the Benjaminites? Whose side is God on?
4. What is absurd about the way in which the Israelites obtain wives for the Benjaminites? Should we keep our vows/promises at any cost?

5. What is the significance of the last line of the chapter? How does this chapter invite us to think about leadership in our communities today?

Chapter 29: Samuel
(1 Samuel 1-4)

1. Why does Hannah want a son so badly? What do you think of Hannah giving up her boy to God's service? What can we learn from Hannah?
2. How is it that Eli could not control his sons? Does God's punishment seem fair to you? How much should parents be held responsible for the behavior of their children?
3. Is it unsettling that Samuel does not recognize the voice of God? How do we fail to recognize God's calling in our lives?
4. Are the Israelites wise to bring the Ark into battle? Does it represent an act of faith? Or is it somehow misguided? Can certain religious objects bring success in our lives?
5. What do you think will happen to the Ark at this point now that it is Philistine hands?

Chapter 30: Tumors
(1 Samuel 5-7)

1. What does this chapter say about the power of other gods? After seeing the fate of Dagon, why do the Philistines not "convert" to the religion of Israel?
2. Could you say that God "uses the cows" to accomplish his purposes? Where else have animals appeared in important ways in the story?
3. Why does God kill the seventy men who looked into the Ark? Are there religious objects or symbols that we should treat with utmost respect?

4. Do you think there will be repercussions for Israel forgetting the Ark? What would you have recommended doing with the Ark?
5. How is Samuel like the previous deliverers of Israel (Ehud, Gideon, Samson)? How is he different? What are the different leadership models we find in these stories?

Chapter 31: Saul, the First King
(1 Samuel 8, 10-11)

1. Are you sympathetic to the people's desire for a king? Why does God "give in" and grant the people's request?
2. How does Israel's desire to be "like all the nations around us" parallel the desires in our own lives? When does trust in human power (a king) become a rejection of God's power?
3. Is Saul's hiding among the baggage a good sign or a bad one? Is it good that he is reluctant? Or does it suggest he is a coward not fit for the job?
4. What other stories does Saul's defeat of Nahash remind you of? How is Saul acting a lot like some of the earlier heroes of Israel?
5. Are you surprised that the spirit of God comes upon Saul and he is successful—even though God was not happy with the idea of a king?

Chapter 32: Royal Trouble
(1 Samuel 13-15)

1. Is Samuel partly responsible for not showing up on time for the sacrifice? Do you think he was intentionally late because he was opposed to the idea of a king?
2. Is Jonathan wrong to act independently of his father the king? How do we determine the difference between "taking initiative" and over stepping one's bounds?

3. Is Saul's punishment (rejection by God) for not killing the king and all the animals too harsh? How does the statement, "To obey is better than sacrifice" apply to our lives today?
4. What does this chapter say about the relationship between politics (the king) and religion (the prophet)? How are those two arenas related in your culture?
5. What do you think of the last line in the chapter? How is the last line ironic in light of the fact that Samuel says God does not change his mind?

Chapter 33: A Shepherd Boy and a Giant
(1 Samuel 16-17)

1. How is Samuel's looking on the outward appearance similar to the way people think today? Why are people drawn to tall, attractive leaders? Is it ironic that David, too, is good-looking?
2. What do you think of "an evil spirit from God" tormenting Saul? Does evil come from God?
3. Music soothes Saul. What are the main functions of music in our world today? Does it continue to have healing power?
4. In his battle with Goliath, who or what is David ultimately trusting in? Is human confidence compatible with trust in divine power?
5. The story of David and Goliath is well known. Why has it captured popular imagination? What makes it so appealing?

Chapter 34: David in the Palace of Saul
(1 Samuel 18-20)

1. Jonathan was in a difficult spot—caught between his friend and his father. How do you think he handled the situation? What would you have done differently?
2. Why does God again torment Saul with an evil spirit? How would Saul be diagnosed today?

3. How do you imagine Michal felt about the bride price paid for her? What kind of relationship might she have had with her brother Jonathan?
4. How do themes of loyalty and betrayal play out in this chapter? How do they play out in our lives today?
5. There are not many texts in the Bible that deal with the relationship of friends. What is your assessment of the relationship between Jonathan and David? What can we draw from it?

Chapter 35: Renegade

(1 Samuel 21-25)

1. Is David ultimately responsible for the deaths of the people in Nob as he asserts? Or is Saul solely to blame?
2. David claims theological reasons for not killing Saul in the cave—he was God's anointed. What other political, military, or personal reasons might David have had?
3. How would you describe David's character in this chapter? What current public figures does he remind you of?
4. Is Abigail a model of moral courage and peacemaking? Or do you think she had other motivations for her actions?
5. What is God's role in this chapter? Is God both present and absent from the story in unexpected ways?

Chapter 36: Among the Philistines

(1 Samuel 26-27, 29-30)

1. David, again, does not kill Saul. What do you think of the reasons he gives this time (God will see to it that Saul dies)? Should we rely on God to do our vengeance? Or should we hope for reconciliation?
2. David is no saint in this chapter. Are there times when difficult circumstances compel us to act in morally suspect ways? Does God approve of such actions?

3. Is David bribing the people of Israel with gifts? Or is this wise politics? How does it compare to contemporary political actions?
4. David orders his men to share the spoils. Should those who risk more—those who went to battle—get more?
5. David attributes his victory over the bandits to God. Should we believe David that God was in fact behind his success? Are there times when we give God credit for things which have nothing to do with God?

Chapter 37: Suicide
(1 Samuel 28, 31; 2 Samuel 1)

1. Why does God refuse to answer Saul? Might there be other circumstances in which God does not respond to prayers?
2. Is Saul right to consult a medium as a last ditch effort? Does this chapter support belief in ghosts and communication with the dead?
3. Do you resonate with Saul's desire to know the future? How do people in our world try to learn and control the future?
4. Should we celebrate or lament the life of Saul? Does he die tragically or heroically?
5. Why does David kill the messenger? Do you think he is genuinely sad about the death of Saul? Of Jonathan?

Chapter 38: Civil War, Again
(2 Samuel 2-5)

1. Asahel breaks the rules of the battle. Are there rules in war? Should there be? Is everything fair in war?
2. Why does David mourn publicly for Abner? How do we distinguish political maneuverings from authentic personal feelings?
3. What role do women play in this chapter? How does their appearance in the story compare to the role of women in politics and war today?

4. This is a bloody chapter. What advice would you give the characters to deter the violence?
5. What do these stories suggest about the relationship between political power and violence? Are all people and regimes that come to power inevitably guilty of moral failure in some way?

Chapter 39: The City of David
(2 Samuel 5-8, 10)

1. God's promise that David would be king is now finally fulfilled. What has David experienced and what has he had to do in order to receive the fulfillment? How can we relate this to our own lives?
2. Do you find the death of Uzzah disturbing? What is God's point in killing him?
3. What do you think of David's dancing? Does it have anything to say to us about dance and bodily movement in worship today?
4. Should David have built a house for God first, or at least asked God if he wanted one? How do we "put God first" in our lives? Does it require neglecting our own needs and desires?
5. How do you think God's promise to David of an everlasting kingdom will play out in the rest of the story?

Chapter 40: Adultery and Murder, Rape and Incest
(2 Samuel 11-13)

1. David uses his power in unthinkable ways with Bathsheba and Uriah. How do leaders today misuse their power for personal gain?
2. Is the punishment for David reasonable? Was the death of the baby intended as punishment for Bathsheba too?
3. Why is Nathan's parable effective? How can Nathan's rhetorical strategy inform the way in which we assess ourselves?

4. How is Tamar's fate like and unlike other women in the story thus far? How is it like the tragic story of some young women in our current world?
5. Was Absalom's murder of his brother Amnon justified? Should David be held partly responsible for failing to address Amnon's sin?

Chapter 41: Father Against Son
(2 Samuel 14-16)

1. How does the wise woman's story help David envision a different future? Does telling stories help us imagine alternative ways of thinking and acting?
2. What habits and practices has Absalom seemingly learned from his father? How can parents set a good example for children? How can children emulate only parents' good qualities?
3. In light of Absalom's usurping the throne in this chapter, should we re-evaluate his motivation for killing this brother Amnon in the last chapter?
4. Do you feel bad for David? Or is he getting what he deserves? Why did David refuse to take the Ark with him?
5. What is your view of David's response to Shimei? What do you think will happen to Shimei if David returns to the throne?

Chapter 42: O Absalom!
(2 Samuel 16-19)

1. How do Ahithophel and Hushai help us think about loyalty and treachery? Do we too often shift our loyalties (or compromise our commitments) in order to be on "the winning side"?
2. What do you imagine David's ten concubines would have to say about the events of this chapter?

3. Can you understand or identify with David's grieving over Absalom—even though Absalom had tried to kill him?
4. What is your assessment of how Joab handled David's grieving? Does he show a lack of sympathy for David? Or does David fail to appreciate what his men did?
5. In your judgment, does David deal with Ziba and Mephibosheth appropriately? Do you believe Mephibosheth's claims?

Chapter 43: Sheba and Bathsheba

(2 Samuel 20, 24; 1 Kings 1-2)

1. What other women in the story does the woman in Abel-beth-maacah remind you of? What women today?
2. What are your unanswered questions about the scene in which David takes a census and God punishes him?
3. Did Bathsheba and Nathan dupe the aging David about the promise to make Solomon king? Or are we supposed to think that David had in fact made such a promise, even though it is not mentioned anywhere?
4. How is Bathsheba's role here different from her appearance earlier in the story (chapter 40)? Do we tend to evaluate the political actions of women and men differently?
5. Are you surprised by David's violent exhortations to Solomon? How does David subtly alter the promise God made to him when he relates it to Solomon?

Chapter 44: King Solomon

(1 Kings 2-10)

1. King Solomon establishes his kingdom through violent means. Would things have been different if he asked for wisdom prior to doing so?
2. What does the chapter imply about the association between wisdom and wealth? Does wisdom always bring riches and honor?

3. What do you think of Solomon's decision regarding the baby? How could it have backfired on him?
4. Solomon builds a magnificent temple. Does this suggest that God likes big, ornate buildings in his honor? What are your thoughts on extravagant places of worship?
5. Does Solomon's prayer have the right focus? What, if anything, should be the difference between public and private prayers?

Chapter 45: Torn Asunder

(1 Kings 11-14)

1. Where else in the story have "foreign women" caused problems for Israel? Where have they helped Israel? How does the story's view of outsiders compare to your attitude toward "foreigners"?
2. What can we draw from Solomon's putting political expediency (marrying foreign women to establish political alliances) before commitment to God's covenant?
3. Why do you think Rehoboam listens to the advice of the younger men? What can we learn from his errors?
4. What does the story of the man of God from Judah and the old prophet in Bethel suggest to us about the difficulty of discerning the true word from God?
5. In light of David's life, what do you think of God's statement that David followed him with all his heart? Do you feel badly for Jeroboam's wife, the mother of the sick (and then dead) child?

Chapter 46: Elijah and Ahab

(1 Kings 14-19)

1. How does the chaos and political instability in Israel compare to our contemporary world? What is typically the root cause of such violence?
2. What does this chapter say about God's control over nature? Do you think God controls nature today? What about natural disasters?

3. What is God's relationship with Elijah? What are the high points and low points? What might we learn from Elijah's life of faith?
4. What do you think of Elijah's killing the prophets of Baal? Is violence in the name of God ever appropriate?
5. What is the significance of the idea that God was not in the wind, earthquake, and fire, but rather in the stillness? Where do you look for God's presence in your life?

Chapter 47: Prophets and Vineyards

(1 Kings 20-22)

1. The name Ahab is sometimes associated with pure evil. What are some of the positive aspects of Ahab in this chapter? Is anyone "pure evil"?
2. Are you surprised by some of the things God does in this chapter? How should we look for the hand of God at work in unexpected ways in our lives?
3. Should Ahab be held partly responsible for Naboth's death, or only Jezebel? Notably, on this occasion God is not upset with the king for worshiping other gods. What exactly is he upset about?
4. According to Micaiah's vision, God intentionally deceived Ahab. Does God sometimes trick people? Or are we not to trust Micaiah's vision?
5. What does the scene with Micaiah suggest about how we distinguish true from false prophecy?

Chapter 48: Chariot of Fire

(1 Kings 22; 2 Kings 1-3)

1. Ahaziah is judged for not seeking God about his health. How should we think about medicine as it relates to faith in God?
2. What are your impressions of Elisha in this chapter? Should he have asked for a double portion of Elijah's spirit? How

do we differentiate between confidence/boldness and greed/arrogance?

3. Do Elijah and Elisha use their powers wisely in this chapter? What would be the criteria for determining a wise or godly use of power? How does this issue relate to our lives today?
4. Again we see King Jehoshaphat of Judah working with Israelite kings. Does that speak well of him? Or should he not associate with those who are not fully committed to God?
5. What do you make of the very end of the chapter (it is a confusing passage which has perplexed interpreters)?

Chapter 49: Miracles

(2 Kings 4, 6)

1. Does the story of the woman in debt at the beginning of the chapter have anything to offer to us concerning faith and personal finances?
2. Do these stories focus on the power of Elisha or the power of God? Does it matter?
3. Why is the woman of Shunem upset with Elisha when her son dies? Do you find it strange that Gehazi and Elisha have some difficulty in raising the child?
4. What is the significance of Elisha associating with and performing miracles for women?
5. Do you prefer these "domestic" stories? Or the ones where prophets are involved with kings, wars, and politics? What can we take from the fact that they are engaged in both spheres?

Chapter 50: Elisha and the Enemy

(2 Kings 5-8)

1. Can you empathize with Naaman's response to Elisha's instructions? How can we learn from his story?

2. What would you have done if you were one of the lepers who discovered the deserted camp? Were they wrong to take things for themselves before revealing the news?
3. What does this chapter say about giving gifts to holy men? Should religious leaders accept large monetary compensation for their service?
4. Elisha is now working among the Arameans. What does this suggest about the scope of his mission and ministry?
5. Elisha instructs Hazael to lie. Why? Where else have prophets been associated with deception? Do you find this troubling?

Chapter 51: Treason

(2 Kings 8-10)

1. Which of Jehu's murders is most shocking? What other events outside the Bible does Jehu's rampage remind you of?
2. In what ways is Jehu's violence commissioned and ordained by God? How do we handle such bloody texts today?
3. Here we see religion and politics closely aligned. Is it good to separate the two? What are the dangers of joining them or splitting them?
4. The story seems to take special delight in the violent death of Jezebel. What do you feel about her brutal ending? What do you think her parents would have felt?
5. What do you think of Jehu's destruction of the prophets of Baal? Clever ploy? Or mean trick?

Chapter 52: Israel Destroyed

(2 Kings 11-15, 17)

1. What can we learn from Elisha's interaction with Jehoash? Is the prophetic word hard to interpret? Are there times when our lack of energy and enthusiasm costs us?
2. What do you think of the dead man who comes to life when he touches Elisha's bones? What might we draw from this about the power and influence of our lives on others even after we are gone?

3. King Amaziah's defeat would seem to present an easy lesson in the dangers of pride. But how do we know when to be confident and trust God for bigger and better things? And when to be content with what we have?
4. Is it sometimes better to surrender to keep the peace, as Menahem does? How do we know when to compromise and when to stand our ground?
5. What are your thoughts on the destruction of the northern kingdom: well-deserved and glad that it is over or sad and shocked to see it end?

Chapter 53: Two Good Kings and One Very Bad
(2 Kings 16, 18-23)

1. Is it appropriate to ask God for signs as Hezekiah does? What is God's response to the king's request? Does this imply that needing more proof is acceptable?
2. Is it surprising that God saves Jerusalem? What is God's main motivation for doing so? When is the last time God (or the angel of God) intervened so directly in the story?
3. Why would God not punish Manasseh? Why wait until later? Is this reasonable?
4. Do you imagine Josiah was happy that destruction would not come in his time or sad for the future of his nation? Would it have helped if Josiah pleaded with God to change his mind?
5. Is Josiah's reform (destroying the idols) and renewal of the covenant a case of "too little too late"? Do we sometimes reach a "point of no return" in our relationship with God?

Chapter 54: Final Defeat
(2 Kings 23-25)

1. It is not clear why Josiah tried to stop Neco. Is this simply a case of poor military strategy? Why would an otherwise good king meet such an untimely death?

2. Could a case be made that Judah would have survived if they continued to pay tribute to the greater powers? How do we know when to resist the powers-that-be and when to submit to them?
3. What do you think motivated Ishmael's actions—religious fervor for God or anger about Babylonian occupation? Are there times when even the highest and purest motives yield bad results?
4. Why does God use other peoples and nations to carry out his will? Should we interpret political and military events today in terms of divine providence?
5. How do you interpret the final paragraph? Is it a glimmer of hope or just a footnote to a sad ending?

ABOUT THE AUTHOR

Mark Roncace is Professor of Religion at Wingate University in North Carolina. His other books include:

Jeremiah, Zedekiah, and the Fall of Jerusalem
Teaching the Bible: Practical Strategies for Classroom Instruction
Teaching the Bible Through Popular Culture and the Arts
Raw Revelation: The Bible They Never Tell You About
Global Perspectives on the Bible
Global Perspectives on the Old Testament
Global Perspectives on the New Testament

If you'd like to read more about the fascinating lives of Biblical characters, consider the work of Diana Wallis Taylor:

Ruth, Mother of Kings: The story of Ruth has captivated Christian believers for centuries, not least of all because she is one of only two women with books of the Bible named after them. Now, Diana Wallis Taylor animates this cherished part of the Old Testament, with its unforgettable cast of characters. Experience Ruth's elation as a young bride and her grief at finding herself a widow far before her time. Witness the unspeakable relief of Naomi upon hearing her daughter-in-law promise never to leave her. And celebrate with Boaz when, after years as a widower, he discovers love again, with a woman he first found gleaning in his field. The story of this remarkable woman to whom Jesus Christ traced His lineage comes to life in the pages of this dramatic retelling.

Claudia, Wife of Pontius Pilate: In a time of turmoil, one woman will search for love and peace--and find it where she never expected. Tugged this way and that by fate's indifferent hand, Claudia's life is adrift--until she meets Lucius Pontius Pilate and becomes his wife. When they move to the troublesome territory of Judea, she does what she has always done: makes the best of it. But unrest is brewing and Claudia will soon find herself and her beloved husband embroiled in controversy and rebellion. Might she find hope in the mysterious Jewish Rabbi everyone seems to be talking about?

Are you interested in studying some of the extraordinary people of the Bible?

Perhaps you'd like David Clarke's *Top 10 Most Outrageous Couples of the Bible.* Improve your marriage—and have some fun along the way—with Christian psychologist David Clarke's latest book, *The Top 10 Most Outrageous Couples of the Bible.* Drawing on the stories of Adam and Eve, Abraham and Sarah, Jacob and Rachel and Leah (yeah, one guy with two wives), and several others, Clarke provides both biblical teaching and real-life counseling expertise to help you see what will work—and not work—in your marriage today. Written with plenty of humor, *The Top 10 Most Outrageous Couples of the Bible* proves that "outrageous isn't a bad thing"—as Clarke says, "It's not always pretty. But it's always powerful."

Would you like to learn more about the language of the Bible?

Try Chaim Bentorah's *Beyond the Hebrew Lexicon* book and workbook. Many Christians long to study the Word of God in the original Hebrew. They will take Hebrew Classes at a college, a synagogue or online and often become discouraged because these classes either teach them to speak Hebrew or spend considerable time teaching complex rules of grammar when all they really want is to find God's heart and message in His Word. As a result, these Christians usually give up and just go to the back of Strong's Concordance, a lexicon, or a Bible dictionary to look up a word. This book is written for the Christian who does not want to learn to speak Hebrew or spend long hours trying to understand complex rules of grammar. It is written for those who want to find a deeper meaning to certain Hebrew words on their own. Even after looking up a word in their lexicon they are still left with a nagging feeling that there must be more. In most cases there is more and this book will give some guidelines in how to drill down into the very heart, soul and core of a Hebrew word. It will take you to a world beyond your lexicon without spending years in a seminary or Bible College. What you will need is a love for the Word of God. If you love it enough, it will reveal its secrets. Hebrew is a language of the heart and if you love God enough, He will reveal His heart to you through the ancient Hebrew Language.

CPSIA information can be obtained at www.ICGtesting.com
Printed in the USA
LVOW07s0309220616

493602LV00003B/17/P

9 781517 723354